CHRONICLE OF CHESTER

The 200 Years, 1775–1975

Other Books by Herbert Hughes

CHESHIRE AND ITS WELSH BORDER
PLAGUE ON THE CHESHIRE PLAIN

Chronicle of
CHESTER

The 200 Years, 1775–1975

HERBERT HUGHES

MACDONALD AND JANE'S · LONDON

First published in 1975 in Great Britain by
Macdonald and Jane's
Macdonald and Company (Publishers) Ltd.
Paulton House
8 Shepherdess Walk
London N1 7LW

ISBN 0 356 08209 1

Photoset, printed and bound
in Great Britain by
REDWOOD BURN LIMITED
Trowbridge & Esher

Contents

List of Illustrations

Frederick Coplestone.
Title page of John Trevor's *Panorama of the City of Chester*, 1843.
The Dee Bridge. (Vignette from Hanshall's *History of Cheshire*.)
Northgate Street West. (Etching by G. Bateman, 1807.)

Between pages 162 and 163
Chester Cathedral.
The Cathedral choir stalls.
Chester Castle.
The old Eastgate.
The Exchange (former Town Hall). (Vignette from Hanshall's *History of Cheshire*.)
Gamul House. (Sketch by Romney.)
Bishop Lloyd's Palace. (Sketch by Romney.)
Bishop Lloyd's Palace. (Contemporary photograph.)
The 16th-century Dutch Houses.

Between pages 194 and 195
Eastgate Street. (G. Pickering's print of about 1829.)
Lower Bridge Street, in the late 18th-century.
The junction of Bridge Street and Lower Bridge Street. (From Romney's *Sketchbook*, 1851.)
Superimposed photograph of the restored High Cross.
Partial destruction of the City Wall.
The 20th-century Police Headquarters framed in the 18th-century entrance of Chester Castle.
Eastgate Street today.
The Roman amphitheatre.
An early print of Bridge Street.

Between pages 226 and 227
Reconstruction of the Roman amphitheatre.
Chester Rows, old style.
Chester Rows, new style.
Lord Thomson and the American Ambassador with issue number 70 of the Chronicle.
Eaton House.
Eaton Hall.
Famous visitors watching the world go by.

Foreword

'I was quite enchanted at Chester, so that I could with difficulty quit it' (Boswell, in 1779).

Perhaps no biographer on earth is more revealing of the human situation – its successes and failures, strengths and weaknesses, comedy and suffering – than an old newspaper. How does the skilled journalist's eye range back over the fortunes of his fellow-men, not only today but from the vacillating vantage point of two long centuries of political and social change?

There can at the same time be few great cities whose strength and continuity of human and family tradition show more tenacity than here in Chester. Around the walls of Committee Room No. 1 at the Town Hall – fading gently into their chocolate background as the dates go back – stretch, year by year, the names of a continuous chain (if this is the right collective noun) of Mayors, from William the Clerk in 1238 to Wilfred Mitchell in 1974, now 'First Mayor of the Reorganised City under the Local Government Act of 1972'.

The supporting names of Chester's Town Clerks, on the other hand, present an astonishingly sparse total by the sheer length of their reigns. After only twenty-six names over four tumultuous centuries (from 1404 to 1799) four Clerks alone (Wm. Richards 1799, John Maddock 1817, John Walker 1857 and Samuel Smith 1886) span a whole century; then only two (James Dickson 1903 and Gerald Burkinshaw 1939) reach to their successor, Malcolm Kermode, by 1969 – an astonishing record of continuous and devoted service.

It is against this background that Chester's own Chronicle has so prospered and grown. Surely there cannot be many journals of such a stature and span. The pattern of daily news and opinion, in such a determined setting, makes an exemplary commentary upon those differences and similarities which are the very essence of human affairs. To take only one example – the city's river port, the very progenitor of its fortunes, steadily declined and silted up, sand upon sand – and what impact did this have upon the body politic? Today

ix

the very street name of 'Watergate' carries new transatlantic connotations of political scandal which bring a haunted smile to every American visitor to Chester. But this in turn will fade and, in maybe a decade, the honour of the name will be clear, as a new generation of tourists begins to arrive.

As I stood last night at midnight at the meeting of Chester's ancient ways, under the names not only of Watergate but Via Principalis, while around me nodded the tall black and white gables of a century ago (mostly, for seasonal renewal brings new leaves to every tree), I wondered what this spot may see in another hundred years. What then will be its main shaping influences? Perhaps our new and alarming awareness of the increasingly sheer and inescapable shortage of fossil fuels? If tomorrow there were suddenly no oil or petrol, how would our cities survive? Would Chester fare better than most? Almost certainly it would, for ancient towns congregated to serve their peoples by closeness and community; the dispersing and almost explosive power of rapid motor transport and allied attractions of suburban living have damaged our city certainly, but not yet destroyed its delicate fabric.

Through the mists I seemed to sense the City Cross again in its rightful place: may we yet see these symbolic stones reassembled here – perhaps even in this European Architectural Heritage Year? If so, what a handsome echo this event will make, answering back to some earlier column in the 'Chester Chronicle'; and may I be there to see! This is why, when, like Boswell, so many of us have been captured and enslaved by this fair city, it is such a privilege now to share in seeing through the devoted eyes of its Editor, Herbert Hughes, the two centuries of humanity that the Chronicle explores and illuminates with a light so sympathetic and so searching.

Chester, February, 1975

Donald W. Insall,
F.S.A., F.R.I.B.A., M.R.T.P.I., S.P.Dip.,
Consultant Architect to the City of
Chester and the Department of the
Environment, for the City's Conservation
Action Plan.

(Author: *Chester: A Study in Conservation*
HMSO, 1968)

Author's Introduction

When, some time ago, I made up my mind, as the twelfth editor of the Chester Chronicle and its associated newspapers, to write a book for the bicentennial I confess I was brought to a stand-still by the seeming complexity of the task and the space of time and events that had to be covered. There are millions of words bound up in the file rooms of the paper, words running from May 2, 1775, to the contents of the latest issue. Some system of selection was necessary and for this I followed the signposts of history and the example of four of my predecessors in the editorial chair, William Cowdroy, James Hanshall, Joseph Hemingway, and John Trevor, each of whom collected and published the city and county annals in addition to performing his regular journalistic work. But all stopped short before the completion of the first hundred years of the paper, and there was a long way to go to 1975.

Since continuity is the life stream of a newspaper founded so long ago, I determined never to lose sight of the first edition, so to say, and to introduce each chapter with a scene of contemporary life and to bring the story, theme, or subject up to date, so that there is at least the semblance of a continuing narrative over two hundred years. I tried to see myself as a reader of the paper at any time from the last quarter of the eighteenth century to the present day.

In thus attempting to turn the past into the present and to sustain the sense of immediacy and continuity, I have used the facts of the files with some imaginative freedom here and there, and I hope the historians who may read this book will forgive me for that. The story of a long-lived newspaper is not told merely by reproducing contemporary extracts accompanied by a crib from the history books. Some such extracts I have given, or woven into the narrative, for their own sake, but in the early to mid nineteenth century there were columns and columns of turgid stuff that make heavy reading today.

The change marked the abolition of the stamp and advertisement duties and the appearance of the provincial daily papers in the rising towns of Liverpool (which took away Chester's maritime trade and at the same time ensured the survival of the old city as an historic entity), Manchester, Leeds, Birmingham, and Newcastle-upon-Tyne. These towns overtook in population and commercial import-ance the old settlements where, outside London, newspapers were first established and had for perhaps fifty years or more a national as well as a local and regional flavour. The significance of this change and how the Chester Chronicle adapted itself in the first Industrial Revolution and the age of reform are discussed in Chapter 13.

Presently the uncertain, turgid writing that succeeded so incon-gruously the grace, style, humour, and invective of the 1780–1820 dec-ades gave way in turn in the later nineteenth century to a settled style of detailed news reporting and well-written, well-informed comment on political and social affairs. This was perhaps the best period of the Chester Chronicle as a city and county journal having a direct influ-ence upon reformative opinion and the improvement of conditions in the factories and workshops which were by this time diversifying the once exclusively agricultural character of Cheshire and the border counties. For its unswerving support of Mr. Gladstone's Liberal Party the Chronicle drew upon its old-time Whig allegiance, demon-strated throughout the revolt of the American colonies and in many turbulent local elections thereafter.

This book, then, is the story of the paper and of the famous old city from 1775 to this European Heritage Year of 1975. How Chester keeps its past-in-the-present and continues to cast its spell on world-tourists and citizens alike is the subject of the last chapter. For the interior history of the Chronicle I have had to go to many sources: the paper, according to the tradition of the Press, is reticent about its own affairs. For example, there is no report of John Fletcher's trial on the libel charge and a good part of his experience in prison I have tried to reconstruct with a hint or two from Tobias Smollett. As far as I know, the book relates, for the first time, Fletcher's re-lationship with Thomas Telford as canal and roads engineer and contractor, and I trust that my claim for the Chester Chronicle's part in the establishment of the flourishing town of Ellesmere Port is justified.

I could have wished to include a chapter on the paper's fugitive but fascinating reporting of Captain Cook's last two great voyages, on the Gordon Riots, and on the French Revolution, but another volume would have been needed. Finally, I am indebted to the

Chester Library staff and to the City Archivist and the Grosvenor
family archivist at Eaton for much help and courtesy; the Editor of
the Chester Courant has opened the files of that even-longer lived
newspaper to me; and I gratefully acknowledge the understanding
I derived, in writing Chapter 4, from the paper in the Chester
Archaeological Society's Journal No. 57 on the 1784 election by
Mr. Frank O'Gorman, of the University of Manchester.

Chester, February, 1975   Herbert Hughes

Acknowledgments

The thanks of the author and publisher are due to the following for kind permission to use brief quotes: to the Longman Group Ltd. (from *English Social History* by G. M. Trevelyan); to the Garnstone Press (from *Farewell to the Assizes* by the Hon. Sir Basil Nield); to Cassel and Co., Ltd. (from *A History of the English-Speaking Peoples* by Winston S. Churchill); to Mrs. Elspeth Huxley (from *Lady Elizabeth and the Grosvenors* and *Victorian Duke* by Gervas Huxley); to Penguin Books Ltd. (from the Cheshire volume by Dr. Pevsner and Edward Hubbard in the *Buildings of England* series); and to John Farquharson Ltd., agents for the Henry James Estate (from the Chester study reprinted by Heinemann in *English Hours*).

Part 1

1

A paper at war
from the start

'A journalist? Good God! Better be careful'

– *Sir Philip Gibbs*

The time is early in the morning of Tuesday, May 2, 1775. The carriers' carts and the postillions of the delivery post-coaches, from the White Lion and the Yacht Inns, are waiting with a knot of curious citizens at the head of the passage leading from Foregate-street, Chester, into the spacious yard of the Hop-pole Inn. Here is the new general printing office – copper-plates wrought off, books elegantly bound, gentlemen's libraries neatly fitted up on reasonable terms – where Mr. Poole and Mr. Barker are setting out on a venture for which they are fully equipped only in the practical printing sense, and the outcome or duration of which they cannot possibly foresee. But other printers elsewhere are going into newspaper production, and Chester could do with another paper, anyway. A war with America looks to be inevitable, and this is a good time to begin. The appointment of an Editor will have to wait until they can afford one, although there is always the risk of libel in these chancy times . . . The sheets have been stamped, the advertisements canvassed, the news collected from a variety of sources, the London correspondent's dispatch carefully read (they are writing some scandalous stuff in London these days, you can't be too careful), a last look given at the latest editions of the Morning Chronicle and the St. James's Chronicle, the carrier agents and the post-coaches ordered. The type has been set up, the pages assembled, and the hand-press is ready for inking. Number One Chester Chronicle or Commercial Intelligencer is about to go to press, surrounded by the inn stables and the hop-warehouses of Mr. Kenworthy and other wholesale merchants who deal at the city fairs. With the constant coming and going of travellers, the inn yard never sleeps, or only for an hour or two in the early morning, and in that between-time the paper is born.

It consisted of four pages folio 19″ × 12″, each of four columns, with a scrolled G. R. and Crown in the centre of the masthead. The imprint said: Chester: Printed by Poole, Barker, and Co., at their New General Printing Office in Foregate-street, where advertisements (at 3s. 6d. each) and letters, essays, etc. (post paid), are received. The imprint added the information that advertisements were also taken in by agents in London, Liverpool, Manchester, York, Shrewsbury, Hereford, Birmingham and Nantwich. (As the years went by, more agents were nominated in Cheshire, Lancashire and North Wales.) John Poole, born about 1735 and a freeman of Chester in 1766, was a printer and also a bookseller and stationer, admitted to the Stationers' Company of the City Guilds in 1769. He appears to have been the principal partner (little is known of Barker) and acted as his own editor. His hand no doubt penned the first leader, which, with news and advertisements, appeared on the front page. The leader, addressed 'To the Public', opened with a trenchant paragraph on the freedom of the Press as the strongest bulwark of liberty (sometimes 'partially perverted to the bad purpose of personal invective' – partially being used in its meaning of party-political), and went on:

> 'To accelerate the commercial and domestic intelligence of this ancient and respectable City, and the neighbouring counties, upon a more liberal and extensive plan, the Gentlemen concerned in this publication have voluntarily associated. In support of so necessary, and (with due deference, let it be added) so laudable an undertaking, it is not doubted but that the assistance of every FREE individual within the circuit of this paper will be cheerfully given. It is particularly wished, and therefore thus modestly requested, that the Gentlemen of the neighbourhood will please to suggest any practicable improvement in the execution of this public-spirited work, which, the Proprietors fully intend, at the risk of any tolerable expense, to render as generally useful and entertaining as may be. To this end any essays or other literary compositions, entirely free from the error above noted, will always be gratefully acknowledged, and faithfully inserted.'

To invite essays and other literary compositions was asking for trouble, as Mr. Poole presently found out. Some of the verses and belleslettres he was obliged afterwards to print were amateurish in the extreme. And what did 'FREE' mean? Enfranchised citizens (of whom there were not many in this 'rotten borough') or those who were not enslaved by party, employment, or under-privilege? Reading thus far the opening leader in the office of the existing newspaper – the Chester Courant in Newgate-street – John Monk, the able and experienced printer and publisher of that newspaper, could not fail to apprehend that some of these words were addressed to him personally. Damn this pompous fellow Poole with his 'more liberal and extensive plan'! A pernicious Whig, most likely, carried away by the eloquence of Charles James Fox. But how, after all, had he contrived to get the rag started? Mr. Monk's ire mounted as he went on to read the last paragraph of the first rival leader – this was surely aimed at him:

> 'It remains to be observed, although with reluctance, that artful insinuations have been industriously propagated to misrepresent the motives of the Proprietors, and secret schemes laid to impede and if possible frustrate their honest design; but as all falsehoods internally carry their own refutation the Company will persevere; and firmly rely on the countenance of the generous public until they shall be found undeserving of it.'

Battle was joined. The Courant had a challenger for the first time since its foundation by Roger Adams in 1732. (It is still going, a venerable but lively mid-week competitor of the Chronicle to this day.) The first Chester newspaper, the Weekly Journal, had been started in 1721 by William Cooke, born about 1690, a freeman of the city and a member of the Stationers' Company. The Journal survived about four years. Next on the scene was the Courant, and now the Chronicle. John Monk no doubt examined the number one Chronicle with calculating care, assessing its advertisement revenue first, for without that it could not live, although circulation was of the first importance. Let's see, he mused, scanning the pages. Two columns of advertisements on page two, house properties on page one – a good start, Mr. Monk has to admit to himself. Can they keep it up? As for the editorial matter, not much to worry about there, as yet. Just the usual stuff about the expected rebellion in the American colonies. But who's this London correspondent of theirs – a euphemism for scissors-and-paste or the real thing? And publishing on the same day as the Courant; something must be done about that before the Chronicle found circulation. Accordingly, the next Courant stole a march and went to press a day earlier, on Monday, and in the succeeding week the Chronicle, of course, did the same, with this open declaration of war in the number three issue, May 15:

> 'In consequence of the institution of this paper, as may candidly be

presumed, an unusual alacrity hath eminently appeared in the more early publication of the other. But whether this extraordinary ma-noeuvre proceeds from a disinterested and zealous inclination to serve the public, or from a preconcerted design to frustrate the ex-ecution of our scheme, every impartial reader will easily determine. Impressed with an ardent desire of gaining the public estimation by every possible mark of attention to their interest, we have determined, with the advice of many respectable characters, to alter the day of pub-lication from Tuesday to Monday . . .'

The newspaper battle diverted the citizens but caused some per-turbation to the Corporation, and at Eaton Hall, the great house of the lords of the manor, the Grosvenor family. A new paper could represent an opposition political interest, and the Chronicle was being closely watched for the tone of its politics. Thomas Grosvenor (brother of Lord Richard) and his 'running mate' R. W. Bootle had been elected to the first Parliament of George III in 1760 as represen-tatives for the city with the support of the Tory Corporation and Common Council and the Courant. Moreover, they had been con-firmed in their seats in three successive Parliaments afterwards with-out opposition. Now that Lord North's (and the King's) misguided and obdurate policies had brought the country to the brink of open war with the Americans, Charles James Fox, Edmund Burke, and the great elder statesman Chatham were preparing an attack on the follies of government. If the war developed seriously and dragged on, there could be a general election, and if the Chronicle supported the Whig (or Independent) interest there could be an opposition candi-date in Chester – against the Grosvenors and the Corporation – for the first time in years. Although, so far as I know, it was not then directly acknowledged, 'the Gentlemen' associated with Poole and Barker in starting the new paper could have been known or sus-pected as representing such opposition. But a lot was to happen before the next election. Meanwhile, it was in the interest of the local establishment to try to stop the Chronicle in its first stumbling tracks. Clearly a hint was dropped at the New General Printing Office about the morality – and legality – of working on Sunday to publish a paper dated Monday, even though the Courant was equally culpable.

Poole and Barker had misgivings, but countered with another address 'To the Public' in the edition of May 22 (number four), a mock-reluctant piece of sophistry in defence of the 'regulation' forced upon them:

> 'One objection, indeed, and that of the most serious nature, occurs
> to us against the execution of this regulation, however desirable it may
> be in other respects. We mean the very disagreeable circumstance of
> working on the SABBATH. But as it proceeds in the present case from
> an act of necessity, founded on the first leading principle of the law of
> nature – SELF-DEFENCE – we confidently flatter ourselves that the re-
> spectable magistracy of this city . . . will dispense with this flagrant
> violation of common decency whilst the same conduct is notoriously
> practised by another less excusable than ourselves . . .'

Incidentally, in this edition 'Price twopence' appears for the first
time below the masthead.

Could the Chronicle stay the course? With only five issues printed,
rumours were spread that it would be discontinued in a short time.
These rumours Poole and Barker lost no time (edition number six,
June 5) in nailing as 'among the variety of schemes formed by the enemies of this undertaking to render it abortive.' Who were these enemies? The Tory establishment in the city? Mr. Monk and the
Courant? Or were the conductors of the new paper beginning to
doubt their own capacity to continue it? At all events the canard that
the paper would shortly be discontinued was firmly knocked on the
head: 'it has no other foundation', the readers were informed, 'than
the obvious interest and wishes of its author that such an event
should take place. It is the determined resolution of the Proprietors
to persevere in the continuance of a paper (commenced solely with a
view to the general utility, unmixed with any desire of private emolument) which, they are happy to experience, has been received with
unanimous approbation by the candid and unprejudiced, through
its widely extended circuit.' No desire of private emolument, indeed,
mused Mr. Monk of the Courant. General utility philanthropists!
Attack being the best form of defence, the Chronicle (August 7)
claimed a circulation of between two and three thousand, a remarkable achievement if true – the London weekly journals of the day
were selling not much more, and some less, in a concentrated population area many times greater – and declared that the paper was
now also regularly sent by coach and carrier to Newcastle and other
towns in Staffordshire, and to Caernarvonshire and the Isle of Anglesey – 'the advantage, therefore, of ADVERTISING in it is too obvious
to need insisting on.'

In the autumn there was a curious development. In their refutation above of the rumour that the paper would shortly be discontinued, Poole and Barker, it will be seen, singled out an unnamed 'author', not several. This 'anonymous author' appeared again in the issue of September 18 (number 21), in which the proprietors issued a general challenge under the heading of

A CARD

The proprietors of this paper offer their respectful compliments to the public, and in consequence of some insinuations which of late have been industriously propagated by an anonymous author, tending to impeach the establishment of this publication, find themselves under the very disagreeable necessity of thus calling upon any one who with temper and decency will point out in what respect they have acted disreputably. If, in answer, the Company cannot vindicate their conduct to the entire satisfaction of the public, who have so generously bestowed their favours, the proprietors will manfully submit to any censure which their behaviour may be thought to deserve. If, on the contrary, this invitation is suffered to pass unnoticed, the public will, it is hoped, conclude that malevolence alone gave rise to the many groundless reports which are the common talk of the day.

And on October 9 (issue number 24), the paper took open issue with Lord Richard Grosvenor, informing its now deeply intrigued readers that the following Card had been sent to Eaton Hall:

Chester General Printing-office,
26 September, 1775.

The Proprietors present their compliments to Lord Richard Grosvenor, and are very credibly informed that his Lordship has publicly declared a resolution of opposing their undertaking. If this information be true, the Proprietors hope his Lordship will favour the Company with his reasons for this determination, as it may probably lye in their power to explain matters so satisfactorily as to induce his Lordship to alter his mind.

The Right Hon. Lord Grosvenor, Eaton.

His Lordship's answer, *verbally* delivered to the messenger, was: 'What they have heard is very true.'

And that laconic answer is all we have; the paper is silent on the subject thereafter, and the Eaton archives are equally reticent. Rumours and innuendoes died away – far graver matters were taking hold of public interest – and by February, 1776, there was a truce, the Chronicle declaring that from the next issue publication day would be Thursday; anyway, it was better for business:

'The advantages of having more than one Newspaper in every great city have long been so happily experienced that all attempts for their establishment in such places have been warmly encouraged. But to render them the more useful, they are generally printed on different days, by which means Advertisements, requiring immediate insertion, are ushered to the Public in proper time and thereby best effect the purposes for which they are intended . . . .'

Very handsome, and note the proud reference to 'every great city' – for such Chester considered itself to be at this time and was so considered by the rest of the country.

The Chester Chronicle started with a war on its hands – a war to get itself established and accepted, and the widening fratricidal struggle with our American colonies. Hostilities with the American 'rebels' had begun when the paper went to press for the first time, but news travelled slowly. So it happened that the first news of the American War of Independence came in a letter from a Rhode Island merchant to his Chester business correspondent. 'What the consequences will be,' he wrote, 'God only knows. A man's person is not safe, and property is sported with in the most unheard-of manner. Ships laden with goods from England are forced, without unlading, to return back by the populace. . . .' That was bad news for the Port of Chester.

John Poole presumably was editing the Chronicle himself at this time, and he was doing the job with some political skill. The paper's opinions, when they could be separated from quotations from the London Press (not always acknowledged), were clearly critical of Lord North's Tories and King's Friends, but in this they reflected the general dissatisfaction of the country with the war policy; a dissatisfaction shared by the local Tories, whose disaffection for the new paper was thus turned by the course of events and the temper of the people. By Monday, August 7 (number 15) conflicting reports of the Battle of Bunker's Hill on June 17 were beginning to come through, and this issue carried an account from New York very different from those of 'authority' which claimed a royal victory – in fact (in the later words of Sir Winston Churchill) the British had captured the hill but the Americans had won the glory. The unsuccessful General Gage was soon to be called home, but before him, disembarking at Plymouth on September 15, came 'General Gage's Lady and upwards of 170 sick and wounded soldiers who could not get any relief at Boston', a circumstance which provoked the St. James's Chronicle, a popular London evening paper of the day published thrice weekly, to concoct this wicked jeu d'esprit: 'We are assured that it is not General Gage's wife who is arrived from Boston, but the General himself in his wife's cloaths. His wife is left behind, invested with the supreme command, and will prove a much more formidable enemy to the Americans than her husband, who has been beaten twice abroad and every day grows more and more contemptible at home.' (No wonder the Government and the authorities feared the newspapers.)

Reproducing that story in the Chester Chronicle of September 25 (number 22), Messrs. Poole and Barker – not without malice, I like to think – concluded their war story for the year 1775, with the exception of a report of the Rev. John Wesley, in a November sermon, describing the dire horrors of war and taking an impartial swipe at the sins of England and America. All in all, the paper had survived its first perilous eight months with credit. Poole and Barker, closely scanning the London papers, editing their metropolitan correspondent, writing and setting up their columns, operating the handpress, seeing to the supply of stamps and paper, overseeing their agents and carriers, stimulating the flow of advertisements, and keeping their books and a weather-eye open for local enemies, could face 1776 with confidence. The American war, whatever else it was, was good 'copy' and good for circulation, and in Chester the expected opposition to the new paper had died away. There was much work and little profit, but a newspaper generates a life of its own, and though Poole and Barker could not see very far down the corridor of time of two hundred years, they were determined to keep their engagement with the Public and provide 'an Intelligent, a Commercial, and an Entertaining Newspaper' for as long as they could manage it.

This flatteringly comprehensive description was used by the Editor in another address to the readers (July 4, 1776, number 63) explaining the necessity for raising the price to twopence halfpenny. All previous announcements concerning the paper had been made by Poole and Barker under their own names jointly, or anonymously as 'the Proprietors'; this was the first appearance of 'the Editor' as a single identity – but I suppose that it was only John Poole after all. Lord North, in his Budget of the previous month, had increased the newspaper stamp duty by a halfpenny. The newspapers he classed with cards and dice as among the luxuries of life. The Chronicle prepared the way for its coming increase in price by reporting the Prime

Minister's specious observations on the Press. From the beginning of the century the newspapers had fought and won a battle with successive governments for the right to report and publish Parliamentary debates, a right silently conceded in 1771 after many courageous journalists and printers had challenged a House of Commons resolution of 1738 declaring such publication to be a breach of privilege. Like so much else in our mythical constitution, the 'freedom of the Press' is a form of words rather than a statute. Parliament gave way to the persistence of the newspaper men and the power of public opinion, but the breach of privilege resolution has never been formally rescinded. When they were not seeking ways to 'use' the newspapers for their own advancement, governments and parties – and the King – continued to resent the prying of the Press, to go in fear of it, and so they tried to curb its influence by taxes on paper – the stamp duty – and later by taxes on advertisements.

As we have seen, the Government's mismanagement of affairs with the Americans was 'getting a bad Press', and when Lord North made his Budget speech in April, 1776, he retaliated with a turn of the screw by adding a halfpenny on the 'taxes on knowledge' and a few well-chosen words. Without entering into the question, he said, of whether newspapers were, as some people thought, of great utility or, as others contended, they were from their licentiousness a disgrace to the country, they certainly were an article of luxury and therefore a fair object of taxation. He had learned from the Stamp Office that stamp duty had been paid in the last year for twelve millions of newspapers – 'no bad proof of the tyranny and oppression exercised over the Press by the present wicked and despotic ministry!' With a final stroke of irony, the Prime Minister presumed that no gentleman would part from so agreeable and informative a companion as his newspaper for the trifling difference of a ha'penny. Undeterred, the papers went on printing everything they could lay their hands on. Occasionally editors or printers were committed to the King's Bench Prison for libel (it happened to the Chester Chronicle, as we shall see), and one Luke Kent, printer of the Hampshire Chronicle, was arraigned for publishing a letter held to reflect on the conduct of Lord Mansfield, the distinguished (and merciful) Chief Justice. The trial Judge recommended the jury to find the defendant guilty by the mere act of publication, but 'the jury' (said the Chester Chronicle, reporting the case with evident approval), 'had an opinion of their own, and, with a manliness becoming Englishmen, disdained to be dictated to in a matter of which they were the sole judges: convinced of the defendant's innocence, they asserted the dignity of an English Jury and pronounced him Not Guilty.'

For the first time the venalities of high as well as low life were getting a public airing in the newspapers, against which there was 'a general cry' of scandal-mongering and licentiousness. The Press defended itself and the Chronicle quoted this London comment: 'Let every sober man lay his hand on his heart and answer whether the licentiousness of newspapers or the profligacy of the times is the true cause of the supposed scandal. . . A newspaper is a mirror, and if Sir John squints or my Lady has wrinkles in her face, she must not condemn the faithful reflector.'

Meanwhile, the Editor of the Chester Chronicle – which while making the most of metropolitan bankruptcies, divorces, elopements, suicides, duels, and gambling debts, faithfully reflected the relative sobriety of local life – was obliged to pass on the extra halfpenny to his readers and to increase the price of the paper to twopence halfpenny: 'this being an advance of no more than the additional duty'. In return he would keep them up to date with the progress of 'this unhappy contest with America', and all matters domestic and foreign. Later the Printer (not the Editor) made it known that he was under the disagreeable necessity of advancing the cost of short advertisements to four shillings and longer ones proportionately, the Ministry having clapped sixpence on the two shillings duty for each insertion.

The citizens of Chester resented the press gang, now active in the city and round about. An officer and eight other ranks of the press gang, taking three men from Chester to Liverpool, were set upon by sixty men of Parkgate, on the turnpike road at Little Sutton. The three pressed men were liberated in a fierce running battle. One press gang man was shot dead and several wounded. The Naval press gang picked up lads from the streets 'as they were about their masters' business, some not fourteen years old', and shipped them off to the Nore. 'Is this a land of liberty where parents have their children dragged from them, masters their servants and apprentices?' indignantly asked the Chronicle. The war came a little nearer home, too, with the assembly for a month's training of the Flintshire and the

Royal Cheshire Militias – all militiamen failing to report to forfeit £20 or go to gaol for six months. The prospect of home service with the militia was preferable to the risk of being picked up in the street or snatched out of bed by the press gang, and the Chronicle reported able-bodied men, unable for some reason to get into the militia, secretly leaving Chester because the city was too near Liverpool for comfort – Liverpool, formerly the little slave creek, now fast growing and the headquarters of those ruthless white-slavers, the Royal Naval Press Gang. The Fleet had a glorious history – and before this war was over Admiral Rodney was to enhance its renown – but an evil reputation among sailors, pressed or voluntary, for bad food, stinking quarters and the most brutal discipline of the lash. Better to take your chance with the army of General Howe at New York – at least, if you came back, you could boast that you had seen that American show place.

Almost the entire content of the paper's four pages folio, with very little space surrendered to only rudimentary headlines, was now given up to politics and war week by week. Since very few of the London papers reached the provinces, regional readers looked to their own paper – where there was one – to epitomise the national and international news and to interpret the politics behind the events. The modern world was shaping fast, and as yet the Chronicle was among the 'national' papers, with a different job to do and (strange as it may seem) a wider field to cover than was its function after the first quarter of the next century or there-abouts.

On August 23, 1776, the Chronicle printed, without recognising them as such, the first immortal words that had come its way. Words out of Philadelphia, the United States' capital, twelve miles from that other Chester on the Delaware River, named by William Penn in remembrance of the Quaker settlers from the old city on the Dee River. These words had been read out in the Court House at Chester, Pennsylvania, on July 8, at the same time as in the State House in Philadelphia, and now the citizens of old Chester were reading them for the first time, new-minted and having travelled as fast as words could travel in those days. What was it all about, this column and a half of very small type on page two? At first glance it looked like nothing more than a high-flown war communiqué. And there it still lies on the yellowing page of the file, the birth certificate of a nation:

MONDAY NIGHT'S POST
Advices from America
In Congress, July 4, 1776
A Declaration by the Representatives
of the UNITED STATES OF AMERICA, in
General Congress assembled.

When in the course of human events it becomes necessary for one people to dissolve the political bonds which have connected them with another, and to assume among the powers of the earth the separate and equal station to which the laws of nature and of nature's God entitle them, a decent respect to the opinions of mankind requires that they should declare the causes which impel them to the separation.

We hold these truths to be self-evident: that all men are created equal; that they are endowed by their Creator with certain unalienable rights; that among these are life, liberty, and the pursuit of happiness. . . .

And so to the end – Signed by order, and on behalf of the Congress, JOHN HANCOCK, President. Attest, Charles Thomson, Secretary.

That year's end the Mayor of Chester, the Common Council and the Chronicle pondered soberly the likely effects of a long and bitter struggle upon the Port and trade of the city. And most unseasonably, at Christmas the citizens were obliged to bar their doors. 'On Saturday a party of sailors beat up in this city for volunteers and on Sunday night a smart press began. Several men were taken out of bed from their wives, and a woman, in endeavouring to prevent her husband being carried off, was dangerously wounded on the arm by a stroke of a cutlass.' That was the last local war report of 1776.

In the following year Chester suffered the unusual experience of an earthquake shock, but what was that compared with the shock of the crushing defeat of the army at Saratoga? Not until December was that disaster known. With the war at sea developing, three privateers sailed from the Port of Chester. One of these, the Empress of Russia, after capturing a Swedish ship of 330 tons, was taken by a French frigate and sent to L'Orient.

On the domestic front the Welsh and Cheshire gentlemen of the Turf who kept luxurious establishments and were the support of Chester Races vented their displeasure in the Chronicle with the Government's bill imposing a tax on servants, and ingenious arguments were used to distinguish and except from tax day servants, outside servants, seasonal servants, jockeys, grooms, stable-men non-resident, and others. For the first time many town readers were

instructed in the order of precedence of the army of retainers necessary to support the consequence of the country squires whose estates
lay all around them: maitre d'hotel, house steward, master of the
horse, groom of the chamber, valet de chambre, butler, under butler,
clerk of the kitchen, confectioner, cook, house porter, chairman, footman, running footman, coachman, groom, postillion, stable boy,
gardener, under gardener, park keeper, huntsman, and whipper-in.
What had the war and the press gang to do with that kind of privileged servility? A city satirist wrote a savage letter to the Editor proposing that added to the list for taxation should be alehouses,
brothels, bagnios, bachelors after thirty, French hair dressers, Jews,
kept mistresses, lawyers, notaries and playhouses.

2

Paper tigers
– and the end of the war

'Such leading articles, and such spirited attacks.' –
'Our worthless contemporary, the Gazette.' – 'That
disgraceful and dastardly journal, the Independent.'

The Pickwick Papers

It is New Year's Eve. The last chime of midnight from all the city
towers and steeples will bring in Seventeen Hundred and Eighty-
Two. John Poole, in his burdened capacity of printer and publisher,
business manager and editor, sits pensively in his little room in the
New General Printing Office in the yard of the Hop-pole Inn, mood-
ily withdrawn from the good cheer and festivity issuing from that
hospitable establishment. Quill in hand, he listens to the confused
sounds of revel from Foregate-street, reflecting that the citizens, God
knows, have precious little to revel about, with the American colonies whistled down the wind and the country in the devil of a mess.
Chester's traditional Christmas Lord of Misrule, indeed! There has
been a lord of misrule at Westminster far too long. And the King's
Friends in Chester haven't much to say for themselves after the disaster of Yorktown. Had not some of them hearkened with shame on
Sunday sen'night to the Rev. John Wesley preaching at the Octagon
Chapel at the Bars against the evils of misgovernment? The paper
has been on the right side from the start, and, thinks John Poole (who
is short of ideas of his own at this moment, a bit wound down as he is,
like the Old Year itself), it will be a good thing to reprint some time
soon that great prophetic speech of the old Earl Chatham. How
much wisdom and foresight there was in it, to be sure. Every word
has come true. And here we are, defeated in arms and kicked out by
the Americans, enemies on all sides, imposts up, and trade withering. John Poole has cast up the Chester Chronicle accounts for the
year, and he is troubled. How much longer can he keep the paper
going? Three hundred and forty-nine editions gone to press in six
years of continuous war! The paper is an unremitting taskmaster,
demanding constantly to be fed with costly news expresses and

eating up the original capital as well as the modest profits of general printing, engraving, book-binding and book-selling. True, the circulation has gone up – there is so much to read about and more and more people able to read – but advertisement revenue has fallen because of the Government imposts, and the costs of production, paper, carriage and candles, to say nothing of wages, add up to a daunting total. Besides, fresh type will be needed soon, and something will have to be done about the press – it is nearly worn out.

On the credit side, the paper is well received – it was a good move to advance publication day to Friday from August, 1776. thus making a nicely rounded week. It compares more than favourably with the illiberal Courant, which neglects no opportunity to injure its younger rival; a new paper not yet firmly established can be destroyed overnight by such means. And Poole cannot honestly say that his Chronicle is firmly established. The political opposition of the first year has been checked by responsible and judicious journalism and the march of events, but it is merely latent until the general election which the obdurate King George will sooner or later have no choice but to concede. There is no love lost between the Courant and the Chronicle and the knives – and the mobs – will be out when the election comes, with the young Mr. Pitt deliberately confusing the old issues, seeking to curb the power of the Crown and to reform the Parliamentary representation, and supporting Mr. Burke across the party lines of Whig and Tory. But these are wayward thoughts: if the paper is to survive John Poole must raise the wind in some quarter or other, and preferably in some fresh quarter. He does not like the way those associates who helped him to establish the paper have lately begun to interfere in its conduct.

Meanwhile, he is the slave of publication, and there is an Address to the Public to be written for the New Year. The quill dips into the inkhorn. Although, heaven help him, he has little skill at it, he will cheer himself up and challenge the satirical poetisers and self-advertisers of the Courant with an Address in verse. And so, in the first issue of 1782 (number 350) we find this execrable stuff:

The Editor's respectful Address

To his good Friends the Editor presents
The customary annual compliments;
Owning as he, in gratitude, is bound,
Their kind support has his endeavours crown'd;
And, shou'd he change the mode of his Address

From prose to rhyme, his Readers must confess
Th'attempt is novel and will prove at least
A wish to gratify the public taste.

Those who the task consider well may guess,
That, with a due attention on the press,
Much lies on an Editor to chuse
Materials proper for a weekly news.
He must inform, instruct, and entertain,
Please every party, yet to no side lain . . .
Thus he, the public censure to avoid,
May do his best, and yet please neither side,
While our affairs to such a crisis tend
'Tis problematic when the times will mend . . .
Black clouds obscure our prospects every way,
Hope that once flatter'd lends no chearing ray,
And those we trust have led us most astray.

May better omens with this op'ning year
Reverse the scene and make our prospects clear;
Then should some happy incidents take place
Which to our land may call back exil'd Peace,
That she, once more, the olive branch may bring,
And dove-like settle here with downy wing:
He will by the Express still duly sent
Among the first announce the great event;
Claiming, on this account, no other praise
But that which an indulged Public pays
For his allow'd exertions to dispense
The earliest and the best intelligence.

If indeed John Poole wrote this, it is charitable to assume that he
did so as a consequence of deciding, after all, to dismiss his darker
preoccupations in the convivial taproom of the Hop-pole Inn across
the coach-yard from his office. The best that can be said of it, is that
the sentiments are worthy and unexceptionable. There is evidence,
too, that he was conscious of having depressed the spirits of his readers by the uniformly bad news he had been obliged to print of late.
But there was another, more compelling, reason for Poole turning
poet – the spur of emulation. He had taken note, we may be sure, of
the announcement in the previous Tuesday's Courant of the publication, price one shilling, of *The Vapourish Man or Hypocrisy
Detected*, a dramatic piece in two acts as performed at the Theatre
Royal in Chester and Manchester 'with universal applause'. This
announcement gave no pleasure to Mr. Poole, for the verse play was

the work of William Cowdroy, at this time a printer and compositor at the Courant and a gifted protegé of John Monk, with whom he had started as an apprentice. Not only did Cowdroy compose type for the rival paper, he enlivened its contents with witty skits and puns. His writing for the theatre had gained notice too; he had a gift for farce, and popular farcical pieces were much in request on the contemporary stage – they lifted the curtain on full-length plays and if locally written with local allusions, helped to establish the credentials of touring companies. And so here was Cowdroy, a fledgeling Dramatic Author, published by his employer Mr. Monk. Worse – John Poole, as bookseller, would be obliged to stock the piffling piece. His customers would be bound to ask for it because although, as he had heard, 'The Vapourish Man' had failed on the stage, the Courant had used every opportunity of puffing it.

Portentously the Courant answered the Chronicle's New Year doggerel with an Ode for the New Year, by William Whitehead, the Poet Laureate himself but one of the least distinguished of the line. He was getting past it and hadn't much to inspire his official muse anyway; the American victory in the war was scarcely a fit subject for a British song of praise. But he did achieve a passable heroic couplet:

> In Britain's voice 'tis freedom calls,
> For freedom dies if Britain falls.

The rest was not much better, if more professional, than John Poole's sad effort. There the thing should have ended, but young Mr. Cowdroy – he was about thirty at this time – perceived a farcical situation in the making and (no doubt with the silent assent of his Editor, Mr. Monk) determined to divert the town with a mounting satirical attack on the Editorial Poet of the Chronicle, seventeen years his senior. A ludicrous battle of paper tigers ensued that was to set the pattern for the unbridled personal and political invective to be employed in both camps at city elections, to the end of the century and afterwards. In 1826, for example, the Editor of the Chronicle called his brother of the Courant 'a pernicious fellow' and the Courant retorted with 'that political sycophant', picturing the Editor of the Chronicle as 'that man who enjoys his pipe and easy chair . . . and who takes his facts at second or third hand from persons interested in mis-stating them, to say nothing of his own blind political bias.' Before that election was over hard missiles – paving stones among them – as well as hard words were flying. (How times have changed, alas – it is many years since the Chronicle and the Courant exchanged a discourtesy.) The incomparable comedy of the editorial combats between Mr. Pott, of the Eatanswill Gazette, and Mr. Slurk, of the Eatanswill Independent in 'The Pickwick Papers' could well have been suggested to the young Charles Dickens, who roamed the country for material and had an eye for everything, by a comparison of the files of the Chester Chronicle and the Chester Courant, and the poll-books published by both, at election times up to about 1830. When the local papers were not pulverising each other they united in savaging the Macclesfield Courier for daring to intervene in the sacred mysteries of a Chester election.

The prototypes of Mr. Pott and Mr. Slurk may be said to have made their first appearance in 1782, and the combat was not a party set-to but a vicious war of words in which each paper sought to discredit the other irretrievably. Ostensibly it was all about such trumpery matters as syntax, prosody and feeble versification, for which readers could be expected to care nothing. But these were merely the pretexts for studied insult, copious innuendo, and a wicked purpose to kill by ridicule. Readers, I have no doubt, enjoyed every word of it. Many of them would know the newspaper men personally, and although no one was directly named in the entire course of the polemic, every personal allusion was perfectly understood and relished. The intense rivalry of the papers was also well known and readers, then as now, were diverted by the spectacle of journalists taking themselves too seriously. As for the protagonists, Cowdroy, I suspect, treated it as a great joke, Monk hoped the Chronicle's credit would be damaged, and Poole, after a hesitant start, warmed to the work and finally claimed the victory. After studying the files of both papers I hesitate, after nearly two hundred years, to say which side won. The evidence is not complete, and there is so much that, tantalisingly, one can never know. Was it, after all, just a glorious spoof, an exercise in the hard-won liberty to publish and be damned, and did the 'enemies' foregather in the pub at night to compare notes? On reflection, I do not think so. The thing was serious enough while it lasted and the Chronicle might well have staggered a year earlier than it eventually did – as we shall see in the next chapter – and this time with no helping hand to sustain it and push it on to its bicentenary!

At all events, Mr. Poole soon had cause to regret that he had ever penned his miserable New Year Address, which was subjected to a detailed dissection by a correspondent in the Courant of January 15. The entire effusion, wrote this correspondent, 'would reflect discredit on the most wretched poetical blacksmith that ever hammered out a couplet'. The Editor of the Courant (or Cowdroy, almost certainly, writing for him) put up a pretence of dissenting from this vulgar judgment: 'Indeed, sensibly impressed with the merit of the whole Address, we cannot withhold our commendation in declaring that the sentiments it contains are so perfectly liberal and just, the versification so easy, flowing and poetical. . . .' Which manifestly they were not. A hint was delicately insinuated that the Chronicle's lines on the national troubles –

> Black clouds obscure our prospects every way,
> Hope that once flatter'd lends no chearing ray,
> And those we trust have led us most astray –

were really a description of the Chronicle's own difficulties after some six years of publication. John Poole was on the anvil, but they were not going to hammer him down. Dredging his vocabulary, he came up with this righteous, telling stuff on January 18:

> 'The writer of the critisism in last Tuesday's Courant is respectfully informed that the Editor's Address alluded to was not intended to display any shining parts, or florid bombast, but the natural impulse of a grateful mind sensible of the many favours conferred. He leaves it to others to commence Dramatic Essayists – to write small-talk so insufferably tedious and insipid that even their best friends are disgusted by the perusal . . . These gentry, preparatory to the appearance of their flimsy works, by self-created mechanical Puffs are ever fond of passing high encomiums on their own productions that they may with greater security fleece the Public . . . Such splenetic witlings, such drivellers in science, aspiring to commence satirists without possessing one particle of the true Attic leaven so necessary to support the character, are perfect nuisances to society, wasting their time, that most valuable of all gifts committed to their care, in as trifling and absurd a manner as Caligula, who spent no small portion of his time in killing flies. If it is vanity that goads them on, they are to be pitied; if poverty, let them remember it is preferable to shame. Be this as it may, the following quotation from a satirical writer will perhaps be thought applicable:
>
>> Some write to shew their wit and some their spite,
>> But want of money makes me write.'

Some interior elucidation is necessary here. The 'Dramatic Essayist' is, of course, Cowdroy. The publication of Cowdroy's farce *The*

Vapourish Man, after its presumed failure in performance, is stigmatised as 'fleecing the public' (John Monk as printer is by association
involved here), and the rest holds up to ridicule the pretentions of the
provincial printer and compositor who aspires to be a playwright. At
this crucial point there is, unhappily, a gap in the continuity of the
communiqués from the battlefield: the issue of the Courant of January 22 is missing from the file. Although this happened not infrequently in both newspaper offices, perhaps it was thought at the time
that this particular issue of the Courant was too libellous to keep for
posterity! Clearly, however, the Courant writer had got down to
business of the most personal order, delineating the character, habits
and appearance of his rival, and the wounding capacity of this performance can be gauged by the outraged riposte in the Chronicle of
January 25. Cowdroy (by inference) is belittled as 'the occasionally
deputed Editor of the Courant' – a reminder that he is still merely a
printer got above himself and that his boss, Mr. Monk, is just 'using'
him. He is roundly accused of spending too much time in public kitchens and at 'the most unseemly nocturnal revels'. To pay for his dis-
sipations he has had to resort to 'plotting artifices' (writing farces) –
'artifices not more pitiful and humiliating in themselves than contemptible in their execution.' As for *The Vapourish Man*, was not
the theatre manager in Manchester rebuked for 'presuming to
obtrude so trifling, surreptitious, and ridiculous a piece of buffoon-
ery upon the town'? And the author had the effrontery to claim the
fullest approbation of the public! Poole wound up magisterially: 'I
shall not pretend to combat this fastidious, self-sufficient Prig in
these particulars . . . I venture to deem him the most lethargic
scribbler that ever presumed to insult the understanding. Though
The Vapourish Man is void of originality, the same cannot be said of its
author; for precept, both wise and honourable, in this instance, pro-
claims him A FIRST-RATE BLOCKHEAD.'

Never, cried the Courant on January 29, did an angry man throw
dirt with less skill and ability than the respectable and liberal Editor
of the Chronicle in his last edition. No doubt that 'gentleman' had
been pained by the character they had been constrained to give of
him and by the truth of the portrayal (presumably in the missing edition). But what was he to expect after accusing a certain writer of
fleecing the public and casting poverty in his face? 'If he, who can be
capable of this, is no richer in pocket than in understanding, and
goodness of heart, we may pronounce him poor indeed, and were his

cheek susceptible of a blush, the bare recollection thereof would certainly tincture it.' (A palpable hit there by the compositor and occasionally deputed Editor, on modest wages, against the substantial master printer and Editor.) Cowdroy sharpened his pen – or perhaps he did not even trouble to write, instead composing the injurious words straight into his compositor's stick: implacable envy and prejudice . . . malevolence . . . such as no man of common decency or common probity could be guilty of . . . false and ungenerous in asserting that *The Vapourish Man* was a failure . . . Here's an extract from a letter to the author from Mr. Joseph Younger, manager of the Theatre Royal, Drury-lane, attesting that the farce was performed repeatedly with general applause in Manchester and inviting him to submit any further piece for possible presentation at Drury-lane itself.

And so on, and on, the quarrel swelling on obscure Latin allusions – these were very learned printer-journalists – and sinking to the trivia of grammar and punctuation. Where did it all start? The combatants had forgotten. And anyway the thing was becoming tedious. 'We appeal to the judgment of the Public whether we are or are not the aggressors', wrote the Editor of the Chronicle on February 1, resting his case. As befits the senior, he concedes a point to his younger antagonist: 'In this contest he is a Volunteer, and to do him justice, handles his weapons most admirably.' Then John Poole had an inspiration, dubbing Cowdroy 'this Colossus of the Courant, bestriding *half* the city'. Gratuitously he tendered him three pieces of advice: one, to seek instant relief from the Itch of Writing; two, to be more careful of personal abuse; three, to write no more bad Latin but to ponder what every schoolboy knew –

> Let all the foreign tongues alone
> Till you can read and spell your own.

There was a half-hearted rejoinder in the Courant of February 5. Clearly the mercurial Cowdroy had had enough of it, and the Chronicle had the last word on February 8: 'It is necessary to make an apology to our numerous distant readers on the conclusion of the wayward dispute we have been reluctantly forced into, calculated only for the meridian of this city . . . But all is at an end with this comma-hunting Quixote – as he now bites the grass it would be cruel to trample on him, and I shall finally conclude with assuring the Public that as we have hitherto happily steered clear of commencing local disputes, we shall persevere in the same line of conduct, reserving ourselves to act on the defensive only.' So ended this curious and instructive passage of arms. But all was not by any means at an end with William Cowdroy. Presently he was to sit in John Poole's chair, not as proprietor of the Chester Chronicle but as the first professional editor – the editor Poole could never afford.

But this is to anticipate. This relation of the war of words has held in abeyance the completion of the Chronicle's account of the war with the American colonies. After the military defeat at Saratoga, British spirits were cheered by the news of Rodney at sea. On Monday, February 13, 1780, there was 'a general illumination' of Chester, as the paper reported, on account of the relief of Gibraltar, the dispersal of the investing Spanish fleet, and the capture of the Admiral, Don Juan de Langara, in an action off Cape St. Vincent on January 16–17. Rodney's despatch to the Admiralty from the flagship Sandwich in Gibraltar Bay reported a classic sea fight of some ferocity, beginning with a general chase and ending with the signal to engage and close. This was the Chronicle's first detailed account of a naval battle under sail and it is full of pride in the fleet. 'At sunset,' ended Rodney's despatch, 'we entered the Gut.' Don Juan was treated with every courtesy, but Rodney refused a parole for him and his officers while British seamen were detained in Spanish prisons.

In April the Chronicle reported at length the resolution of city and county deputies throughout the country (Cheshire excepted) calling upon Parliament to curtail the 'fatal influence of the Crown – enormous, compactly accumulated, all-devouring'. Mr. Fox supported the deputies in their general desire to reduce the influence of the Crown, shorten the duration of Parliaments, procure a more equal representation, and put an end to 'the accursed war with America'. In the House of Commons on April 6, a Mr. Pitt, on the famous motion that 'it is necessary to declare that the influence of the Crown has increased, is increasing, and ought to be diminished', invited Lord North to resign, since his continuance in office was enough alone to prove the influence of the Crown. The motion was carried by a majority of 18, and this was the first sign of the coming power of William Pitt the Younger, striking a blow for Parliament and People and combining the more enlightened and progressive elements of

Whig and Tory. At this historic moment for democratic reform, the Chronicle (number 261) had to report loyal and feudal Cheshire opting out. A meeting of 'Gentlemen, Clergy, and Freeholders' at the Shire Hall on April 11 declined to support the reform of Parliament movement, Sir Thomas Broughton having expressed reservations about the intentions of those who would reduce the influence of the Crown. The accumulation of taxes had been one of the many grievances advanced in the Parliamentary petition, and the proposed increase in salt duty (one of Lord North's devices to help pay for the cost of the war, now running at sixty-three and a half million pounds) caused the 'saline gentry' of Northwich, as the Chronicle called the salt manufacturers of that Cheshire town, to put up the price immediately and make 'pretty pickings' before the extra duty came on. Perhaps this was one self-interested reason for Cheshire staying out. There was, however, another reason for the county's resistance to change. Cheshire and Chester had been together a County Palatine from the time of the Conqueror; it was governed almost independently of the Crown until the reign of Henry III, and managed to keep some powers and privileges until these lapsed in the time of Henry VIII. Separate jurisdiction continued in some minor form until 1851. In 1780, then, Cheshire could expediently demonstrate its loyalty to the Crown because it did not want a Parliamentary reform that would interfere in its individual style of local government – including the method of electing the city officers, many times challenged, and a near-feudal representation at Westminster. Mr. Burke had these matters in mind when, on July 3, as the Chronicle reported, he presented a bill in the House of Commons 'for the more perfectly uniting to the Crown the Principality of Wales and the County Palatine of Chester, for the more commodious administration of justice within the same, and for abolishing certain offices now appertaining thereto.'

Four columns of field despatches filled a page of the paper on June 8, 1781. Lord Cornwallis reported the defeat of the Americans in the Battle of Guildford Courthouse on March 15, as a result of which the British were able to move north to Virginia and the peninsula of Yorktown in Chesapeake Bay. This success, following the capitulation of Charlestown in the previous June and Rodney's command of the sea, caused some British hope of an honourable settlement in the 'unnatural' conflict. This could have been the turning point. George Washington was himself moody and dispirited, so much so that John Hancock, the New England leader, wrote him a remarkable letter, published in the Chronicle of July 13 (number 325):

> '. . . You say that our finances are low, and our paper money not cur-rent; that the troops are discontented, and in some parts almost famishing; you likewise tell us of innumerable desertions, and that the disaffected are many. All these, Mr. Washington, may be true, and it is what we are to expect. But Great Britain herself has dissatisfied men in her army, her navy, and her senate. We have convincing proofs every day of a kindling rebellion in the very heart of that proud empire . . . We know your abilities and have a strong confidence in them; you are loved and admired by the army; and even your enemies allow you merit. If you desert us it may do us essential mischief. The English con-sider you as our sheet anchor; and your resignation would indeed be a triumph to them. You must not therefore at this time think of it. The idea is very dangerous and if published would sow discontent through-out the army. Lucrative motives, we are certain, are no objects to you, or you might name your terms. The gratitude of America is, however, superior to the promises of Congress; and when the day of peace comes, her glorious General will not be forgot. As to the conquest of Charlestown, it is indeed an immense loss to us; but the victory of Britain in Carolina will be short lived. We have friends who are work-ing such a mine as will blow up their triumphal schemes. And if Provi-dence favour us, the news of the surrender will come to their ears a day too late for their rejoicing in London. I have already given you a hint that must raise your expectations – the explanation will surprise you.'

The 'friends who are working such a mine' were the French, whose fleet under Admiral de Grasse outmanoeuvred Rear-Admiral Graves, landed 4,000 troops to support the Franco-American army, and cut off Yorktown from Chesapeake Bay. Cornwallis's army was locked in, the blockade was complete; no reinforcements had come from Sir Henry Clinton in New York, and on October 19 the British surrendered. The news reached London on November 25. The Chronicle published Cornwallis's despatch in two columns of small type on December 21 (number 348). In bland and inconsequential terms Cornwallis accounted for the irretrievable loss of America. No explanation of why he had waited in Yorktown for two months, allowing Washington to recover his spirits and his wits and to com-bine with the sea strategy of the French admiral. No explanation of why Clinton lingered in New York until it was too late. Admiral Rodney, who fully intended to bring the victorious de Grasse to battle, must have read that despatch with impatience and perhaps contempt. The land war was finished and the United States of America owed no more allegiance to his Britannic Majesty.

When we shared the thoughts of John Poole as he sat at his desk in the Chester Chronicle office on the eve of 1782, in the opening paragraph of this chapter, the knowledge of these and other events was in his mind, and he was concerned not only for the future of the paper. Three months later he recalled his New Year resolution and on March 22 (number 361) reprinted in full, Lord Chatham's speech in the House warning the ministry and the country of the consequences of the American adventure. The surrender of Yorktown – stigmatised as 'humiliating, degrading, and distracting to those who remember the glory of former days' – at last brought about the fall of the King's Friends after the House had voted by a majority only of one to continue the war. 'His Majesty's Ministers are no more', said Lord North in the Commons on Wednesday, March 20, and the Marquis of Rockingham took office, with the Earl of Shelburne, Fox and Burke in the new ministry. It was at best a caretaker construction. The future was gloomy and unpredictable. Then, out of the immensity of the oceans, tremendous news came flying. Admiral Rodney had engaged and broken the French fleet in the West Indies and captured the commander, the same Count de Grasse who had cut off Cornwallis's army at Yorktown.

The Chronicle of May 24 (number 370) was a total war edition, all victory, with Rodney's despatches and a copious account of the Battle of the Saints, derived from many sources, including the enemy. When Rodney returned home he got a hero's welcome. 'The battle,' he said in his despatch, 'lasted with unremitting fury from seven in the morning of April 12 till half-past six in the evening, when the setting sun put an end to the contest . . . The enemy's whole army, consisting of 5,500 men, was on board their ships of war. The destruction among them must be prodigious, as for the greatest part of the action every gun told.' The action off Cape St. Vincent had been something to write about, but that was merely a preliminary to the stunning affair of the Battle of the Saints, which was probably the first great naval engagement to be reported so fully in the public prints. It provided the only occasion, so far as I can determine, that the Chester Chronicle devoted an entire edition – true, only four pages – to one subject. Not even Trafalgar some years hence got such good treatment.

The Chronicle gave an account of how Chester celebrated the victory, but that story is best told by the paper's third Editor, Joseph Hemingway, in his 'History'. At this time the old Bridge Gate had not long been taken down (in 1781), in the Mayoralty of Joseph Snow. It was, says Hemingway, an arched gateway, flanked with two strong round towers, on one of which was erected a lofty octagonal tower – which served as a cistern for supplying the city with water – called Tyrer's Waterworks. At the south or Handbridge end of the Dee Bridge stood a gatehouse with an arch in the centre. Construction of the new Bridge Gate was begun in May, 1782, in the Mayoralty of Pattison Ellames and finished in December, in the Mayoralty of Thomas Pattison. (I list these Mayors because, as events happened, their names became fortuitously linked with that of the heroic Admiral.) Mayor Ellames laid the first stone on May 21, with a brass plate sunk into it, inscribed, 'At this time France, Spain, and the States of Holland leagued with the British American colonies (now in open and ungrateful rebellion) are endeavouring the destruction of the empire of Britain, her freedom, her religion, her land, and her honour, in support of which blessings her armies and navies are bravely contending in every quarter of the globe. May the God of Armies go forth with them'. Who composed this florid, lapidary stuff? It must have been the Town Clerk or Clerk of the Pentice, one Thomas Brock at this time. 'At this precise moment,' continues Hemingway, 'the gratifying news arrived in Chester of the signal victory of Admiral Rodney in the West Indies over the French fleet, when the record of that memorable event was indorsed on the back of the same plate, in the following terms 'The great and joyful news was announced this day of the British fleet, under the command of Admirals Rodney, Hood, and Drake, having defeated the French fleet in the West Indies, taking the French Admiral de Grasse and five ships of the line, and sunk one. The battle continued close and bloody for eleven hours.' So the Bridge Gate stands today as Chester's memorial of the Battle of the Saints.

The paper of February 7, 1783, contained four columns of provisional treaties signed on January 20, and in September the peace treaty signed at Versailles established the Independence of the United States of America. The final touch was reserved for January 4, 1784, when the U.S. Congress at Annapolis ratified the definitive articles of peace and friendship between the United States and his Britannic Majesty. The number of the Chronicle in which this appeared was 462, and the first war report was in issue number one. But it was more by good luck than good management that the paper survived to finish off the story, as you will see in the next chapter.

3

The paper's dead,
long live the paper!

The time is early in the morning of Friday, August 8, 1783. John Poole, printer, stationer, bookseller, and up to this moment newspaper proprietor, sits in the same office where we first found him about the same hour on Tuesday, May 2, 1775. But this time his thoughts are very different. The difficulties that were beginning to beset him on the eve of 1782 are now insurmountable. He has failed. The Chester Chronicle is nearly bankrupt and the last edition – number 431 – is waiting on the press. Soon the 'meridian of the city' (remember his words) will read the paper's obituary notice in its own columns. It will be read aloud by incredulous citizens in the White Lion and other places of resort, and the post-coach will carry the news to London and Holyhead and to all Cheshire and the neighbouring counties. The war paper has not survived the war, people will say. And there will be rejoicing in the office of the Courant. Monk and Cowdroy will make the most of it, of course. Sad and defeated as he is, John Poole is powerfully mortified by the thought of the approaching triumph of the Courant. It is a bitter business, all the more so because he knows that he has not failed as a journalist or as a printing craftsman but as a commercial manager short of capital and deserted at the finish by the associates whose money he has lost and whose meddlesome advice has deteriorated at length into an intolerable interference. (The paper, said a later writer, recalling this time, was debilitated by 'the prescriptions of too many doctors'.) After much agonised thought and re-writing Poole has completed his last Address, the proof of which lies before him on the desk. It says:

Chester, Friday, August 8.

To the PUBLIC
The Editor of this Paper begs leave
to inform them, that finding the
printing of it to be a losing concern,
on several counts, he is determined to
discontinue the publication of it from

this day. He esteems himself much
obliged for the kind indulgence and
favours shown to him by the Public and
shall ever retain a grateful sense
of the obligation.

All persons who have any demands
on this Printing-Office are
requested to send in their accounts
in order that they may be immediately
discharged; and those who stand
indebted to it, in any sums of money,
are desired to pay the same to Mr.
Charles Hamilton, Attorney at Law
in Chester, who is authorised to
settle all accounts.

So that's the end of it. At least the record of all the good, honest,
hopeful work is there – the files have been dutifully kept – and all
accounts will be honourably settled. He hopes to keep some of his
loyal printers and compositors and what remains of his former business. Now there is nothing more to do but go to press and go home.

Virtually, but not quite, from that time John Poole drops out of the
story of the paper which he founded, bravely continued for some
eight embattled years, and so nearly foundered. Across the great
divide of two hundred years he is a shadowy figure, and yet I have a
clear impression of his character: resolute, conscientious, public-
spirited, persevering in a period of many troubles, politically astute,
but journalistically something of a drudge compared with his readier
rivals. He did not successfully achieve the 'local touch', but the
Chronicle's wider reporting of the American War of Independence,
whatever the source of the information, was substantial and consistent. The colonies, we are led to conclude, were needlessly thrown
away by political ineptitude and military incompetence – and that,
whatever the Americans may think, is the verdict of history. What influence the 'London correspondent' had on the way the news was
compiled and presented we cannot know, nor even if he actually
existed, but I suspect that Poole, like other provincial newsmen of the
day, was under a weightier obligation to the famous Morning
Chronicle, which, edited by William Woodfall, was among the first
and most influential of the London papers (it survived until 1862 and
was the principal rival of The Times in the nineteenth century). In
choosing 'materials proper for a weekly news' (as he himself said), it

is possible that Poole was not much more than a diligent scavenger of the public prints that came down to him by the postboy. But if this was so – and it was not entirely so, for I think he had many sources of information – he contrived to maintain an independent and individual line that has been the editorial attitude ever since, and for that he deserves to be remembered by his successors.

At this moment, however, he had no expectation of any successors. Going home in the small hours of that Black Friday he resolved to keep within doors while the city talked about the death of his paper. But later in the day he had a shock. One John Fletcher, a young man in his late twenties, brisk and business-like, called upon him. Without preamble he said he was prepared to continue the Chronicle without break of publication. After reading the announcement that morning he had lost no time in consulting and coming to an arrangement with his (Poole's) former associates, and he now sought Poole's agreement also for the acquisition of the entire going concern of the New General Printing Office. Time was pressing. An immediate decision was necessary because he (Fletcher) intended to put an advertisement in next Tuesday's Courant – if they would accept it – to say that the Chronicle would be published as usual on the Friday. In this way the 'triumph' of the Courant would be forestalled. Mr. Hamilton, the attorney, was ready to make the transfer. If Poole really wished the Chronicle to continue, this was the only way, and Fletcher ended by saying that he would move in forthwith as proprietor and editor, and prepare the next edition with the printers. Poole, deeply astonished and at the same time relieved, agreed to everything – he wasn't given any time to think about it. Over at the office of the Courant elation was killed stone dead by the receipt of Fletcher's advertisement. He paid four shillings for it over the counter and quickly departed before Mr. Monk had a chance to decline it. And this Mr. Monk could not very well do, unless the thing was a hoax. But he had heard of Fletcher and surmised that this piece of audacity was in character. There was nothing for it but to print the advertisement and carry on the battle with the Chronicle under its new management. Things were moving fast in the local newspaper world. But what, after all, did this fellow Fletcher – a schoolmaster of some sort, wasn't he? – know about printing and publishing? The Chronicle, edition number 432, was cried in the streets on Friday as usual and eagerly bought up. John Poole paid his twopence halfpenny with the rest of his old readers and was delighted to see his personal imprint still there, even if it was for the last time. The paper explained its swift reprieve, or internal revolution, in this way:

Chester, Friday, August 15.

To the PUBLIC

John Fletcher having purchased of the late
Proprietors of this Paper the Stock of
their office, will, in compliance with the
requests of his Friends, continue to publish
and circulate it as heretofore, and execute
any orders in the Printing or Copper-plate
branches in the most correct, neat, and
expeditious manner, and on terms to merit
the continuance of the favours of the
generous Public. The heavy imposts on
Advertisements, Stamps, and Paper will, he
hopes, be a sufficient plea for requesting
payment for Advertisements at the time of
insertion; and to obviate the great
inconvenience attending the collecting of
payment for papers sent into the country,
desires that it may be made quarterly in
Chester; or to such Receivers as he shall
appoint in the different districts – and
in order to render this publication of
general information, utility, and
entertainment, a portion will be allotted
for the literary compositions and
information of the learned and ingenious,
whose favours will be gratefully
acknowledged, and every opportunity
embraced to certify his due sense of the
obligations conferred on their obedient
servant,

JOHN FLETCHER

From the start Fletcher meant to cut expenses and incur no bad debts for advertisements; it was to be strictly cash across the counter, like his own adroit transaction with the Courant. The contributions of 'the learned and ingenious' would help to fill up the paper at no cost, and for years thereafter they shared the back page with the Parliamentary debates and extracts from literary memoirs. Of a scientific turn of mind himself, Fletcher encouraged all kinds of enthusiasts, inventors and projectors – inspired by Mr. Watt and Mr. Arkwright and the pioneering engineers of turnpike roads and

canals – and a good many cranks and crack-brained savants as well
as original thinkers, not to mention some very minor poets, got into
print in the Chronicle. One of the first things Fletcher did was to buy
a new account book from Poole at a cost of two shillings. It is open
before me as I write, and the first entry is for the first week of publication under the new management, August 15, 1783. It is from the
account book, neatly inscribed by a scrivener in flowing copper-
plate, and not from the paper itself, that we get the inside story of the
discomfiture of the Courant and the delight of the Chronicle people
that their jobs were secure and the paper was going on. Although an
account book is not the place for a touch of human insight, the circumstances were sufficiently unusual, and here it is, alongside a
column of sober figures: 'This being Our first Publication we were
necessitated to advertise the Continuation (which the former Proprietors had declin'd) in Mr. Monk's Paper, encourage the Dis-
tributors by a Treat of Ale and send to Liverpool for Stamps for the
Publication; which together increased our weekly Expenses. Mr.
Monk was so much elated with the prospect of its Discontinuation
that this Day was intended for a Festival to his Men, in Triumph of
his Victory, which was render'd a Day of Gloominess and Dejection
by the Republication.' On the other side of the ledger we learn that
'the treat in ale' cost three shillings, a skin of vellum thirteen shillings, printing 775 copies of the paper £5. 18s. 9d., newspaper tax and
duty on fourteen advertisements £1. 15s., rent of premises 5s. 8d., and
sending papers to Lancashire by coach 2s. 2d. The four shillings paid
for the advertisement 'in Mr. Monk's paper' is there also, and it was
this item, the celebratory drink, and the stamps from Liverpool that
'increased our weekly expenses' to some £9. 3s. 7d. On the revenue
side the sale of papers brought in £7. 0s. ½d. and advertisements and
printing orders £5. 7s. 5½d. a total of £12. 7s. 6d. Such were the modest
economics of newspaper production in the late eighteenth century.
(You had to be a more enterprising manager than John Poole had
been to make a profit at all.) The names of carriers and agents in
Cheshire, Lancashire and North Wales are preserved in the ledger,
and week after week there is a regular entry under servants' wages of
7s. 6d. paid to 'Peter', no doubt one of the first of a long line of copy
boys.

The cumbrous 'Commercial Intelligencer' presently disappeared
from the masthead, to be replaced by 'General Advertiser'. Issue
number 433 (August 22) was the first of John Fletcher's own imprint.

CHESTER:

To be Let, and entered upon at Midsummer next,

A Handsome fashed HOUSE in Nicholas-street (now in the holding of Mr. Thomas Hitchcock); with a brew-house, coal-house, a large garden at the back of it, and a road into Weaver's-lane, with room for building a stable, coach-house, ware-house, or other necessaries, if required.

For further particulars, inquire of Mr. Spurstow, in Eastgate-street.

Above Property advertisement in the Number One Chronicle. *Right* Famous words first printed: the American Declaration of Independence occupied over a column and a half in the Chester Chronicle of August 23, 1776. *Below* In this corner of the Hop-pole Paddock, now a car-park, it is conjectured that the first Chronicle office stood, in the shadow of the City Wall and the Cathedral.

MONDAY NIGHT'S POST.

ADVICES *from* AMERICA.

In CONGRESS, *July* 4, 1776.

A DECLARATION *by the* REPRESENTATIVES *of the* UNITED STATES *of* AMERICA, *in* GENERAL CONGRESS *assembled.*

WHEN in the course of human events it becomes necessary for one people to dissolve the political bands which have connected them with another, and to assume among the powers of the earth the separate and equal station to which the laws of nature and of nature's God entitle them, a decent respect to the opinions of mankind requires that they should declare the causes which impel them to the separation.

We hold these truths to be self-evident; that all men are created equal; that they are endowed by their Creator with certain unalienable rights; that among these are life, liberty, and the pursuit of happiness. That to secure these rights, governments are instituted among men, deriving their just powers from the consent of the governed; and whenever any form of government becomes destructive of these ends, it is the right of the people to alter or to abolish it, and to institute new government, laying its foundation on such principles, and organizing its powers in such form, as to them shall seem most  likely to affect their safety and happiness. Prudence indeed will dictate that governments long established should not be changed for light and transient causes; and accordingly all experience hath shewn, that mankind are more disposed to suffer, while evils are sufferable, than to right themselves by abolishing the forms to which they are accustomed; but when a long train of abuses and usurpations, pursuing invariably the same object, evinces a design to reduce them under absolute despotism, it is their right, it is their duty, to throw off such government, and to provide new guards for their future security. Such has been the patient sufferance of these colonies, and such is now the necessity which constrains them to alter their former systems of government. The history of the present King of Great Britain, is a history of repeated injuries and usurpations; all having in direct object the establishment of an absolute tyranny over these states. To prove this, let facts be submitted to a candid world.

He has refused his assent to laws, the most wholesome and necessary for the public good.

He has forbidden his governors to pass laws of immediate

THE CHESTER CHRONICLE;

OR, COMMERCIAL INTELLIGENCER.

I.   TUESDAY, May 2, 1775.   No. 1.

To the PUBLIC.

IT is univerſally allowed, that the freedom of the preſs is the ſtrongeſt bulwark to the liberty of every ſtate, wherein the ſubject hath any ſhare in the legiſlature.—This truth of this remark might, if queſtioned, be illuſtrated, and proved, by many inſuperable arguments;—the moſt obvious of which is the great utility, evidently, reſulting from the publication of News-papers in the free country;—"a land" to uſe the words of a living Oracle of the Law)—" perhaps the only one "in the univerſe, in which political, or "civil, liberty is the very end and ſcope "of the conſtitution.—Experience, indeed, hath taught us, that this, as well as other human inſtitutions, is ſometimes, through inattention, improper influence, or other ſecret motive, rendered leſs uſeful than it might be.—Or (which is ſtill more reprehenſible) partially perverted to the bad purpoſe of perſonal invective.

LONDON, April 25.

THURSDAY NIGHT's POST.

From the LONDON GAZETTE.

Madrid (Spain), April 2.

COUNTRY NEWS.

CHESTER CANAL NAVIGATION.

BRICKLAYERS.

For the Benefit of the Creditors.

Above The old (and infamous) Northgate Gaol, common gaol of the city from mediaeval times. *Right* Bridge Street Row East in the early 19th century, with a wrongly spelt sign indicating the Chronicle office, removed to Fletcher's buildings, the present site, about 1827, some time after the fire in the Hop-pole yard which damaged the first printing office.

Right John Fletcher (1756–1835), who rescued the Chester Chronicle from a shaky start and set it firmly on the way to its double century. *Below left* Section of the restored Nine Houses, in one of which lived William Cowdroy for a time. *Below right* Romney's sketch of the 17th-century house in White Friars; it is still there, not much altered.

'Here's a saucy thing.' must have been the pleasantly titillated reaction of some readers, for on the front page there was a long, bawdy anecdote, source unacknowledged, about Charles the Second, beginning, 'This monarch was violently addicted to women, and only valued them for sensual pleasures, which appeared more openly in his public commerce with the mistresses he admitted to court and privately in the nocturnal debauches his Majesty entered into, in company with some of his courtiers, in the extravagant pursuits of illicit pleasures amongst the common prostitutes of the town. . . .' Old stuff, to be sure, but vastly entertaining. Evidently there was to be a fresh liveliness in the Chronicle, something nearer to the taste of the time. So it proved, but this anecdote of the Merry Monarch was merely adventitious, inserted to catch attention or perhaps for no other reason than to fill up the paper in a disorganised week. Fletcher was soon to demonstrate his understanding of how to run a newspaper successfully in far more significant ways. He had political instincts, zeal for the public service, a practical mind and aptitudes, and a constant engagement with what was going on. He was above all a man of his time, of the Industrial Revolution, in which he was caught up not only as a journalist but as a speculator, self-taught engineer, and works contractor. He had a many-sided life outside the office, and for fifty years he kept his paper and his four successive editors well informed of the news that he was often himself helping to make: civic affairs, road building, canal construction and the masterly projects of his friend, the great Thomas Telford.

A self-made man . . . the architect of his own fortune . . . rose, by the force of his genius and talent alone, to considerable eminence among scientific men . . . the history of his life is curious and instructive. In such words those who knew or remembered him described John Fletcher at the end of his long life. Uniformly the emphasis is on his self-taught native capacity. He had, so far as we know, no apprenticeship to the craft of printing. Yet he became a master printer and publisher. Without any previous experience he ventured upon the publication of a newspaper. Printers, it must be remembered, were (at least in the provinces) usually the first journalists, writing and setting up their own copy. When Fletcher appeared suddenly in the Chronicle office there was something illogical, even mysterious, about it. He was an outsider, neither printer nor scribe. From Halton in Cheshire, where he was born in 1756, the eldest child of Thomas Fletcher, a husbandman (or agricultural labourer), he came to

Chester in 1782 or earlier and lived in Parson's-lane (Princess-street afterwards and so known today) as a schoolmaster. Whether he conducted a school there or had a job in some other school or 'academy' is not known. His own education could only have been got at the village school in Halton.

It was, then, improbably enough, the schoolmaster who was designed to become, almost over night, the proprietor and rescuer of the Chester Chronicle. The thing required courage, nerve and extraordinary self-confidence – and some money. Where the money came from was not publicly acknowledged until much later, and then only inferentially. Like Poole before him, Fletcher had his friends and backers, but he never allowed them to influence his conduct of the paper. Fletcher from the start was his own man, and he made his own fortune (leaving an estate of £20,000 at his death) and sustained the Chronicle into a 'healthful maturity', as the most notable of his editors, Joseph Hemingway, wrote later on. But before he established himself, and when, like Poole, he was acting as his own editor, he found himself in gaol for libel. This experience, to be related in the next chapter, taught Fletcher something about himself and also that there was more in the conduct of a newspaper than sound business management, although without that, to be sure, there would be nothing to conduct. Thereafter, sadder and wiser and perhaps just a little frightened, he appointed editors to look after the paper's contents in news and opinion and to do the writing so much better than he could do it himself.

In Fletcher's time the first-generation printers who went into newspaper production gave way to a second generation of editors who, while still allied to printing as a trade, were journalists in their own right. Such were William Cowdroy (from 1784 or 1795), who has already appeared in these pages, James Hickson Hanshall (from 1809), Joseph Hemingway (from 1824), and John David Barry (from 1830). Each in turn edited the Chronicle in Fletcher's lifetime. Cowdroy he called in from the Courant in time to 'oversee' the paper while he himself was in prison, and his last appointment, that of J. D. Barry, he made forty-six years later. All four were men of literary talent and two were well-read scholars and historians who enhanced the prestige and authority of the paper and made Fletcher's name as a publisher. It was Cowdroy who started the Chronicle's remarkable corpus of editorial writing about Chester and Cheshire in which history is illuminated by contemporary description, personal observation, social, economic, and political study, and character sketching of the more distinguished or eccentric citizens – all undertaken at the same time as the exacting conduct of the paper itself. *The Directory and Guide for the County and City of Chester* by William Cowdroy, was published by Fletcher in 1789 from Poole's old printing shop in the Hop-pole Inn yard. In it are many felicitous touches, descriptive of the city as it was then, and the street names and details of trades and occupations are valuable source material. Hanshall took up the story from Cowdroy in 1816, when from the Chronicle printing office in the yard of the Hop-pole Inn was issued *The Stranger in Chester,* a duodecimo volume intended for the pocket of the traveller but packed full of interest to the citizens. It offered 'an accurate sketch of local history' and a chronology of notable events drawn from the records of the Corporation and elsewhere. There is a folding frontispiece woodcut of the frowning north side of the Northgate Gaol, then not long taken down (see the chapter headed On Gallows Hill and Tyburn Tree), and a sketch of Telford's Pontcysyllte Aqueduct recently erected across the romantic Vale of Llangollen.

'This little literary bantling' Hanshall called his book. It is a concise historical guidebook which set the pattern for many successors but is matched by few either in elegance of writing or as a picture of their time and place. The changes that occurred in the city in Hanshall's own experience are instructively noted. One of the few extant copies is in my possession and it was Fletcher's own, durably bound and with blank interleaves for notes. Most of these leaves are filled up with a diary kept by a traveller from Liverpool to North Wales, who called upon Fletcher at his house in Parkgate-road. The house is there today, its exterior little altered, standing upon a rock and surmounted by the glass cupola used by Fletcher as a conservatory. Hospitably received, the visitor bought Hanshall's little book from his host and afterwards inscribed in it, in a scholar's neat, clear, economical hand, a traveller's tale which hands down to us – from a fortuitously original source – an intimate study of the Chester Chronicle's great man at his own fireside and afterwards escorting his friend of a few hours on a tour of the city, parting at the inn door at one o'clock in the morning. Here it is, this delightful domestic sketch of a chance encounter more than a century and a half ago:

'Hearing of this publication, and our stay being so short, we wished to obtain it, that we might if time would permit see any particular objects which we were yet unacquainted with. We went to a Mr. Fletcher, the printer of this book, who we were informed lived at the end of the street leading to Neston. We went to the place we were recommended to, expecting to find a dwelling house and shop where the printing business was carried on. We were, however, agreeably surprised on ascending several steps cut out of the solid rock to find ourselves in a most beautiful garden well stocked with flowers and with a profusion of hollyhocks of all colours which gave it a very Chinese and yet handsome appearance. From the side of his house projected a hot house, and as you entered in on your right and left were greenhouse plants neatly arranged one above another, and vines filled with grapes surmounted the whole. On entering the house, a very handsome carpet covered the floor, and the room filled with good furniture added to a most extensive library of books, induced me to apologise for my intrusion, naturally conceiving our director had made a mistake. But finding that he really was Mr. Fletcher, the printer of this book, I told him that I hoped our returning at seven o'clock in the morning which we intended would apologise for our troubling him on the Sabbath Day. He informed me that he was not a seller of the work, but only the printer, but he thought he had one which he had got bound for himself, with blank leaves for remarks; and after some trouble he found it amongst his books and kindly let us have it on my paying him a little addition for the binding and paper.

'After a further conversation, he very politely invited me to sit down and take some wine with him. I refused this kind invitation, but expressed a wish to walk round his garden where I had a friend waiting for me. He immediately met my wishes and his lady accompanied us, to whose management its beauties were owing. A pump close to the garden wall 26 yards deep cut out of the rock was very convenient both for it and the house. He made us a present of some garden seeds and showed us his little workshop adjoining in which he made most of his instruments of measuring land, etc. We informed him what we had seen, and he promised if we would favour him with our company he would show us the remainder of the city. We complied with his polite and pressing invitation. We were then shown into a front room in which there was a bay window, from whence you had a delightful view of several of the mountains of Wales, especially one in Denbighshire on which they had erected a round building to perpetuate the Jubilee year of the reign of his present Majesty. Nearer lay the sea coast of Wales, Flint Castle, Parkgate shore, Neston, and, under the window, the canal and richly cultivated fields, where formerly the River Dee ran. The house is built in the form of a summer house and on the top is a cupola of glass from whence there must be a still more extensive prospect. During our tea we found Mr. Fletcher to be a most intelligent and scientific man. He had cut the present line of canal, he had laid out the racecourse, and built the grand stand, and had undertook most of the public works, and made the new road from Wrexham to Llangollen and so on to Ruthin. He had also the making of the embankment to the magnificent aqueduct over the River Dee which he strongly recommended us to see. After accompanying us through the remainder of the city, and it had got quite dark, we all adjourned to the inn and the clock had struck one before we separated, enjoying very rational and instructive conversation; and I shall always feel delight in reflecting on the few happy hours I spent in this stranger's company, and they add a greater zest when contrasted with the conduct of a certain gentlemen at Holywell to whom I introduced myself. . . .'

The inn where, circulating the social glass and deep in rational and instructive talk, the friends heard the chimes at midnight was the White Lion in Northgate-street, only a short walk from Fletcher's house. Here the traveller and his companion had been set down by the coach that Sunday morning about the time of matins at the Cathedral, to which they immediately went and heard the Dean preach to 'a very respectable congregation', assembled for a service of ordination conducted by the Bishop. 'After dinner,' says the diarist talking to himself (and us) in the leaves of Hanshall's book, 'we perambulated the town and walked round the City Walls. During our walk we overtook a very intelligent and communicative old gentleman. He pointed out to us the very many changes in the appearance of the city which had taken place in his time. He informed us that he had recollected salmon at one penny per pound, and formerly it was provided by a clause in the poor apprentices' indentures that their masters must not give them salmon above two days in the week, so little then was this excellent fish esteemed. We need not fear that any poor apprentice will be surfeited with it now. The covenant is now obsolete, for at present salmon is as dear at Chester as at any other town near the sea.' Though a rare old town, Chester seemed to the travellers 'very gloomy and heavy'. Many of the newer buildings were very good but because of the narrowness of the streets they could not be seen to advantage. Be that as it may, they continued their journey the richer for the hospitality, company and conversation of John Fletcher. And it is from these notes, written up in the coach and in the inn at night, that we first learn of the scope of Fletcher's activities outside the newspaper office. What title Fletcher had to call himself engineer and man of science we shall presently see. Curious and instructive as the history of his life was afterwards said to be, he left no personal record of it, although he printed the literary works of his editors and by that means ensured that their names would live longer than his own.

The next production of the Chronicle press also came from the pen of James Hanshall. This is the copious *History of the County Palatine of Chester*, published in 1823. If it falls short of expectation, says Hanshall, subscribers will perhaps recollect 'that it has been arranged and written during the Author's indispensable attention to the various laborious but important duties connected with the editorial management of a popular Provincial Newspaper.' (To that in my turn I give a personal silent assent.) It is a big book of over 600 pages set in double column, with many woodcuts, plates, vignettes, and plans. As a work of history and scholarship, it is overshadowed by George Ormerod's monumental volumes, published in 1819, and by the Cheshire volume in the *Lysons' Magna Britannia*, published in 1810, but Hanshall is more readable today. As the narrative draws nearer to his own time – and everything is brought up to date to the year of publication – the interest quickens with vivid scenes of mob clamour and industrial unrest drawn from the contemporary reporting of the Chester Chronicle, from which it appears that the paper in the early nineteenth century was less liberal in its attitude to the condition of the common people than it had been in the last quarter of the eighteenth. Hanshall was, I am sure, a man of feeling and sensibility, but all the same, as a patrician Chester editor of his time, he had little sympathy with those who took to the streets in defiance of authority – the Luddites and the cotton spinners of East Cheshire working in the 'satanic mills' of the Industrial Revolution. The idea of a human revolution evoked only one response in the county capital: it must be put down. William Cobbett (of the *Rural Rides* and a fellow journalist of some reforming power) is vilified by Hanshall as a 'notorious renegade' whose presses deluged Cheshire with seditious and blasphemous pamphlets, inciting to mob violence and the 'desperate attempts of deluded and wicked men'. Chester's duty – let nobody forget it – in times of insurrection and rebellion was to send troops to quell the rioters and carry off the ringleaders to the Castle Gaol.

Fletcher would endorse the views of his editor. By this time he had served as one of the two Sheriffs of the city and had been accepted into the city establishment, his own rebellion of 1784 against the

Corporation authority forgiven and forgotten. After the Civil War –
a long time ago – Chester was always happier celebrating than fighting, and Hanshall turns with relief from the dark troubles on the con-
fines of the county to the splendour of the city's loyal, expensive and
obsequious welcome, on August 15, 1814, to Lord Combermere (Sta-
pleton Cotton), Cheshire's own noble soldier and dashing cavalry
commander, and Lord Hill (Rowland Hill), triumphantly returned
from the Peninsular and French wars. The Mayor and Corporation,
in scarlet and blue gowns, turned out at the head of a procession of
trumpeters, guildsmen, societies Brotherly, True Blue, and Amica-
ble, the warriors in a crimson-lined coach adorned at the four corners with eagles of burnished gold, the London Royal Mail coach
drawn by six dark bay horses, the military, and the citizens. The
great bells of the Cathedral were clashed and fired. And afterwards
at the Royal Hotel the banqueting table groaned under the weight of
a costly feast, the centre-pieces of which were two fine fat bucks from
Eaton and Oulton, the gifts of Grosvenor and Egerton, and 'an
immense turtle'. That was the style: there was always the inclination
and the wherewithal for eating and drinking at election times and
every other possible occasion in the loyal city, and Hanshall tells us
about it with the help of his industrious scribes of the Chronicle.

Joseph Hemingway was editing the paper a few years later when
the city seized another opportunity for festivity, but this time a little
too late to make the very most of it. In December, 1829, it became
known from the Chronicle's country intelligence that the great Duke
of Wellington, still trailing clouds of glory after Waterloo, was in
Cheshire, the guest of Lord Combermere at Combermere Abbey for
the christening of Combermere's second son. The post-coach carried
a letter from the city to the Abbey:

Town-hall, Chester, December 21, 1820.

My Lord. – It is my pleasing duty, at the unanimous desire of a meeting of the inhabitants, convened for the purpose of testifying their respectful attachment to the person and character of the Duke of
Wellington, to solicit the honour of your company, and that of the
guests at Combermere Abbey, to a public dinner in this city on the 27th
instant, or such other day as may be convenient to your Lordship and
his Grace. May I presume to suggest that the latest day to which his
Grace's visit in Cheshire can be extended will be more preferable, as it
will afford the committee more time to invite those public characters
who will rejoice to do honour to his Grace and your Lordship.

I have the honour to be, my Lord,
Your Lordship's obedient humble servant,

WILLIAM SELLER, Mayor.

Accordingly, a splendid cavalcade of coaches lined up on the margin of the mere beside which the Abbey stands, and took to the country roads from Wrenbury village and thence to the Chester turnpike. It was Wednesday, December 27. From the paper's restrained report, in which nothing like the euphoria of the earlier occasion is evident, I have the impression that for once the Corporation had not done as much as it might have done to honour these brave comrades in arms. Could the reason have been political?

Here was the Duke himself, who had stopped the Corsican tyrant, with Combermere and Hill once more (although it was true Combermere had not led the cavalry at the final destruction of Bonaparte's army; he was lucky, for Uxbridge, who was preferred to him in the command, lost a leg in the action) within the city walls, attended by most – but not all – of the county's landed and political interest. But for want of time or other cause a signal mark of distinction had been neglected. Hemingway, recalling the event in his History, is scarcely more explicit than the paper. The Duke, he says:

'took up his quarters at the Albion Hotel, from whence he made a short excursion to the Castle, inspected that building, armoury, etc., and afterwards proceeded to the Exchange, where a most sumptuous banquet had been prepared. Colonel Barnston presided at the festive board, which was surrounded by about 150 guests, amongst whom were Lords Combermere, Hill and Kenyon, Sir W. W. Wynn, Sir James Lyon, Sir H. M. Mainwaring, Col. Thomas Cholmondeley, Major-General Beckwith, and others. During the evening, and indeed while he remained in Chester, his grace received every mark of respect that could be shewn to a character whose eminent services in the field of honour had entitled him to the gratitude of his country. It has been spoken of as a subject of regret that the usual compliment of presenting the Duke with the freedom of the city was omitted; but I am inclined to think that the omission arose solely from a mistake or misapprehension in some of those individuals whose business it was to attend to the necessary proceedings, and not to any intentional disrespect.'

The comment is characteristic of Hemingway's good sense but less complimentary to his candour. You will note that absent from the celebrations was Earl Grosvenor, a staunch Whig at this time and therefore the political foe of the Duke. This explains a good deal. But the fact remains that the city has never made 'a usual compliment' of bestowing its freedom. When Prince Charles, Prince of Wales and Earl of Chester, was so honoured in 1973 his name stood only thirty-sixth on the roll. At all events, the Iron Duke was suffered to decamp from the city without the freedom. Chester afterwards gave Comber-mere a statue. The Field Marshal sits for ever astride his cavalry charger outside the entrance to the Castle Square.

Hemingway, succeeding Hanshall in 1824, was the first editor to remove with the paper to the new Chronicle Office at Fletcher's Buildings in Bridge-street Row East, brought into use in 1827, and he was the last, of course, at the original printing office in the Hop-pole Inn yard. Here, he notes in his History, the Chester Chronicle was printed and published for half a century, within the same passage as 'Mrs Rutter's carrying warehouse'. The removal to a more commo-dious building became necessary, sooner or later, after the fire in the Hop-pole yard on January 27, 1809. The confined neighbourhood in which the paper had been born and carried to a 'healthful maturity' of some fifty years is vividly recreated for us in the Chronicle's own account of this fire:

> 'On Friday morning at six o'clock a most tremendous fire broke out in Mr. Kenworthy's warehouse in the Hop-pole Yard, close adjoining our printing-office, which threatened the immediate destruction of the whole range of building, but by the prompt and effectual assistance of the populace, and the arrival of the engines, which were well supplied with water and directed with great skill by Mr. Porter, it was fortu-nately stopped in its progress about 8 o'clock, after destroying the warehouses where it broke out, containing a great quantity of goods, Mr. Bather's shop above with all his materials (and we are sorry to add, neither were insured), two warehouses belonging to our office containing a valuable stock of paper and about 4,000 stamps (fortu-nately insured), two stables occupied by Mr. Williams, and the stable opposite to where the fire began, which were only insured for a small sum. Mr. Williams, the landlord of the Hop-pole, we are sorry to add, lost a considerable quantity of hay and straw, but we are happy to say that he is enabled to accommodate travellers as usual. Those who know the situation and construction of these premises deem it next a miracle that the progress of the devouring element was stopped. Our types and materials are thrown into great confusion by their hasty removal, but that will be speedily remedied.'

The editorship of Joseph Hemingway, though relatively short, brought the Chronicle into its modern period, when the paper said farewell to the eighteenth century and the small four-page edition which contrived, none the less, to print news from everywhere and give a fascinating picture of its time, as my later chapters will, I hope, show. After the French Revolution, Trafalgar and Waterloo, the character of the Press first established in the historic towns began to change, largely influenced by the diminution of the importance of such towns in the national life, by the foundation of daily newspapers in the large new provincial centres of trade, industry and population, and by the development of the London Press and its quicker delivery throughout the country with the coming of the railways. And so, as time went on, and national and provincial daily and evening papers gained in power and influence and wide circulation, the Chronicle concentrated more upon its region, Chester, Cheshire, Flintshire, and the other border counties, and developed along its own lines into the big family of papers that collectively form the Chester Chronicle and Associated Newspapers of today. But of that more later. We have not yet by any means done with John Fletcher, who made all this possible, and the third and greatest of his editors, Joseph Hemingway, who lives on in his *History of Chester*, a classic of its kind which also marks the beginning of the modern city co-existing with the old and completes the Chronicle editors' independent and sequential study of the past and their own times – a body of work of which few newspapers can show the like.

Hemingway began his *History* about 1829, while still occupying the editorial chair of the Chronicle (to which he had been 'translated' from the same seat at the Courant). It seems probable, however, that he brought it to completion after he had left the paper. Writing to an old friend from his house, 44 Nicholas-street, in November, 1831, he says, 'I have been chiefly engaged as Editor of one of the Chester papers, but about two years ago a rheumatic affection in my feet rendered so active an employment inconvenient, and since that time I have employed myself in writing and publishing a History of Chester which has answered my purpose as well as I expected'. (That rheumatic affection was the gout.) The work was first published in eight parts and in 1831 it was handsomely printed by Fletcher at the Chronicle Office in two volumes octavo. The copy that I have is the original, with etchings by George Cuitt. The name of Hemingway is synonymous with Chester, said Frank Simpson, F.S.A., in 1924: 'He was a man of considerable literary attainment. Had it not been for his work, much of the contents of his *History of Chester* would have been lost to us. It is undoubtedly the most popular history of the city up to the present time, is more reliable than the majority of those written today, and is the one most frequently quoted.' That judgment, by the most diligent collector of gleanings of old Chester in this century, holds true now: Hemingway is never likely to be superseded, only added to and, here and there, amended. His early research, though enlarged and sometimes controverted by later scholarship, is basically as conclusive as any study of the far past can ever be, and he does not deal in fables unless as good stories to be told. Like Hanshall before him, he makes use of the contemporary record of the paper, selecting his materials with even greater skill, and in his pages there is a living picture of Chester and its citizens in the 1820s, 1830s and earlier. 'Materials are abundant', he wrote in a letter, 'but if the present generation pass away, difficulties of an insuperable nature will interpose' – and so the personal observation, knowledge and curiosity of the journalist is transmuted into literary history which has stood the test of time. All subsequent writers on the same theme must go back to Hemingway and it is fortunate for posterity that he wrote at a time when the eighteenth-century city was undergoing its first modern 'redevelopment'. With him we walk the streets of the old town as they were beginning to change from fabulous antiquity into some semblance of the streets as they have since become. No other writer – and I cannot think of higher praise – until the great novelist Henry James set down his impression of Chester about 1869, has expressed so imaginatively and factually the idea of the weight and density of the past pervading the present as it does in human settlements of such long-ago foundation as this city.

Moreover, the old local journalist and the great writer looking at the same scenes some forty years later shared the same thought: they were at one in questioning the quality of life that was to be lived behind those grotesque, close and decaying façades, many of which lingered in Henry James's time. Hemingway, for all his feeling for the past, was not, as we should say today, a conservationist merely. He insisted on the acknowledgment of the necessity of change and improvement; people cannot live and work in conditions of decay, however picturesque. Look around, he says, and you will see irresistible proof of the mutability of all human affairs and fabrics. Of Eastgate-street, in the much-read 'Perambulation of the City' – not again attempted in such detail until 1971, when Dr. Nikolaus Pevsner published his examination of all the building stock as it stood at that moment – Hemingway writes: 'There are about half a dozen old houses on the north side of the street, forming the front of Pepper-alley, which overhang their base, and moreover project three or four yards further into the street than the shops and houses lower down. If the necessities or the parsimony of the owners of these premises, however, will not allow of their removal, it may be expected that ere long the all-destroying hand of Time will accomplish this desirable object. Below these, on this side, the houses and shops are pretty regular and well built; but on the south side, new-built dwellings are so intermixed with old ones as to give the street a motley and gro-tesque appearance.' And he instances the 'demi-palace' shop of Messrs. William and Henry Brown, lately built, adjoined in the street on one side by a small chandler's and on the other a butcher's shop, 'like a brace of country clowns'. He is neither romantic nor sen-timental about the unique Rows, where changes 'are daily taking place', in his day as in ours. 'Very considerable improvements have occurred within the last thirty years, for whenever ruin or decay ren-ders a re-erection necessary the spirit of the times . . . imposes a more modern and elegant form of construction.' Then, as now, there was some misgiving, and probably with good reason, about the style of commercial innovation in these famous old galleries. But, 'formerly in front of the Row was fixed a clumsy wooden railing, with immense pillars of oak supporting transverse beams upon which the houses, chiefly built of wood, rested, and which leaned forward over the street in a terrific attitude. These old erections, to the no small morti-fication of the admirers of antiquity, are fast decreasing in most parts of the city, though several of them yet remain, particularly in Water-gate-street.'

In Bridge-street he notes the 'awkward confinement of low close rooms yielding to the more healthful taste of modern building'. Paltry shops and dark gabled houses 'nodding over their base', he considers ripe for improvement because they are unfit to occupy and, besides, 'the density of buildings within the Walls, and especially in those parts considered eligibly situated for trade, almost precludes an increase of good retail shops; while our dwelling-houses and population are rapidly augmenting without the Walls and in the suburbs'. Judiciously he adds, however, that within some of these antique dens, fortunes have been made by tradesmen dedicated to

sober industry and perseverance – and the achievement of civic honours. Compare these observations on low, close rooms, nodding
gables leaning over the streets 'in terrific attitudes', and paltry shops
and work places where it is possible to make money but not to dwell
in any decency with this searching passage in Henry James: gables
'cruelly quaint, dreadfully expressive. Fix one of them with your
gaze, and it seems fairly to reek with mortality. Every stain and cre-
vice seems to syllable some human record – a record of lives airless
and unlighted . . . I am quite unable to think of them save as peopled
by the victims of dismal old-world pains and fears. Human life,
surely, packed away behind those impenetrable lattices of lead and
bottle-glass, just above which the black outer beam marks the suffo-
cating nearness of the ceiling, can have expanded into scant freedom
and bloomed into small sweetness.'

That was old Chester. Those were the interiors in which the candle-
light glimmered at night. Hemingway was all for letting light and air
into them and his commercial sense is right up to date, as in this note
which might have been written yesterday: 'The shops in the Rows
are generally considered the best situations for retail trade, but those
on the southern side of Eastgate-street and the eastern side of Bridge-
street have a decided preference. Shops let here are at very high
rents, and are in never-failing request. They are equal in elegance to
those of Manchester and Liverpool; and there is at least one in Eastgate Row, Messrs. Brown's, which . . . would not suffer by comparison with the magnificence of Regent-street.' How modern it all is,
and foreshadowing the future. To his biographical notices of notable
citizens, Hemingway adds a chapter on eccentric characters,
observed with an acuteness, humour and understanding which a
later generation would call Dickensian; and he brings the whole
massive 878-pages-long work to a close with a relation of the city's
turbulent political annals, civic and parliamentary – a masterly performance, scrupulously fair, in which the malice of party and the follies of the mob gratuitously inflamed by Whig and Tory booze, are
seen at work in the gerrymandering of a 'rotten borough'. And at this
point we must go back to John Fletcher, freshly in command of the
Chester Chronicle, and join him in the famous election campaign of
1784, then a year or so later in gaol, and still later reading the Riot
Act at the end of his first Mayoralty in the notorious election of 1826.

4

A thirsty election –
and then a libel

'We shall have no occasion to trouble you more,
Except for some money to pay off the score,
For we can't drink much longer excepting you pay –
We may drink the Black Cow dry, as Cheshire folk say . . .'

To Thomas Grosvenor, from his friends in Chester

It is the early evening of Thursday, April 8, 1784, and John Fletcher of the Chester Chronicle and John Monk of the Chester Courant (he has served the office of Sheriff in 1776–77) are among the company assembled at the house of the Mayor, Thomas Amery. All know why they are there; the Sheriffs (traditionally responsible for the peace of the city), other of the leading citizens, aldermen of the City Guilds, the newspaper men, the election contenders, the Hon. Thomas Grosvenor of Eaton and R. Wilbraham Bootle of Rode, in the Tory interest, and John Crewe of Bolesworth, the Independent, and their party managers. The Mayor has summoned a meeting after the riots in the streets that morning. Although it is difficult even for intelligent men to distinguish the difference between the candidates, Whig or Tory – for they are all professed loyalists – this is a contested election, bound to erupt sooner or later into factitious tumult. Earlier in the day rival mobs flaunting banners, armed with clubs and staves and flown with drink had clashed at the Exchange and the Coffee House in Northgate-street. Incensed by the NO BRIBERY flag hoisted by the supporters of Independency and Mr. Crewe, partisans of Thomas Grosvenor (hired for the purpose, it has been put about) had rushed to the attack. Disgraceful scenes followed. There had been a hand-to-hand battle at the Exchange, where the municipal windows and those of the tradesmen's shops and houses close by had been smashed and much mischief done. (The Grosvenor agent, Mr. Duke, was to note later that he had received a bill from a Mr. Williamson 'for surgery' after the affray and had refused to pay it.) The meeting, though genuinely concerned for the peace of the city, is charged with suppressed feeling, and the Mayor, as spokesman for the Corporation which is tied to the Grosvenor interest, chooses his words

48

carefully, avoiding all offence and imputing no blame. But. : . as they all knew, this was the first parliamentary contested election in Chester for many years, and at this crisis in the nation's affairs, after the late war with the Americans and the recent confusions and uncertainties at Westminster, it was incumbent upon the loyal city to give a responsible and sober judgment.

At this point the Mayor pauses; he cannot help but hear the raucous shouting and ranting of ribald songs in the street outside. He goes on . . . excess of party spirit . . . inconceivable that Mr. Grosvenor or Mr. Crewe could be privy to bribing or hiring mobs . . . appealed to both sides to impose restraint upon their followers and conjure them to keep the peace and order of the city . . . a repetition of that morning's incidents must be equally injurious to the interests of all parties and a danger to life and property. And so on. . . . There is a silence in the room, broken at last by protestations from both parties that the public peace had not been first broken by them – it was the other side that gave the offence. And all are thinking, what does the Mayor mean by a 'sober judgment', with so much free drink flowing? Whatever the distresses of the country, all know, not least the Mayor, Mr. Fletcher and Mr. Monk, that this is an old-fashioned Chester domestic contest between the house of Eaton and the Corporation on one side, the Rest on the other, and the not so 'free men' of the city in the middle. But the Mayor is right. By the standards of a long, embittered past of election warfare, this contest has been polled peacefully enough until now. A precarious and acrimonious truce is patched up over a glass of wine and the meeting breaks up. John Fletcher goes back reflectively to his office in the Hop-pole Inn yard. He has an article to write for the next morning's Chronicle, and he is in some confusion of mind.

This is the Chronicle's first election, the election long anticipated by the paper's founder, John Poole. At that time, eight years ago, Fletcher remembers from his study of the files, the equivocal reception the new paper had had from the Eaton family, entrenched in the city representation at Westminster, and the Corporation, accustomed to do the Grosvenors' bidding, whatever politics they espoused. Sure of the Courant, they anticipated opposition from the Chronicle when the time should come. The time has come, but in the unexampled political confusion brought about with great subtlety by the young William Pitt – who has won the confidence of the King even after opposing his Majesty's disastrous personal government in the conduct of the war – where does opposition lie? Who is Whig and who is Tory? At times Pitt has been one or the other, and so have Grosvenor and Bootle, the sitting Members for Chester. True, Charles Fox heads a Whig opposition in the present contest, but Fox outside his own constituency of Westminster is discredited for making a cynically opportunist alliance with Lord North after condemning with unbridled invective, in debate after debate in the House of Commons, the King's own Minister for the loss of the American colonies. Fox in the past has championed many liberal and independent causes, and for that he has the thanks of the Chronicle, but his late perfidy has forfeited all confidence, and Fletcher has been astonished to see Thomas Grosvenor presiding in February, and Wilbraham Bootle, his fellow Member for Chester, with him, at a meeting of a group of independent Members of the House in support of an alliance of Pitt and Fox. This the Chronicle has condemned out of hand as 'this odious, dreaded union', and Pitt himself will have nothing to do with it. Chester has endorsed the paper's opinions with its loyal petition to the King signed by 891 hands. Though returned by patronage and absence of opposition, rather than by suffrage of the citizens, to three successive parliaments, Grosvenor and Bootle have been good constituency Members, sometimes Whig, sometimes Tory in their openly expressed opinions, and now they are for Pitt, the only man who can impose some unity upon the nation and restore its self-respect. And so the Chronicle is for King and Constitution and Mr. Pitt, and that means for Grosvenor and Bootle.

But . . . here's the rub, reflects Fletcher, trying to see his way through the complexity of national policy at odds with local politics, Mr. Crewe is for the same principles and yet for Independency in the Chester election – he is the first candidate to come forward in many years to challenge the Eaton-Corporation oligarchy which by self-perpetuation has made the parliamentary and municipal representation its own as of right and denied the freedom of the city's 'freemen' to choose their own. And all because of the dubious legal interpretation of royal charters. That Crewe should have the hardihood to offer himself at all, thus precipitating a contest with its heavy expense in 'treating' and other political chicanery (and, as has been seen that morning, the destruction of the peace), has been received by the controlling junto as presumption and effrontery and injurious and ungrateful to Mr. Bootle, whose share of the vote for the second seat is principally imperilled. What can Mr. Pitt, who among other things seeks to reform the system of representation throughout the country, think about this situation in Chester? And how much longer can the house of Eaton and the Corporation by secret co-alition and election by 'select body' be suffered to control all power in the city without the consent of the citizens? A rotten borough, indeed, and a so-called freeman borough at that! That the Grosven-ors have performed many good works for the city is not in doubt. Unfailingly generous to the poor, of whom there are many, charit-able at all times, the house of Eaton opens its purse and exerts its in-fluence for civic service in better schooling, improved medicine and institutional care of the sick. These are great matters for which the city has reason to be grateful – there is much unrelieved suffering and indigence in other towns. But the price of Grosvenor patronage is the feudal allegiance of a subject citizenry and a self-electing biddable Corporation.

It is improbable, thinks John Fletcher, that Mr. Crewe can wrest a seat from the grip of the Grosvenors. Certainly he has been first in the field and there are many freemen who wish to be independently represented. But to unseat the Hon. Thomas, powerfully supported by his brother Richard, Baron Grosvenor in 1761 and now in this present year of 1784 to be Earl Grosvenor, will cost more than Crewe can afford. And to challenge Wilbraham Bootle, the other Member and Eaton nominee, is no light matter either. Crewe has not the political experience of either Member and the only recommendation he has is that he offers an alternative to truly 'free' men. The time is not yet come to free the city from its overlords, but here is a beginning and the Chronicle must encourage the Independents and at the same time acknowledge the good service of Grosvenor and Bootle in the House of Commons. Since the issue of the contest is not seriously in doubt, the time to conduct the argument for unshackled representa-tion will be *after* the poll. . . . . From all of this it might appear that John Fletcher had decided to abdicate or at least compromise his paper's liberal principles in this, its first election, by sitting on the fence. But there was a real dilemma for the new proprietor and edi-tor, and how he managed matters we shall see.

Chester had its first exciting whiff of a contest in the February 13 Chronicle when John Crewe addressed himself from Bolesworth

Castle 'to the worthy and independent freemen of Chester'. Totally unconnected with any party, he declared, he would in the event of a dissolution offer himself as 'your free and independent choice'. So the thousand or so registered freemen (the only people entitled to vote at parliamentary elections out of a population at this time of about 15,000) learned that the Grosvenors were to have a fight on their hands and soon the party canvassers would be rounding up those freemen, some 400 or so, as yet unregistered, and urging them to hurry and 'be made free'. As for the citizens at large, a contested election meant unlimited free drink day after day while the polling lasted. No contest, no booze – for making nonsense of that Mr. Crewe's health was drunk in many a town tavern that night by the 'friends' of both sides. Polling began on April 5 and continued until April 16. Crewe, first in the field, had, as he thought, made sure of many 'friends' before the sitting Members appeared in the city upon the dissolution. On March 26 his supporters followed up the advantage with a snap advertisement in the paper:

To the Worthy and Independent
Freemen of the City of
Chester

You will quickly see your Members
amongst you to canvass. – They
cannot come down ignorant that it
is the determined resolution of
the City to send up One Member by
the Free Choice of the People.
If they are hardy enough, therefore,
to resist this very reasonable
resolution,

REMEMBER!
that it is owing to them, not to
Mr. Crewe, who comes invited to
your service, that the peace of
the City is disturbed; and that
the contest is not whether Mr.
Crewe shall be elected – but
whether you are for ever to remain a
BOROUGH OF THE HOUSE OF GROSVENOR.

Civicus.

The city had a bad history of rioting at contested elections, parliamentary and municipal, with bought votes, non-resident freemen brought to the polls, thousands of pounds spent on drink, and some fatal injuries in the streets, and if there was trouble this time Mr. Crewe was making certain that it should not be laid at his door. And trouble clearly was expected. 'Every alehouse is a scene of contention,' said the Chronicle on April 2, 'and every voter's mind a harbour for outrage and violence, party spirit has risen to such a height.' But, with the exception of the mischief of April 8, the subject of the Mayoral meeting with which this chapter opened, the election of 1784 – so important for the country – staggered along in Chester in a fairly peaceable alcoholic haze. 'This contest,' wrote Hemingway in his *History*, some 47 years later, 'is computed to have cost £30,000, when wine, the *chief favourite* of cobblers, tinkers, and labourers during an election, was not more than half its present price; and one-third of this sum has been placed, by common rumour, to Mr. Crewe's account.' In other words, the Grosvenors were the principal paymasters in standing generous treats to freemen and non-freemen alike. Such entertainment was traditional and not looked upon as barefaced bribery: it was, simply, 'treating'. Some Grosvenor supporters downed the Grosvenor drink and gave their other vote to Crewe – and vice versa.

But even the Grosvenors' purse – continuously enriched by the development of their City of Westminster lands and properties – was stretched on this occasion, the landlords of the Chester inns claiming much in excess of the order from the Eaton agent, Mr. Duke, of 'a barrel and a gallon' in the canvass period. When the bills came in they amounted to £14,000. Mr. Duke, whose account book is in the Eaton archives, pruned away at false and extortionate claims which were at odds with the merchants' record of supplies to the innkeepers, and got the sum down to £8,500. Even so, his accounts show that he met bills for 1,187 barrels of ale, 3,756 gallons of spirits, 4,600 bottles of gin and 27,624 bottles of wine. What a grand, gratuitously slaked thirst! The Feathers Inn, the Exchange Coffee House, and the Red Lion had the biggest share, but Mr. Duke was not too strict in his inquiries here, for these houses were well known as popular resorts of the freemen and their friends. Even the keepers of the Northgate Gaol and the House of Correction had the nerve to tap the election largesse, sending in bills which were, of course, indignantly repudiated. 'The very idea of the City gaols being made use of as Drinking Houses is a gross absurdity' – so the righteously prudent Mr. Duke entered in his invaluable account book. The victuallers did, however, pay their shot in return: twenty-one of the twenty-three innkeepers and sixteen of the eighteen wine merchants voted for Grosvenor and Bootle, as the poll books subsequently showed.

To return to the hustings: when at last the Tory propagandists got to work, the first thing they did was to question the truth of Crewe's professed independence of all parties. He was known to have supported the Whigs, and, moreover, one of the Members for Cheshire, likewise named John Crewe, was the confidant of Charles James Fox himself. These John Crewes were not related, but that was no matter; here was enough circumstantial evidence to warrant fixing the opprobrious label of Foxite on the Chester challenger. But Crewe was not having any of that. In the Chronicle of April 2 he dissociated himself from any taint of disloyalty, reasserted that the family of Eaton could have no equitable claim to recommend both Members for Chester, and exhorted the freemen to seize this opportunity to emancipate themselves. 'I am, from principle, a supporter of the Just Prerogatives of the Crown and of the present Ministers, and NO FOXITE;' he declared. This took what political steam there was out of the campaign. All the Chester contenders were now clearly seen as having no political difference whatever: 'Although,' as Hemingway wrote later, 'Mr. Crewe was known to belong to the Whig party and his opponents to the Tory party, yet neither did he, nor they, affect to rest any claim upon their respective principles – the principal criterion by which the electors could be distinguished was by their adherence or hostility to the house of Eaton and the Corporation.'

This after-reading of the contest was openly stated at the time, in the same April 2 issue of the Chronicle, by an independent freeman signing himself Liber. 'The political principles or personal qualities of the late Members,' he wrote, 'are not the ground of the present opposition. As the freemen of this city are necessarily distinguished by the descriptions of those who are attached to or dependant upon the Grosvenor family and the Corporation and those who are not, the only question is whether the latter are of sufficient consequence to have a representative of their own, or whether they must acquiesce (however reluctantly) in the choice of the former.'

John Crewe made it plain that he had no quarrel with the sitting Members save that they were monopolising both seats in the same interest, Eaton and the Corporation; and his opponents, for their part, said no more against his principles or his loyalty but contented themselves by treating him as an interloper and by, as we have seen, copiously 'treating' the citizenry on their own account. Crewe's early canvass was so far successful that on the eighth day of polling, April 13, he had the same number of votes (397) as Bootle, Grosvenor's 'running mate', according to a list in the Eaton archives. On that day the Crewe party created a diversion. Roger Barnston, a member of their campaign committee, entered the contest on the Independent ticket ostensibly to draw off the second votes from Bootle and to diminish the Grosvenor lead – the Hon. Thomas had not faltered since the sixth day, when he had overhauled Crewe. The diversion was too late, and at the close of the poll on Friday, April 16, the result was declared at the Exchange

Grosvenor	713;
Bootle	626;
Crewe	480;
Barnston	38

on the votes of 1,104 freemen. (With such a limited franchise in a population of some 15,000 it could not be said that the parliamentary borough of Chester was a democracy, nor indeed could it be said of any other borough in the eighteenth century.) In the paper of April 23, Crewe sadly thanked his supporters. It was not in their power, he said, 'to prevent the effects which have arisen from the broken promises of pretended friends, and from the threats of a body of men, who (a few worthy individuals excepted) seem determined to maintain, by all means, that absolute control which they have too long usurp'd over their fellow citizens'. So John Crewe was disappointed in defeat. The election was over, the Eaton-Corporation sway was confirmed, and the citizens, happily seduced by wine and spirits over a heady fortnight, went back to buying their own beer.

Mr. Crewe's freedom principle had been sunk by the weight of patronage and, paradoxically, the best result had been achieved. Chester had been held for Mr. Pitt – which was the Chronicle's intention – and sufficient consideration had been given to the Independents, who, anyway, were for Mr. Pitt also. Now, the election having been safely decided, the moment had come to dredge the mud of local politics lying deep and thick below the surface of the contest. This exercise was carried on with much vigour and a mixture of rancour and enjoyment in the papers until May 28 and afterwards in the poll books customarily published by the papers. To what purpose? To give both sides the facility of scoring off each other in print, to expose secret plots, strategems, and coercions, and to prepare the way for the next time. And the next time, municipally, was only a few months off: the election of the Mayor and Corporation officers – by the secret decision of the internal 'select body' or by the free vote of the freemen representing the citizens at large? Was Chester to be stigmatised by the name of rotten borough? The Chronicle of April 23 published a trenchant polemic signed 'Honestus' in which the citizens were invited to consider their condition and whether they were in truth in any better position than the citizens of the rottenest of rotten boroughs. What was a rotten borough? 'Honestus' defined it as a place where, 'the right of election being unjustly and absurdly confined to a few persons, and those perhaps in low circumstances, they voluntarily and without shame offer the representation to any who will give the most money for it'. Then there were other boroughs in which 'it is in the power of any rich man, by the purchase of houses or contiguous estates, to dictate to them, and to pull down one and set up another at his pleasure'. Was not the situation of the citizens of Chester in some respects similar to these? 'You have heard much of late of coalitions. Behold here as palpable a coalition between the House of Eaton and the Corporation as ever was between North and Fox!'

Then with great candour and considerable literary skill 'Honestus' took the lid off the contest lately ended. In reading what follows you must keep it in the context of its time, before the reform of Parliamentary and municipal representation achieved in the next century; as such it is an example of fearless eighteenth-century journalism:

> The representation of this place in Parliament has excited the ambitious desires of a neighbouring family who some years ago were fortunate enough to overthrow the interest of their opponents and to fill the Corporation with creatures of their own. A connection being then formed between Eaton Hall and the Council Chamber, their possessors have ever since been using every possible means to secure each other's continuance in power. The former have strengthened the common cause by taking a lease of King's Lands which an unlucky accident threw in their way, and the latter have invariably endeavoured to exclude from their fraternity every man who was not faithfully devoted to the interest of their patrons, who now, thinking themselves secure of their object, have treated us with all the indifference and even contempt which such a confidence naturally inspires, seldom deigning to honour us with their presence and speaking of us in terms too degrading for any free-born mind to bear with patience.

The conduct of this hopeful junto, and that of their abettors, through the late contest between them and the friends of freedom, has been quite correspondent with the principles upon which it was formed. When you call to mind the various tricks that have been played and the scandalous partiality that has been discovered in the admission of free-men – the mean threats that have gone forth against tenants and shop-keepers – the unbounded promises by which they have allured the unwary, not to mention practices of a still more flagrant nature – their connivance at, if not encouragement of, a premeditated Riot in which not only the lives of many of their fellow citizens might have been lost but the property of all endangered; and particularly the shameless conduct of some who, tho' bound by oaths of office to strict im-partiality, openly sided with one party – I say, when you recollect such things, can you want any further proof that these are a set of men who will stick at nothing to gain a point, that their designs are arbitrary, tyrannical, in short, utterly subversive of the rights and privileges of freemen, and that it is our duty as Englishmen to oppose them?

They have been called upon to support by fair argument the pro-priety of their claims, and how have they answered us? With idle songs and illiberal ridicule, or by attempts to divert us from the real ground of the dispute by repeatedly enlarging on the merits and independence of Mr. Bootle, tho' they well know the opposition was not meant per-sonally against him, but against the Eaton interest. We are ready to give him all the praise his Parliamentary conduct deserves, nor have we any other objection to him as a representative but his voluntarily plac-ing himself in a situation which necessarily casts a shade on his charac-ter as an independent man. He himself has publicly avowed, on a former occasion, that he was introduced by the interest of his col-league, and no man of common sense will believe that he has forsaken it without more demonstrative and unequivocal proofs than have hitherto been given. On the contrary, we are well convinced that by his success the Eaton interest is confirmed, and the introduction of one of the younger branches of that House in his stead (an event probably not far distant) will remove every particle of doubt as to the inglorious bon-dage in which we are held.

The most forthright charges in this article were of jobbery in the admission of freemen and intimidation of tenants on Crown leases or Corporation tenures. And 'an event probably not far distant' proved to be no later than the parliament of 1790, when R. W. Bootle gave place to Robert Grosvenor. When John Fletcher compiled the Chronicle's poll book of the 1784 election he included this and a sub-sequent article by 'Honestus'. Had he written them himself? That they expressed his opinions there can be little doubt, but the writing, in my opinion, was not his, although he was his own editor at this time. Had 'Honestus' given grounds for an action for libel? Certainly he had called in question the impartiality of the Corporation officers without specifically naming any individual, but the Corporation was no doubt satisfied with the result of the contest and for the time being had had enough of litigious appeals against what Hemingway afterwards called their 'pertinacious obstinacy', in continuing to elect their own officers by the 'select body' only.

If idle songs and illiberal ridicule were more to the taste of the entrenched party than fair argument, the Independents would show that they, too, could write an idle song to some purpose. It took the form of a spirited piece of verse satire purporting to come from the other side and containing, incidentally, some further revelations of the conduct of the contest. From the lively pen of 'Factotum' there appeared in the Chronicle of April 30:

THE TRIUMPH OF SLAVERY
A Rhapsody

Come ye Slaves of Chester city,
Whether grave, or gay, or witty,
While the muse has something pretty
In the praise of slav'ry.

Now my boys we've won the day
And self-interest bears the sway,
Let us give a loud huzza
In the cause of slav'ry.

Now Crewe's Plumpers see their folly
And are looking melancholy,
We will sing and still be jolly
In the cause of slav'ry.

'Spite of Freedom and of Crewe
And of Independence too,
We have shown what we can do
In the cause of slav'ry.

Tho' they beat us in the riot,
Now we've made the Plumpers quiet,
Thanks to our strong drink and diet
And our vote for slav'ry.

Tho' they say we brib'd our men
And made th'Exchange a pris'ners' den,
We'll lock up and bribe again
In the cause of slav'ry.

If they call us by a summons
To the bar of the House of Commons,
We'll be staunch as any Romans
In the cause of slav'ry.

Let them call, for prove we can
That to execute our plan
Cost near twenty pounds a man,
Ev'ry vote for slav'ry.

Let the Plumpers we have beaten
Say we're sold to th'House of Eaton,
Let them banter, let them threaten,
We'll be true to slav'ry.

Gro'v'nor's paid for Chester ground
'Bove an hundred thousand pound,
And shall have it, we'll be bound
In the cause of slav'ry.

As to voters when they're wanted,
Right or no right, when we're scanted,
They shall have their freedom granted,
Viz., to vote for slav'ry.

We've above one hundred made
Who had no just right, 'tis said,
Never mind, they lent us aid,
In the cause of slav'ry.

We've a long train of dependants,
Bailiffs, chairmen, and defendants,
All firm foes to Independence,
Voters all for slav'ry.

We've a Printer and a Poet
Who has wit and wills to show it,
And a champion, you all know it,
In the cause of slav'ry.

Tho' Factotum's pen they draw,
We don't mind them of a straw,
We can give them Poet's law
In defence of slav'ry.

Let them still go on abusing,
Plumping, threat'ning, and accusing,
And to shew their right of chusing
Call us tools of slav'ry.

While we've beef, good wine, and ale,
Never mind them, let them rail

Or go sing the Mourning Peal
And lament o'er slav'ry.

Threats of future opposition
Ne'er can alter our condition,
We're so strong a Coalition
In the cause of slav'ry.

Drink about, a fig for Crewe,
We have shown what we can do,
And drawn them through the Spigot too,
So huzza for slav'ry!

Since 'The Triumph of Slavery' was, so to speak, a double satire in
the guise of a bragging self-justification by the victors, it deserves to
be remembered as the subtlest contribution to the 'literature' of the
1784 contest in Chester. In the modern city the contest has a 'memorial', though few of today's citizens realise it as they pass under its
elegant pillars. The Grosvenor Hotel, which began life as the Royal
Hotel, owes its origin, as Hemingway records, 'to electioneering
warfare; it was distributed into a number of shares and built soon
after the memorable contest of 1784 by the political friends of Mr.
Crewe, in whose possession it remained, with some occasional
changes in the proprietary, till 1815, when the whole concern was
purchased by the Right Hon. Earl Grosvenor'. Poor Mr. Crewe – he
was unlucky also in his property speculations. And I suspect that
John Fletcher had some of those original shares.

No sooner had Mr. Pitt come to power than he began vigorously to
lay on the taxes, so many and so various that in September Fletcher
printed, price sixpence, an 'Abridgement' of the Acts of Parliament
imposing taxes on paper, candles, bricks, tiles, windows, horses,
hackney coaches, beer, letter post, soap and starch, hats, smuggling,
silk and gauze and pawnbrokers. Although the newspapers took
exception to the tax on paper ('pressing of the press'), they had fun
with Mr. Pitt. The Chronicle (number 485) published 'A proposal
for laying a Tax on Bachelors', in which it was argued that male celi-
bacy 'is one of the growing evils of the age, productive of vice of
almost every species, injurious in many cases to the party himself,
and a living act of injustice to the other sex, to the state, and to posterity'. All bachelors over 25 should be taxed according to their
means and station until such time as they married. (Mr. Pitt was a

bachelor and at this time aged 25.) The Minister's first Budget was apostrophised in the paper thus:

Master Billy's Budget
Sing a Song of Taxes

Ye boobies of Britain who lately thought fit
The care of the State to a Child to commit,
Pray how do you like your young Minister's budget?
Should he take your last farthing, you never can grudge it.

What little we may by industry have made
We must pay for a licence to set up a trade;
So that every poor devil must now be tax'd more
For dealing in goods that paid taxes before.

*   *   *   *

Then last, that our murmurs might seize him the less,
By a tax upon paper he'd silence the press:
So our sorrows by singing can ne'er be relaxed,
Since a song upon taxes itself must be tax'd.

Meanwhile in Chester the time of the election of the Mayor and Corporation officers was drawing near, and the citizens, with the parliamentary contest fresh in mind, expected the ruling party to maintain itself in office by self-appointment; this was the customary operation of the Eaton-Corporation oligarchy so much resented by the independent freemen and others. What would the Chronicle do about it? That was the question in all minds. The first thing, we may guess, that John Fletcher did, was to study the conflicting Royal Charters which were basically the cause of all the trouble. The Great Charter was given to Chester by Henry VII in 1506; it created the office of Recorder and ordered that the Mayor, Sheriffs, and all aldermen, common council-men and officers should be elected by the citizens. This charter was ratified by Queen Elizabeth in 1574 and by James I in 1605. Charles II in 1664 renewed and confirmed the previous charters, but, after serving a writ on the city for abuse of privileges, issued another charter in 1685 displacing the elected Mayor by the direct appointment of Sir Thomas Grosvenor and removing several council-men. At the same time the new charter empowered the select body within the reformed council henceforth to appoint all the Corporation officers without a vote of the citizens. Thus was established the Grosvenor control of the council and of the representation, and the council thereafter persisted in quoting the charter as its warrant for current practice in the election of officers, although the claim was challenged in the Court of King's Bench and elsewhere by citizens zealous for the restoration of their rights given in the original Great Charter. The second charter of Charles II was the cause of much mischief in Chester then and afterwards, and it made a martyr of John Fletcher.

On October 29 (number 490) the Chronicle reported:

> Friday last being the annual election of the corporate officers of this city, the following gentlemen were appointed in office for the ensuing year, in a mode contrary to the express terms of the Charter and in opposition to the sentiments of the citizens (Mr. Richardson excepted):
>
> Mr. Henry Hegg, Mayor;
> Mr. John Meacock and Mr. Richard Richardson, Sheriffs;
> Mr. John Bennett and Mr. Thomas Edwards, Coroners;
> Mr. Thomas Edwards and Mr. John Hallwood, Treasurers;
> Mr. John Larden and Mr. Thomas Jones, Leavelookers.

The council had, then, once again denied the citizens their right of election of the city officers and had acted arbitrarily under cover of the second charter of Charles II in direct opposition to the common rights of the Great Charter. In stating this the Chronicle was not at fault, for it was clearly the fact, and to say that the appointments were made 'in a mode contrary to the express terms of the Charter and in opposition to the sentiments of the citizens', with the exception quoted, was all true in substance and fair comment in the public interest. But then Fletcher made a blunder and fell into a trap; he decided to attack the Recorder, Robert Townsend, a veteran of some thirty years in office. The irony of the thing was that Townsend, as the council's law officer, owed his office to the original Great Charter, the electoral provisions of which the council were flouting. This was not lost on Fletcher, of course, and if he had had the skilful pen of 'Honestus' he would have known how to make his criticism stick without the use of words injurious to an individual, and that individual a lawyer.

In the heat of the moment, and thinking perhaps that the mutually licensed invective and abuse of the late parliamentary contest was still current, he wrote and printed below the report of the council appointments, an article which he was presently to expiate in prison. The article follows, and the modern reader will understand the interior allusions better by reference to the explanation of the charter laws given in a preceding paragraph above:

> It must excite abhorrence in every liberal mind to see him, who is placed to determine the election rights and franchises of this city, step forth the avowed enemy to the exercise of those privileges which were granted by the Crown for the wisest purposes; when the great Paramount of Justice was called upon by the Advocate of the injured Citizens, with what prevaricating arguments did the self-created Recorder endeavour to stifle their complaints and suppress their legal demands, 'to know by what authority they exist as a body and exercise dominion over them'? Was it denied because you were conscious of not being justified in your proceedings, or as the aged Lawyer of 75 years, whose recollection sanctioned the unjustifiable mode? 'He could remember 50 years, and the election was always the same as it is now, and no doubt was always so conducted, for this city was founded and governed by its officers before the existence of Charters, and they have handed down this prescriptive mode to the present time.' But, good Mr. Recorder, as your memory is so collective of ancient usage and ancient history, you perhaps have not forgotten that this city is privileged by Charter, which points out the extent and duration of your authority and by what means and manner you must acquire it. You must know that the present mode of election is contrary to Charter, is repugnant to the principles of the British constitution.
>
> As a member then of that body how durst you stand forth an advocate of tyrannical usurpation, and as a man advance positions in the face of an insulted people which you cannot but know to be without foundation of truth? But this is consonant with the whole tenor of your proceedings. And what other explanation can be formed when impotent ignorance presides on the bench and partiality dictates decision? What can be expected from a set of men placed by their oath to administer justice as well to the poor as to the rich, to hear their complaints and redress their wrongs (who in a Court of Justice, with the boldest effrontery, tell you that your requisitions shall not be heard), but every species of oppressive insolence?
>
> Notwithstanding a report has been propagated that the citizens had abandoned the idea of any further proceedings respecting their right of annually electing the whole body of the Corporation officers, we are desired to assure the public that the claim will be firmly prosecuted as speedy as possible, the subscription entered into for that laudable purpose meeting the approbation of the public in general by almost daily additions thereto.

The citizens' claim was indeed prosecuted. On April 20 of the succeeding year, according to Hemingway, a motion was made in the Court of King's Bench calling upon Mr. Amery, an alderman, and Mr. Monk, a common councilman, to show cause by what authority they acted as such, not having been elected by the commonalty. But for Fletcher the damage was done when the Chronicle went to press on Friday, October 29, 1784. A writ for libel was on its way, and months of anxiety stretched before the paper's proprietor and editor.

This memorable year of 1784 was remarkable for something else which had nothing to do with politics, national or local, but which is related to a too familiar aspect of life today. The Chronicle in August reported a trade dispute – a genteel dispute by any modern standard – and readers were informed of it not in the news columns but by advertisement. The journeymen, carpenters and joiners of Chester went on strike and, anticipating the tactics of the 1970s, put their case before the public. Inserting a notice in the paper of August 6 (number 478), the carpenters said: 'Our wages are so very low, being only eight shillings, eight and sixpence, nine shillings, and some few hands nine and six per week, that we find it impossible to provide sufficient support for ourselves and families – more especially as we are obliged to find all our tools out of those wages and in the winter are under the necessity of sometimes being unemployed a day or two a week, a season of all others when our wants press most hard upon us.' All they wanted was a rise of a shilling a week all round. The cost of living was going up, the price of provisions had doubled in the last fifteen years, and yet 'our wages remain the same' and even fifteen years ago, 'we may reasonably suppose that the masters of those days did not allow their men more than sufficient for themselves and families'. The city carpenters concluded with the hope that no hands from the country districts 'will offer to supply our places, tho' ever so much pressed to do so'. No intimidation, but no blacklegs, please!

In the following week the carpenters' announcement was repeated, and in the same column immediately below, five employers offered the men 'proper encouragement and constant employ', at the same time contradicting (their own word) the carpenters' statement of earnings and uncertainty of employment in the winter. Nine, ten, eleven, and twelve shillings a week had been given, asserted the masters, and very few men had lost a day's work. Evidently an accommodation was reached in the next seven days. In the paper of August 20, the carpenters reasserted that none of their fraternity was engaged at ten shillings, only one at eleven shillings and one at twelve shillings per week, 'and these are looked upon as possessing abilities of a superior nature not generally expected in a journeyman'. Very skilled workers in fact. But . . . 'we cannot conclude without tendering our public thanks to those masters who have cheerfully advanced the wages, and assure them our best abilities will be exerted to serve them with fidelity'. They were good craftsmen in those days – twelve shillings a week for the highest skill – and these ancestors of the Amalgamated Society of Woodworkers certainly knew how to present their case with confidence and good humour.

5

Prison–and 40 turbulent political years

'There is nothing in the place that looks like
a jail, or bears the least colour of restraint . . .
Here the voice of misery never complains; and,
indeed, little else is to be heard but the sounds
of mirth and jollity.'

Tobias Smollett

The time is Christmas Eve, 1785, and the place the King's Bench prison in St. George's Fields, London. There are worse lodgings, even on Christmas Eve and a Saturday night at that. A mile away the tide of life ebbs and flows across Westminster Bridge. Look into the faces of the people passing ceaselessly to and fro, fitfully illumined by the smoking flambeaux. Almost every one expresses a feverish festivity, a forced gaiety. The patricians in their carriages and the well-found merchants and tradesmen are far outnumbered by the London poor. Mr. Pitt has done but little yet to relieve the poverty and distress in the capital. Indeed, he has been hooted in the streets and his effigy burnt because of the injurious taxes he has laid on. And the weather all month has continued bitterly cold. John Fletcher, proprietor of the Chester Chronicle, is up from the country, a temporary guest of his Majesty within the high prison walls. His pensive reflection at this moment is that there are many outside the gate who would be better accommodated within at this season. For himself, he considers the events that fixed him here for what he expects to be the longest half-year of his life.

When, after many delays and a protracted hearing, the Court of King's Bench on November 17 gave judgment against him in the action for libel brought by the Recorder of Chester, Robert Townsend, and ordered his confinement in prison for six months, with a fine of £50, Fletcher determined to answer the unforgiving obduracy of his prosecutor by serving the sentence without complaint. Had he not in his affidavit before the Court, accepted sole responsibility for writing and publishing the libel – to which none was privy before publication save the compositors who set up the type – offered to pay

66

Telford's aqueduct.
Above Soaring piers at
Pontcysyllte. *Right* The
canal and the towpath,
arrow-straight across the
River Dee and the Vale
of Llangollen.

Right The Canal Bridge and the Water Tower on Chester City Walls, 1802.

Above The canal basin at Chester where the Ellesmere Port link (Telford and Fletcher) joins the main stream of the Shropshire Union. *Right* The first grandstand on the Roodee racecourse, erected in 1817 by subscription and contracted for by John Fletcher.

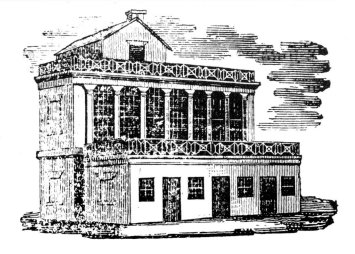

Above The Holyhead and Chester Mail Coaches lost in the snow at Dunstable. *Right* The flying postboy. *Below right* Advertisement for the London and Chester post coach. *Below* Advertisement for the new Royal Mail Coaches.

Top The Dee Bridge seen through the arch of the Bridge Gate, with the Dee Mills before they were finally taken down about 1910. On the right is the many-windowed gable of the Bear and Billet Inn. *Middle* The Port of Liverpool ('a creek in the Port of Chester') in 1724. *Bottom* Port of Chester notices of ships sailing between the London wharves and the Old Crane, Chester.

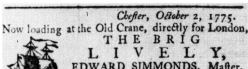

Chester, October 2, 1775.
Now loading at the Old Crane, directly for London,
THE BRIG
LIVELY,
EDWARD SIMMONDS, Master,
Burden 160 tons.
Will be clear to sail the 17th of October instant. For freight apply to the Master, on board the said brig, or to
HUGH JONES, Broker.

CHESTER, December 18, 1775.
Now Loading at SYMOND'S WHARF, London,
For this City and Parts adjacent, The
LORD GROSVENOR,
WILLIAM TYLER, Master,
In contract, to sail in 28 days. Any persons having goods to ship, are desired to give immediate and positive orders to their correspondents for this ship, as the last day of her taking in goods is fixed for the 14th of January next.
HUGH JONES.
Who has for sale a parcel of choice Irish Butter.

the Recorder's costs in the proceedings, to give five guineas to the Chester General Infirmary, and to publish an apology in the paper? All in vain. The writ was issued and not withdrawn. If Mr. Townsend chose to construe a careless word as personally libellous of himself, so be it. The cause of the elective liberties of the citizens of Chester must not be abandoned because of a careless word, nor the clear duty of the Press to uphold the public right against the whim of a Minister or a self-appointing and self-consenting Corporation, be foregone cravenly to appease authority. In the event of his imprisonment, it was necessary for John Fletcher to look to the conduct of the paper and to appoint an independent editor who was also experienced in business and printing. He knew the man and had no difficulty in persuading William Cowdroy, Mr. Monk's gifted apprentice, to leave the Courant and become the first acknowledged editor of the Chronicle.

Upon all this – the trial, the judgment, the separation from his good wife Mary, his confidence in William Cowdroy, and the dispositions they had concerted to carry on the paper and to keep readers informed about the proprietor in prison – John Fletcher ponders this Christmas Eve. Cowdroy, he suspects, means to make a newsworthy martyr out of him – a martyr in a long-standing popular Chester cause, a sufferer for all the deprived citizens. The new Editor's announcement of the judgment in the paper of November 25 has been skilfully calculated to arouse sympathy in the breasts of the readers of the Chronicle and to ensure their continuing loyalty to the paper:

> The chief apprehension we are under from this judgment is that the length of the confinement may probably affect Mr. Fletcher's health. We can, however, assure the numerous friends of this paper, as well in this city as throughout its widely extended circuit, that the business will be carried on during his imprisonment (notwithstanding the vain hopes and malevolent propagations of a few individuals to the contrary) under the immediate inspection of Mr. Cowdroy; and it would be impeaching the humanity of the public to suppose for a moment that the present unfortunate situation of Mr. Fletcher will not induce them to continue those friendly offices they have hitherto so kindly and liberally shewn to him. Any order, therefore, he may be favoured with, will be thankfully received and executed with elegance, accuracy, and dispatch.

Masterly! Business must go on, and the trial has been a costly affair. Entering the prison gate one morning early in December, and hearing the clang made by the turnkeys locking it behind him, John

Fletcher confesses to himself for the first time a certain queasy apprehension at the loss of his liberty even in a cause so dear. What a mischance in life – and yet one that many courageous scribes and printers have suffered before me! But now, and on Christmas Eve, he thinks with astonishment: what cause has there been for apprehension? The prison, save that you can't get out of it until your time is up, is scarcely a prison at all. It has a vigorous life of its own. Everything is to be had if you can afford to pay for it, and even for the indigent prisoners there is a begging-box and charitable funds to supply their wants. Treated from the start as one of the better sort of Crown prisoners, he has been assigned one of the twelve so-called state rooms somewhat apart from the rest. The stone floor is cold and the walls are of plain brick, but the lodging is comfortable enough – many poor devils outside, free only to suffer want and misery, would think themselves well off here. Butchers, green grocers, chandlers, and hawkers enter the prison every day at will and cry their wares. A public kitchen cooks the food. There is a tap-room for drink, a 'garden' for exercise, and the services of a doctor and a clergyman are maintained. The prisoners, on condition of good conduct, are free to occupy and amuse themselves as they please. A curious mixed lot they are, to be sure, and some of their devices for passing the time are ingenious or dubious in the extreme. The only restraint is that they cannot pass the turnkey into the free air of St. George's Fields. But he, John Fletcher is one of them, and as a journalist and man of the world he must profit from the experience. There is more to learn here than in a regiment of foot, and under better conditions, too. For the 'privileged' Crown prisoners books and newspapers are brought in, and if a man wishes to be private he can shut the door against inquisitive fellows or, if he has a mind to be sociable, he can entertain company, provided he keeps his wits about him.

Pleasantly surprised and somewhat bewildered at the reality of the King's Bench prison – so different from his expectation – John Fletcher retires to his room with the copies of the December 9 and December 16 Chronicles just arrived by the Chester-London post-coach. There is also a package, no doubt from his wife Mary, but that can wait; the newspapers must come first. Cowdroy and Mary have evidently considered together and the Editor has composed a deliberately affecting Christmas epistle on the retired and solitary condition of his proprietor, bereft of wife, friends, and the comforts of home at such a time. Fletcher looks round his neat prison 'apartment', sinks into his much-used but welcoming chair, and reads with mounting amusement and admiration:

> The several consolatory letters we have received respecting the present confined situation of Mr. Fletcher must be extremely flattering to his mind. It is not, however, either our province or our wish to accord with the requisitions of some of them, lest they might be deemed exceptionable to the mental tranquility of . . . . ., his friends and advisers. The eye that looks through the medium of candour and moderation will view all the circumstances in their true colours. Every man who is condemned by his peers is supposed guilty. Till he has passed that tribunal no imputation can affect him. But having done so, it becomes, in our opinion, a libel even to question the justice of the sentence, though we may sometimes lament it. To err is human, to forgive, divine; and whether or not, after the very singular, honourable, and, indeed, humiliating concessions made by Mr. Fletcher immediately on being told of his error, he merited the exercise of that godlike attribute, is a question we cheerfully submit to be answered by any man whose breast has ever flowed with the milk of human kindness.
>
> Let not the few real enemies to Mr. Fletcher's concerns (if such there are behind the curtain) suppose that we have said thus much with the smallest view to awaken their compassion. No! Sentence is given, and in God's name let it take its course. As he bore the prosecution, so he received the sentence and will suffer the imprisonment. Why should they not, therefore, enjoy the exultations of this great triumph unenvied, and wear the laurels of this mighty conquest without restraint? The glory, and above all the intention of the deed have been long ere this (to use the language of Sterne) registered in 'heaven's chancery', and He, whom we daily call upon to forgive us our trespasses as we forgive others, will, in that court and by that balance, most certainly and infallibly weigh, judge, and reward them.

Reading this with much satisfaction (not shared by Mr. Townsend), and thinking, not for the first time, that things are not always what they seem, especially when a ready writer goes to work on them, John Fletcher turns to the December 16 paper, in which his wife has taken up the grievous tale:

> The kind and generous support I have already received under the heavy inconvenience of my husband's distant confinement and large fine calls for such acknowledgments on my part that I am at a loss how to express them. My intention, however, I trust, will be admitted as an apology for the feebleness of the attempt; it being not less my duty than I feel it to be my earnest wish to make every return my poor ability will suffer me to do. And although to a compassionate breast an act of goodness is its own reward, yet I cannot help saying that I feel the obligation more sensibly from the manner in which it has been bestowed.

The smallness of my deserts has increased the merit of the bounty and rendered the generosity of the act doubly amiable. Under this conviction, while I cannot but lament the incautious error that unhappily gave the offence, it affords me the inexpressible satisfaction to find that the unkind and unmerited endeavours of a very few individuals will be defeated by the fostering hand of a benevolent public. –Printing Office, December 15. – Mary Fletcher. N.B. – M. Fletcher takes this opportunity to acquaint her friends and the public that the Chester Royal Almanack is now published, and may be had at the printing office in Foregate-street. For the particulars of the contents of this Almanack, see the Advertisement.

Well done, Mary, a puff for the Almanack! But friend Cowdroy has written the thing, of course. What will he think of next? Now for the package, which Fletcher opens very carefully, for it exhales a peculiar smell. Like the papers, it has come up in the boot of the stage and suffered the jolting of a day and a half on the midwinter roads. What's this? Faugh! A damn'd stinking pie! And here's an anonymous letter with it inscribed 'To Mr. Fletcher in the King's Bench, from a well-wisher, Pulford'. Pulford! So that's it, a tenant of the house of Eaton executing a pestilential commission for his masters and the Corporation. Stay, when has he heard the like before? Yes, John Wilkes it was who received a similar political pie when he was incarcerated in this same gaol. At least there is good precedent for the dirty plagiarism. Cowdroy will know what to do about this. Meanwhile, affronted feelings are out of place – after all, it is Christmas Eve and the rotten jest is on him. The prison keeps up all-night revels and the memory of that odious pie evaporates in the general treating and hospitality and good cheer and the appetising aromas from the public kitchens, where a gigantic roast is in preparation as if to last all of the twelve days of Christmas. Outside the prison gates the snow piles up and the post-coaches are delayed by heavy drifts, sometimes for several days. It is not until a fortnight later that Fletcher has his next batch of papers and letters from home, with a number of genuine presents from true friends.

In the Chronicle of December 23, Cowdroy has written a well-directed paragraph recommending Christian compassion to the notice of the unforgiving, and on December 30 he has concluded an appeal for food and warm clothing for the poor of Chester with these words 'Nor let those who are in bonds, in the different gaols of this kingdom, be forgotten.' Not even the dullest-witted readers of the Chester Chronicle can miss the point. And here, for the diversion of the town, is the Editor's Christmas pantomime of Mother Goose, written this time not for the boards of the Theatre Royal (where Mr. Cowdroy's witty sketches and topical songs are so well received) but in the style of the broadest satire for the open columns of the paper:

'We are desired to mention the sincere thanks of Mr. Fletcher for the several complimentary presents he has received in his confinement during this festive season, and we trust we shall be excused expressing them in so public a manner when we say that more than one have come from the hands of anonymous persons, consequently any other mode of address is impracticable. Among the rest of the favours we cannot help observing is a pie weighing exactly 24 pounds, the contents of which do as much credit to the bounty of the donor as its richness does to the hands of the cook that made it. In an Eastern tale we read that a man, having been condemned to a severe punishment for a very trivial and venial offence, contrived to send his prosecutor a pie with the heart of a tiger in it – a just and keen rebuke for the implacable cruelty he had exercised towards him.

'We shall not presume to say whether this may be thought at all applicable to the present instance, but leave every candid, humane, and intelligent mind to make its own comments upon the singularity of this present. It seems, however, necessary briefly to state that it contained three domestic rabbits devoid of brains and equally remarkable for having each of them, as we are informed, a bladder of gall preternaturally large, with ears so unusually capacious that, were we inclined to speak ludicrously, they might be deemed a new species of trap to catch the artless words of poor, inoffensive printers; also a goose without a heart which, were it not for spoiling the pie, we could heartily have wished had been an old gander. N.B. – The letter accompanying this present being dated Pulford, we rather suspect that it is the donation of a tenant of the worthy gentleman who is lord of the manor; and who might perhaps think Mr. Fletcher not undeserving at this inclement season the crumbs falling from his master's table, altho' he was so peculiarly unfortunate as not to succeed in his application to that respectable character for m——y and forgiveness. It may not be impertinent to remark that Mr. Wilkes,* when in the same prison, had a pie sent him weighing precisely 45 pounds.'

On January 6, 1786, William Cowdroy studies a long letter from John Fletcher in which, after discussing the affairs of the paper, the absent proprietor declares a New Year's resolution that henceforth the Chronicle shall be silent about his imprisonment. His confinement, he writes, is sufficiently irksome to any man of sense and feeling, but supportable, and such that, with good health, he can bear

---

* John Wilkes, journalist, politician, Lord Mayor of London, and editor and printer of The North Briton, was twice imprisoned for attacking Ministers as 'tools of despotism and corruption' and for obscene parodies published in that famous journal.

with fortitude and resignation for the rest of the term. Therefore he thinks that it would be politic and seemly to say no more about it in the paper until his release, diverted tho' he has been by that which has been said and especially by the deserved discomfiture of the other side in the episode of the pie. He has had a disorder of the digestion of late and has been obliged to keep to his room. . . .

Considering this sober advice, and weighing the last words, the Editor decides there is still something to be said, in conjunction with a piece of news that has just come in. Taking up his quill he writes: 'We are extremely concerned to hear, by an account received yesterday from London that Mr. Fletcher's health has, within the fortnight past, suffered very materially. The dampness of the apartments in the King's Bench prison at this season of the year (being all of them flagged and arched with brick), has brought on a rheumatic complaint, attended with a pain in his stomach, a disorder to which he has been formerly subject; but, within these few days, has attacked him with such unusual violence as to confine him to his apartment. It is some consolation, however, to hear that he is not at present dangerously affected'. That would do nicely for poor Fletcher; he would recover all right. And now for the Recorder, a last ironical word, neatly subjoined to the above paragraph in the paper of the same date: 'It is with regret we mention that a report is generally prevalent in this city that Robert Townsend, Esq., our worthy Recorder, about ten days ago had been unfortunately robbed of the sum of £30, but by whom this act was perpetrated has not as yet been discovered. When merciless depredators can thus become so valiant in villainy as to attack even the administrators of justice, what may not the more subordinate ranks of life expect in these times of general misery, indigence, and distress?' Fletcher would approve of that, surely!

No more is heard of Mr. Fletcher for the rest of that winter. The paper is silent on his ordeal, if such it is, and Fletcher himself keeps no record of his thoughts and feelings and how he occupies his time in this lost half-year of his long life. But is it lost? He has now the time and the leisure to turn over in his mind many plans and projects that are quite separate and distinct from the newspaper. For the Chronicle he has no apprehension. It is in better editorial hands than his own. William Cowdroy is an accomplished and many-sided journalist and a personality of ready acceptance in all companies. The paper is now more popular than it ever has been and the Chester news sometimes runs to two very full columns compiled with much skill and written in a lively, engaging style. To the controversial politics and social foibles and extravagances of the day Cowdroy brings a touch of humour and shrewd satire, so that the paper is increasingly read for pleasure as well as instruction; and in matters of local debate he is not lightly to be challenged. Secure in the knowledge that all goes well at home, Fletcher reads the days of his confinement away, and his reading is chiefly in the newspapers, about the canals and roads that are linking all parts of the country together and about the inventions of the new age of industry and manufacture. There is a deal of unrest in the country about the conditions of work in mills and factories, but inventive, speculative minds are busy with the expansion of transport and trade as never before. John Fletcher, a self-made practical man of his time, sees instinctively the opportunities in this irresistible progress – and he sits down in his prison 'apartment' to continue the correspondence that he keeps up with his scientific friend Thomas Telford, the engineer whose roads, canals and bridges are to revolutionise the communications of the entire country in the next forty years.

The six months have been served and the day of release arrives. Fletcher will have nothing to do with the Editor's pressing desire that he should return triumphantly into the city with a public escort of his friends and the citizens, and so on May 12 the Chronicle announced:

> 'The period of Mr. Fletcher's confinement having expired, we hear that it is in contemplation among many of his friends to congratulate his return by publicly escorting him into the city. Altho' such a mark of attention would be highly flattering to a mind rendered sufficiently gloomy by a long and rigorous confinement, yet we are authorised to say that, feeling himself, as he does, unconscious of the smallest claim to such honour, he humbly trusts they will forego their kind intentions. And (as neither himself nor his few enemies have any great cause for triumph) he wishes to avoid every appearance of public exultation – which at best can but afford a momentary gratification to some and may probably give lasting offence to others, whom, as a servant of the public, it is not less his duty than he knows it to be his cordial inclination on all occasions to oblige.'

Thus Cowdroy artfully contrives a last public rebuke to those 'few enemies' for what they have done.

Chronicle number 575, May 26, contains the last, the very last, word on the prisoner of the King's Bench. The paragraph is signed by John Fletcher and is in every way worthy of him:

> 'I cannot omit the first opportunity which presents itself since my enlargement of rendering my most cordial thanks to those friends who have so kindly and liberally contributed their support to my business during my long confinement. Deeply impressed as I am with a sense of obligation, it is my earnest wish to make every grateful return in my power, and hope my future conduct will evince to every unprejudiced mind the sincerity of my professions. A period being put to my imprisonment, I trust that a period will also be put to a recollection of the error which gave rise to it. And as I am not conscious of having ever entertained the smallest enmity to the gentleman whom I hastily and incautiously offended, I trust that every resentment will expire with my punishment and be no longer remembered.

Fletcher's manly sentiments certainly, but Cowdroy's writing, surely.

This episode of the 'martyrdom' of John Fletcher hardened the determination of others to prosecute the cause of citizen suffrage against the Corporation. Even while Fletcher was in prison a number of the independent freemen, supporters of Mr. Crewe in the 1784 election, with Mr. Ralph Eddowes at their head, decided upon legal proceedings to establish the validity of the Henry VII charter, copies of which were published and circulated. 'There was no difficulty,' says Hemingway in his History, 'in persuading the people to concur in an object which flattered them with an extension of their rights and privileges.' The hearing came before a Judge and special jury at Shrewsbury on August 8, 1786. Mr. William Hall, the new Town Clerk or Clerk of the Pentice (against whose appointment Fletcher had animadverted in the previous August) upheld the legality of usage under the Charles II charter by which aldermen and common councilmen were chosen by the select body – that is, by the Mayor, aldermen, and common council themselves. The independent freemen argued precisely the opposite case, asserting the citizens' right granted in the earlier Great Charter, as they called it, to elect their civic representatives by free vote, and in particular calling upon Mr. Amery, an alderman, and Mr. Monk (of the Courant), a common council man, 'to show cause by what authority they acted as such, not having been elected by the commonalty'.

The jury's verdict was: 'We find the Charter of Charles II to be bad.' Here, at last, was a famous victory, and the Chronicle of

August 11 (number 586) expressed its satisfaction in terms judicious and measured, in contrast to the blistering attack of yesteryear:

> 'We cannot omit this occasion of expressing our cordial approbation of the very decent and orderly conduct of those independent freemen who have been the uniform and steady friends to this most interesting cause, and we earnestly trust, as they have hitherto distinguished themselves by every just and commendable exertion in the restoration of their rights, so they will embrace the success of it with a manliness and moderation which at once must evince their goodness of sense and entitle them to the thanks of every friend to the peace, harmony, and freedom of the city.'

In other words, the judgment was not a signal to the citizens to march upon the Exchange and forcibly eject the Corporation. But even that extreme measure was to be attempted, as we shall see. After years of ruling the roost in their own way, and with a powerful vested interest at their back, the Corporation were not caving in. They appealed for a new trial, which came on, again at Shrewsbury, on March 20, 1787, and the previous judgment was reversed, the Court of King's Bench confirming. Mr. Eddowes, now involved personally in £2,000 costs claimed by Alderman Amery, appealed to the House of Lords. After a hearing of seven days, beginning on February 5, 1790, the Lord Chancellor reversed the judgment of the King's Bench. But Mr Eddowes, whose counsel unaccountably neglected to apply for costs, had a big bill to meet.

Was this, then, the end of the closed, secret Corporation of Chester? Hemingway gives the answer: 'However elated were the anti-Corporation party on this decisive victory, which, according to their calculation, was to be immediately followed by popular elections, they still found themselves met by the body corporate with an unyielding resistance. Notwithstanding the decision in the Lords, the Corporation still adhered to their usual system and resolved to take up another defence in support of their proceedings. . . .' And so on, year after year, until the Judges of the King's Bench and the House of Lords Appeal Court must have groaned at the very name of Chester.

For some thirty-eight years Fletcher and Cowdroy and then Fletcher and Hanshall worked together producing a well-informed, well-written paper, throughout a period of great events: the Pitt ministries, the French Revolution, the challenge of Napoleon, Nelson's Battles of the Nile and Trafalgar, and the final field of Waterloo. It's all there in the files, with occasional 'editions extraordinary' running to eight pages for momentous news arriving by the postboy on publication days. But, as if oblivious of the course of history and the changes within the Whig and Tory parties – still alike, however, in representing predominantly the landowning interest – the citizens of Chester at election times, parliamentary and municipal, continued to engage in their own private warfare, reducing politics to the simple formula of Independents versus the Corporation and the House of Eaton; and it did not really matter whether the Independent or the reigning Grosvenor was Whig or Tory.

Having fought and suffered in this battle, Fletcher was now keeping a careful neutrality. For one thing, he was a man of business engaged in many enterprises and a member of the Common Council, and therefore involved in the once-detested Corporation oligarchy. Sagacious – or expedient – impartiality was therefore the tone and colour of the Chronicle at this time. Besides, these were difficult days economically for newspaper printers and publishers – the expansive years of the later nineteenth century were yet to come. Although circulation had been maintained at about 20,000 copies a year, Stamp duty had been raised to twopence a sheet in 1789 (rising to a record fourpence a sheet in 1815), thus taxing the loyalty and the pockets of readers at sixpence a copy in 1808, sixpence-halfpenny in 1810, and sevenpence in 1815. The 20,000 copies were bought by those who could afford them, but the actual readership, at second or third hand, was many times that number.

It was also the custom of literate people in the community to read the news and comments aloud in the news rooms of inns or other places of public resort in town and country. Subscription libraries also began at this time. Fletcher became one of the principal patrons of a public library established in 1817 in Bolland's Entry and afterwards enlarged and removed to the then new (and present) Chronicle Office in Fletcher's Buildings. He gave 20 guineas for its support and presented a collection of books, including the Edinburgh Encyclopaedia. (This library is not to be confused with the City Library originally established in White Friars and removed in 1815 to the Commercial Buildings and News Room in Northgate-street.) The portrait of Fletcher now in the civic gallery at the Town Hall formerly hung on the wall of the library room in the newspaper office.

At the turn of the century John Fletcher was in his fifties and as fully and variously occupied as at any time in his life. He described himself professionally as a merchant and the Chronicle Office was a web of agencies and enterprises, not least remarkable being the sale of lint, the production of which had been perfected in Liverpool in 1810. An advertisement in the paper of November 16 in that year informed the public that Mr. Fletcher had been appointed agent for this universal panacea for immediate application to wounds, burns, scalds, and bruises. Orders could be placed at the Chronicle Office, where samples of the new invention could be inspected, and delivery would be made by the newspaper carriers to doctors, hospitals, factories and workshops, and private families. Fletcher was not above dealing also as agent for other of the more empirical nostrums extensively advertised in the paper and described in a subsequent chapter. Fletcher of the Chester Chronicle was indeed a protean character with a capacity for work to match his restless versatility. He was at the public service as printer and publisher, advertising executive, sales agent, promoter, land surveyor, engineer and contractor, employing or hiring craftsmen and journeymen of all kinds. He was at the centre of local politics and business, and the paper had contacts throughout North Wales and the North-West of England, public advertisements and general news appearing regularly in its columns from Lancashire and as far afield as Caernarvonshire and Anglesey.

He was in constant communication with scientists, inventors, and 'aeronauts' of the day and ready to publish treatises on any feasible or marketable new idea for the improvement of machinery and manufactures and the advancement of commerce. A frequent visitor to the office was the by now celebrated Thomas Telford. He would arrive by stage from Shrewsbury and remain closeted with Fletcher, their heads together over plans for the grand construction of the Ellesmere Canal. One day in July, 1796, Telford came into the office on a different errand, to deliver a verse he had written on the death of his even more celebrated countryman, Robert Burns. Telford was a masterly worker in stone and metal, but not much of a poet. His memorial lines, such as they were, but written from the heart, duly appeared on the back page of the next Chronicle. Other frequent callers at the office were Common Councilmen whose business was to discuss civic affairs, devious plots and strategems, and who was in and who was out. In these cabals Fletcher no doubt calculated his advice for almost certain repetition in similar conversations at the office of the Courant, where by 1790 there had been a big change,

John Monk, now an alderman, retiring in favour of his elder son Edmund. The long and notable Monk succession ended in 1832. Edmund died in 1800, was succeeded by his younger brother John Monk the second, who died in 1817, and the paper was continued for the next fifteen years by the latter's widow. For seven years Joseph Hemingway acted as Editor of the Courant for Mrs. Monk before accepting Fletcher's invitation to assume the editorship of the Chronicle.

Earlier Fletcher had lost his old friend, John Poole, founder of the paper, who died about 1798, leaving a printing business to his widow and his son Thomas; and in 1785 he had had a more significant loss in the departure of William Cowdroy, his trusted Editor and sustainer when in prison, to establish the Manchester Gazette with a partner, Thomas Boden. Whether the loyal Cowdroy somehow contrived to help his old chief part-time in the conduct of the Chronicle from this time we do not know. It is not likely, and more probable that Fletcher himself again occupied the editorial chair until 1809 or 1810, when he appointed John Hickson Hanshall as Editor upon completion of his indentures as a printer about that time. (For some years in between, however, Fletcher had the assistance of one Thomas Cutter, to whom he gave the sack, as we shall presently see.) As I have written earlier, Fletcher was fortunate in his four Editors, for the first of whom he clearly had much affection and admiration. Cowdroy had not Hanshall's or Hemingway's scholarship, but he was a true journalist, and a stylish, imaginative, and humorous writer. At his death in 1814 there were many tributes to him, and his memory was not soon forgotten. Hanshall, who succeeded him (after the discarded Cutter) wrote of Cowdroy 'He was a man of infinite humour. His company was courted by all classes, who paid alike the tribute to his invincible wit. For many years he conducted the Chester Chronicle with what ability the recording voice of public opinion can now speak with admiration.' That was written two years after Cowdroy's death, which occurred at the age of 62, by a much younger friend and colleague whose mentor he had been.

Charles H. Timperley, in his *Dictionary of Printers and Printing* (1839), wrote 'Mr. Cowdroy was a man of rare genius, a poet, a wit, a facetious companion, an unshaken patriot, a firm friend, a kind father, and a truly honest man . . . At Chester, while he employed himself as editor and compositor of the Chronicle, he displayed the singular faculty of composing his paragraphs without writing them, and some of his happiest efforts in prose and verse were produced in that manner.' Some of these happy efforts I have quoted in these pages.

In the spring of 1807, and with many affairs on hand that required him to work almost as tirelessly as one of the new steam engines, John Fletcher was faced with a political development that called for some diplomacy by the Chronicle. On the 'glorious sixth of May' (as it became known in a party song) General Thomas Grosvenor and Mr. John Egerton of Oulton were elected Members for Chester. An Independent had been admitted to the hitherto closed circle of the city representation without a contest! How had it happened? The other sitting Member, Richard Drax Grosvenor, the General's brother, had declined the renomination, and the attempted substitution of Colonel Hanmer, son of Sir Thomas Hanmer, to continue the Eaton interest was frustrated when some members of the Corporation had the resolution to back an invitation to Mr. Egerton which was subsequently supported by the Corporation Assembly. It was claimed that Col. Hanmer was unknown in Chester, whereas Mr. Egerton and his family had a long, close, and honourable connection with the city, all of which was true. The Grosvenors had made a mistake in counting on the acceptance of their second, substitute, candidate, and in under-rating the Independent interest inside the Corporation. Mr. Egerton was in, but the citizens at large still had had no say in the transaction: local politics had become a cabal within a cabal. The Chronicle reacted to the affair with a studied assumption of detachment. It reported verbatim a speech of General Grosvenor to the Common Council on May 4, two days before the election, in which the house of Eaton's credit was restored with much skill and complaisance by a practised Parliamentary hand. 'A worthier and more unexceptionable gentleman does not exist than Mr. Egerton of Oulton, for whom I entertain a most cordial regard and respect', said the General generously, adding with circumspection 'I regret that his intention to stand was not made known to you before Colonel Hanmer's declaration. Much trouble and anxiety would have been saved. Now speak your minds, gentlemen!'

The Chronicle, which in the light of its history might have been expected to be openly in the Egerton camp, was still striving for what we today should call a consensus of opinion when, on September 25 of the same year, it reported the presence of Earl Grosvenor himself – Robert, the second Earl, succeeding in 1802 his father Richard, who had opposed the start of the paper back in 1775 – at the Corporation Assembly of the previous Friday. The head of the house of Eaton was evidently in no mood for compromise whatever the Corporation (of which he was an alderman) had seen fit to do. He declared his determination (said the Chronicle) to 'support with all his wealth and influence the interest of his house in the representation of the city.' There was no mistaking the tone. Mr. Egerton (and the Corporation) had been warned. But after the rebuke, the feast. The paper added 'No reply seems to have been made, or offence taken, as they adjourned with his Lordship to the Feathers, where a most elegant dinner was provided.'

In its next edition the Chronicle continued to take the heat out of the affair with a comment on the Courant's report of what had happened in the Assembly. There it was said, according to the rival paper, that Mr. Egerton was returned contrary to the wishes of the Corporation. 'Nothing of the kind,' retorted the Chronicle, repeating that all that had been said was that although Mr. Egerton had been preferred to Colonel Hanmer, 'some other gentleman might perhaps hereafter be preferred to Mr. Egerton.' What was happening? The papers were changing political sides. The Courant, affronted by the Chronicle's coolness in this extraordinary demarche in local politics, made some warm comment or other that drew from Fletcher an undisguised insult. On October 9 he reminded his 'Brother Editor' that he was 'the medium, not the means, of public opinion, a situation sufficiently dangerous and disagreeable when party contention is carried on, without engaging personally in the dispute . . . But we will not break a butterfly on the wheel.' Both parties booked advertising space in the Chronicle of November 6. Below an announcement of the intention of Mr. Egerton and his friends to dine at the Royal Hotel in celebration of the Sixth of May appeared this: 'The friends of Mr. Egerton having advertised their intention of dining together on Monday next, the inhabitants of Chester are requested to be on their guard against any attempt to induce them to take a step that might hereafter be construed as a pledge of their choice of a representative in Parliament.' That advertisement was certainly inspired by Eaton Hall. Colonel Roger Barnston, in the chair at the grand dinner of Mr. Egerton's friends, had no doubt about it: 'An advertisement which appeared in the Chester Chronicle of Friday last I trust has been answered to your satisfaction', he said (and the Chronicle reported). 'I am happy to find so illiberal a publication has received what it so justly merited, the contempt of the independent freemen.' The diners and winers then sang 'The Sixth of May', 'Hearts of Oak', and 'Away with Melancholy.'

When, in October, 1809 (by which time Hanshall was editing the paper), the independents in the Corporation nominated their own candidates for Mayor and Sheriff, who were defeated on the vote, the Chronicle deplored the violence and commotion attending the business and openly sided with the 'official' Corporation (and Grosvenor) interest. The Courant took the opposite stance and forfeited the long-standing Grosvenor patronage it had enjoyed. At this distance of time it is possibly only to guess at the causes. One of them was a shift in politics by the Grosvenors themselves. They were, as we have seen, Tory (or at least Pittite) at the 1784 election and continued their allegiance to Pitt until his death in 1806, when the second Earl joined the Whigs, remaining (as the Eaton biographer, Gervas Huxley, has written) 'steadfast to his liberal Whig outlook for the rest of his long life, befriending the victims of the Peterloo massacre, contributing to the Anti-Corn-Law League, presenting petitions in the Lords in favour of Catholic Emancipation, and voting for the Reform Bill.' In the battle for Reform he had the unqualified support of the Chronicle, which was, however, less liberal than the Earl about Peterloo. On the other side, the Egerton interest, though nominally Independent (in the local sense of challenging the Grosvenor monopoly of Chester's two Parliamentary seats) was uncompromisingly Tory. It was by a Tory Mayor, William Seller, that the Duke of Wellington was invited to Chester from Combermere, as related in Chapter Three, to receive the honour of a civic banquet at which Colonel Barnston, the Egerton 'chief of staff', presided and from which Earl Grosvenor was significantly absent as a mark of his distaste for the gallant Duke's politics.

And so it may be said that the papers changed sides without changing their politics. The Chronicle's Whig coat was now worn by the Grosvenors and the Courant's Tory coat was on the backs of the Independents! As for Fletcher himself, although it was 23 years since he had gone to prison for Free Men and Independency, he had not forgotten the experience, and he was by now thoroughly disillusioned by the malice of faction. The virulence of party strife dishonoured the city, which was becoming notorious for its relentless feuding over a handful of unrepresentative votes commanded by candidates who, whatever their other differences, were alike in being hereditary landowners. (The Egertons and Grosvenors were, indeed, related, the second Earl having married in 1784 Lady Eleanor Egerton, only daughter of the Earl of Wilton.) Even more turbulent election scenes were to follow, and though newspaper sales were increased by party passion, it was the duty of responsible men to seek to put an end to these broils . . . Such thoughts were in Fletcher's mind when on November 17, 1809, he signed and printed a remarkable revelatory column in refutation of a charge in the previous issue of the Courant that he had basely deserted the party of his old friends.

The Independent party, said the Courant, had nurtured the Chronicle in its infancy, when it was in danger of perishing – was all to be sacrificed now to a more splendid patronage? Returning from a business trip to London, Fletcher took up the challenge. Addressing Mr. Monk personally (presumably John Monk senior had inspired the attack), he wrote: 'The curiosity of the charge is that *you* should bring it against *me*, you who were reared and supported by a party, and even that 'splendid' party which you now so wantonly abuse in language and ways that make your friends cry shame. Had I, who never received a splendid patronage, done this my offence would only have been a breach of justice and decency. Yours, Mr. Monk, is that founded on the basest ingratitude.' Fletcher went on to admit that John Poole and his co-founders of the Chronicle had indeed represented the Independent party. Their object was to establish a paper to 'curb and correct, as it ever shall, the insolence and partiality of the Courant.' But all their endeavours were frustrated by the 'splendid patronage' received by the older paper.

> I purchased the Chronicle and was persuaded by my friends to attempt what the united efforts and interest of the party could not accomplish. As this act of my life cannot be justified by the maxims of prudence, I plead guilty of rashness and indiscretion, for sacrificing my ease and happiness for chimerical fame and an uncertain object. But I trust my friends will forgive me when they are told I was severely punished for my temerity. In the long struggle for the honourable existence of the concern I endured such labour of body and anxiety of mind as few could bear and none will envy. I had no friend to assist me against a powerful party and Mr. Monk, who contemplated my destruction daily. An opportunity soon offered to increase my difficulties and distress . . .

This was the action for libel. 'During all this painful and

distressing litigation not one of the Independent party rendered me any assistance or support (beyond the encouragement of business), nor in my confinement did any individual of the party give me any pecuniary aid or friendly consolation . . . This is a true account of my early life . . . Ever since that period I have steadily performed what I conceived to be my duty to the public. The threats of foes, the favour of friends, have had no effect on my political opinions or conduct. I have frequently opposed both when my mind convinced me they were wrong. I never have received any patronage, pay, or promises from any man or party whatever to influence my conduct.' The Courant, he went on, had always been in the pay of the party adverse to the interests and principles it now espoused. 'It is now, behold, become a flaming Independent patriot, and if its warm friends do not guard it, will soon terminate in smoke!' Fletcher confessed that his 'unknown friends' had subscribed to pay the £50 fine imposed upon him; and made ambiguous allusions to the machinations of his acting editor Cutter,* who had apparently ingratiated himself too deeply with the Independent party for Fletcher's liking.

The Courant-Chronicle duel did not end there. The Courant on November 21 had another thrust at Fletcher's 'malevolent assertions', declaring in its turn that Mr. Monk 'has never been honoured with a single favour from Earl Grosvenor, nor had he ever received a shilling from him or his connexions, as pay for the Courant.' The paper, however, disavowed any intention of deliberately wounding Mr. Fletcher by reminding him of his imprisonment. The quarrel spilled over into the correspondence columns of both papers, with the Chronicle now openly on the Grosvenor side (Whig) and the Courant battling for the Independents (Tory). The house of Eaton's former opposition of the Chronicle was forgiven and forgotten in face of the attack now mounted and sustained by the Courant on its erstwhile 'splendid patronage.' The Grosvenors let it be known in 1810 that Sir Richard Brooke would, in conjunction with General Grosvenor, oppose Mr. Egerton at the next election. January 27, the birthday of the heir, Lord Belgrave, was chosen for the announcement, which was made at all the public houses of the city, the Eaton family, as many times before, standing treat to the freemen and citizens. Not to be outdone in hospitality, Mr. Egerton dined his friends and supporters sumptuously at the Royal Hotel. When the

* Cutter on January 2, 1810, advertised in the Courant but not the Chronicle that he was starting a new paper, the Chester Herald, to be published 'early every Saturday morning, the market day'. It died on January 10, 1813.

election came on in October, 1812, the Michaelmas Fair was in full swing and the citizens had a double incentive for drinking and fighting, and the papers were no less intemperate in their editorial exchanges. 'The contest was a severe and costly one' (said Sir Philip Grey Egerton, writing up the family archives in 1869), 'but it resulted in the return of Mr. Egerton by 27 over his opponent, Sir Richard Brooke.'

At the election for city officers in the same year there was the clamorous and unprecedented scene (even for Chester) of two Corporations crowding the Town Hall Exchange for the ascendancy, one being in possession of the insignia, sword and mace as symbols of office, the other set up by the Independents to dispossess them. John Fletcher, as the official Corporation nominee for Sheriff, found himself challenged by the nominee of the party for whom he had once gone to gaol! The challengers attended the Cathedral and 'walked the markets' as a rival Corporation and pressed their claim to a further trial at Shrewsbury which went against them. The citizens of Shrewsbury must by this time have grown accustomed to Chester's dirty linen being washed at their Assize. Before the next Parliamentary contest a second attempt had been made to establish a third newspaper in the city. The Chester Guardian appeared in 1817 to support the Whig party, with an editor brought down from London, one Gorton, 'a man of superior talent', wrote Hemingway later, 'to whom was assigned a salary which few provincial journals could bear.' Perhaps the Grosvenors were concerned by the size of the Tory vote in the city and the undoubted popularity of Mr. Egerton. But the new paper, London editor notwithstanding, was seen off by the Chronicle and the Courant and died in 1823.

In June, 1818, Lord Belgrave entered the lists with General Grosvenor and in the nomination with Mr. Egerton (now Sir John, he having succeeded to the baronetcy in 1816) was one John Williams, a barrister. This time General Grosvenor's majority over Mr. Egerton was 130, and this return, said the Oulton records, 'was petitioned against on the ground of bribery and corruption, but the committee resolved that the sitting members were duly elected.' Sir John tried again in 1820 and nearly brought it off, reducing General Grosvenor's majority to 18. But, again according to the Oulton records, expenses were enormous and caused the sale of estate property and timber. (The Egertons suffered a severe loss a century and some few years later: the Chronicle in February, 1926, reported the total destruction by fire of the family mansion, Oulton Hall, part of the site of which is occupied today by the famous motor-racing circuit.)

The partiality of the papers was demonstrated in their conflicting accounts of a violent clash on the Dee Bridge involving the veteran General Grosvenor on the Saturday night of the poll in the 1820 election. According to the Chronicle the General and his friend and adviser, Mr. Long, had left the hustings to return to Eaton in a coach and four. As it left the city by the Bridge Gate the coach was stopped on the Bridge by a mob of the Independents. The General and his companion were dragged out and roughly used, and the coach was flung over the parapet of the Bridge into the river. The Grosvenors conducted a rearguard action back into the city and found refuge in the Bear and Billet Inn just within the gate. The Chronicle blamed the Independents for premeditating this outrage, but afterwards the prudent General, with the election in his pocket, played it down in a public letter, saying the postboys were drunk and could not manage the horses! That was Sir John Egerton's last election. He died in 1825, when John Fletcher was Mayor of Chester for the first time. The Grosvenor–Chronicle concord was sealed in October of that year, when the Eaton family accepted Fletcher's invitation to the Mayor's dinner and Lord Belgrave replied to the toast of his newly-born son, Hugh Lupus, who became in good time the first Duke of Westminster.

Fletcher had an eventful first year as Mayor. Election warfare in the streets and at the Exchange reached such a height of tumult in June, 1826, that Fletcher, exercising his Mayoral authority, went to the windows of the Exchange and read the Riot Act. This having no effect, he called in the 49th Regiment of Foot and, flanked by Aldermen Massey and Harrison, marched at the head of the troops to the hustings, to the relief of the Sheriffs and the Town Clerk, the latter of whom had been hit on the head by a stone. General Grosvenor, who had at last declined the Eaton nomination in favour of his kinsmen Robert Grosvenor and Lord Belgrave, nevertheless was in the eye of the storm, as in the previous contest. He turned up to cast his vote as an alderman of the Corporation and alighting from his carriage at the Exchange, where the hustings were set up, was surrounded by a mob of the Independents, 'rendered infuriate' by the appearance of their redoubtable enemy. The Chronicle of June 23 reported the 'infamous violence' that ensued, Joseph Hemingway now writing (he had succeeded Hanshall as Editor in 1824). 'A variety of rumours as false as they are ridiculous have been propagated respecting the General's conduct. Among the rest, it has been asserted that he taunted the populace with having upon a former occasion injured his carriage and then insultingly inquired whether they would dare to repeat the outrage?'

Whatever the truth of that, dirt, mud and stones accompanied the General into the hustings. The Grosvenors rallied to protect their old champion as he came out and were met with stones ripped up from the pavement. The battle swayed from the Exchange to Abbey Square and St. Werburgh-street and in the other direction along Northgate-street to the Cross and thence to the Royal Hotel at the Eastgate. In a final riot on the eleventh day of the poll the Sheriffs were pelted with rotten eggs, a dead rat, and other missiles, paving stones 'flew like hail', skulls were cracked with clubs and sticks, the planks of the hustings were thrown down, and Lord Belgrave was obliged to beat a retreat through the back way. Many people were injured, women and children among them, and all the windows of the Exchange and the nearby Coach and Horses Inn were smashed. John Fletcher then decided to put an end to the commotion. The Chronicle blamed the Independents for causing the trouble and the Courant blamed the Grosvenors, who won the contest by 18 votes. But it didn't do them much good. The Tory Government continued in office after the election.

What was Hemingway's real opinion about this contest and about the party strife that had continued without abatement for the past 25 years, much to the injury of the city? As editor of the Courant he had written on one side of the question, as editor of the Chronicle he was now writing on the other. (Without a certain agility of mind you could not prosper as a Chester journalist in those days.) It was Hemingway the historian, recalling the battle-stricken streets, the feuds and animosities, and the neglect of business, who told us the truth. His own sympathies were with the Independents on the ground that 'resistance is praiseworthy when either a real or supposed invasion of our rights is attempted' – and that had been Fletcher's opinion as we remember him at the beginning of this chapter. But at all times the Chronicle deplored the evil effects of party warfare, although on occasion it must be confessed its writing heaped fuel on the fire. Hemingway observed with sadness the deterioration of 'good neighbourhood' among the citizens of all degrees and the bitterness engendered by artificial faction hardening from one generation to the next into a settled hate. Politics in Chester induced idleness, dissoluteness, and dependence in the citizens and reduced the stature of public men to that of puppets dancing on the party strings.

The conduct of the last election had been the worst of all and the behaviour in the streets such as never to be tolerated again – so wrote the Chronicle after the customary poll-book inquests. A family council of the Grosvenors had the same thought. Reform was in the air, and they were supporters of reform and of the great Whig administrations that brought it about. (There is a paradox here which should be sufficiently explained by this relation of the extremely 'domestic' character of politics in Chester.) At all events, in January, 1829, the Chronicle received a communication from Eaton Hall promising that one of the Grosvenor MPs would retire at the dissolution of the present Parliament, 'that in future only one branch of the family will be offered to the choice of the citizens, and that no other individual presenting himself as a candidate will receive either support or opposition from the house of Eaton.' Lord Belgrave repeated the assurance at a meeting of the Corporation, confessed that the family had thought about the subject deeply, especially after the occurrences of the last election, and declared 'The interests of our venerable city, long torn by factions, require a unity of action for the preservation of its remnant of trade and commerce' – a timely reference to the declining Port of Chester and the consequent ill-effects upon the city's trade and manufactures. A few years hence the Reform Bill began the changes in Parliamentary and local representation that finally ended the 'closed Corporations' of which Chester surely had been an historic example. I cannot claim that the Chester Chronicle's political record was uniform and unequivocal. But it set out as a Whig paper and continued in that colour through the great days of the Liberal Party, and the Grosvenors, too, were true to that allegiance until, in the 1880s, the first Duke of Westminster broke with his friend and leader Mr. W. E. Gladstone on Home Rule for Ireland and refused to endorse the Liberal candidate and sitting Member for Chester in the general election of 1886. But this passage is part of the Chronicle's strong Liberal Radical period, to be studied in Chapter Fourteen.

6

Thomas Telford and
John Fletcher

'Telford . . . o'er the vale of Cambrian Dee
Aloft in air at giddy height upborne
Carried his navigable road.'

Southey

The scene is the Vale of Llangollen at Pontcysyllte in Denbighshire, North Wales, and the time is the spring of 1793. Two men are standing high on the hillside with the opulent spread of the Vale in full view and the River Dee running far below in its craggy bed. The men are Thomas Telford, aged 37, engineer, and John Fletcher, aged 37, of the Chester Chronicle. Born in 1756, they have pursued their careers each with a sympathetic understanding of the other's difficulties, especially in early life. They have made their own way in the world and each is largely self-taught. Telford remembers how as a boy of 14 he worked as a stonemason on the making of Edinburgh's famed Princes-street and New Town and he has come a long way since then, applying his Scots genius, tenacity, and capacity for hard study to engineering science and then to the building of roads. But his great works are still to be, and he has perhaps the noblest of them in his mind as he surveys the wide verdant Vale this spring morning. By his side John Fletcher catches the creative gleam in the eyes of his friend. As one who has also taught himself how to survey and measure land and to contract for the cutting and maintenance of stretches of the new canal works in Cheshire, Fletcher has to confess that he does not know how the task before them is to be accomplished, although they have many times talked about it at the Chronicle Office in Chester, at Shrewsbury, where Telford has his base, and in London, where there has been much negotiation and Acts of Parliament have been passed for the construction of the Ellesmere Canal. The idea is to link the Mersey, the Severn, and the Dee, for the mutual benefit of agriculture and commerce, and there below lies the most formidable of many problems – how to come to terms with Nature by carrying the canal over the Vale and over the river. Water over water.

An aqueduct is the only answer, of course, but an aqueduct the like of which for height, length, lightness, and strength has never been attempted before. No wonder Fletcher, by comparison just a gifted, commercially-minded amateur in these matters, is daunted by the mechanics – cutting a canal is one thing, building an aqueduct is another. But, long-sighted in business as we have seen in his conduct of the newspaper, he will help with the contracts and the oversight of the work, of which he has had some experience in his twenties in the construction of the Chester-Nantwich Canal, opened in 1779. Out of that venture he made precious little profit, although the Cestrians and the county people, in the grip of the prevailing canal mania, rushed to buy shares at a hundred pounds which were later to be sold at less than one per cent of their original value. But there is a future yet for the Chester Canal. Little did Fletcher think, when in May, 1779, he wrote for the Chester Chronicle an article signed 'Projector' proposing for the first time the extension of the Chester Canal to the Mersey, that Telford would enlarge the idea and incorporate it into the grander concept of the Ellesmere Canal. But so it is, and here they stand, fourteen years later, Fletcher silent and thoughtful, Telford's mind racing. Old methods and materials will not do, except for the foundations, the piers, and the embankments. How can men lay stones at this height? There must be some wholly original way of constructing and erecting the water-trough.

How he performed the miracle was seen in the ten years from 1795 to 1805. On January 17, 1794, the Ellesmere Canal General Committee ordered that the plan for the aqueduct at Pontcysyllte with three arches as prepared by William Turner, of Whitchurch, should be adopted. Advertisements inviting contract tenders were published in the Chronicle and other newspapers in Cheshire, Shropshire, and North Wales, and on August 10, 1795, Mr. Telford, general surveyor and agent to the company, was directed to proceed with the work, and with the other sections of the canal. Along the stretches Chirk, Llanymynech, and Weston Lullingfield, and Tilstock Park–Nantwich, and the construction of the Chirk and Pontcysyllte aqueducts, Fletcher had a considerable hand as subcontractor and engineer with his partner John Simpson. With many others they worked to the directions of the engineers, Telford in charge, assisted by William Jessop, Matthew Davidson, and Thomas Dadford. Hemingway in his *History* expressly names John Fletcher as one of the engineers employed on 'this extensive work,' and details of his contracts are given in the canal documents now held at the British Transport Section of the Public Record Office in London. Fletcher's contract for the Chirk, Llanymynech, and Weston work was £10,835 5s. 2d; for timber and quicksetts and other materials, £525; and for the Tilstock Park to Nantwich section Fletcher and Simpson received £33,504 4s. 4d. for contracts performed. Fletcher's claim (in Chapter Three) to have had 'the making of the embankment to the magnificent aqueduct over the River Dee' was, I think, a misapprehension by his friend the traveller. It is more probable, from the size of the contract, that his work was for the Chirk aqueduct over the River Ceiriog, also under Telford's direction. The canal accounts state that William Davies executed the earthen embankment (presumably at Pontcysyllte) and that John Simpson executed the masonry – and Fletcher would be his partner in that.

How Telford solved the problem of the Pontcysyllte water-trough and transformed the first design by William Turner is now engineering history. That the Chester Chronicle's proprietor had a part in the story and made an even bigger contribution to the creation of Ellesmere Port with the opening of the Wirral Line of the Ellesmere Canal in 1795 is less well known than it deserves to be. With the exception of his anonymous 'projection' of 1779 (unless, possibly, Telford himself wrote it), he made no personal reference in the paper to his own mercantile and engineering operations, except by contract advertisements for materials and labour; and the elucidation of the canal documents in the Public Record Office requires much labour and more knowledge than I have of canal shares, finance, and mortgages, and the piecemeal distribution of the work among many contractors, each responsible for a canal section and its maintenance. But enough has been established, I trust, for this book. All this part of Fletcher's various activities has now been rescued from oblivion.

Piecemeal most of the canal work in the eighteenth century and afterwards certainly was, but not the construction of the Pontcysyllte aqueduct. It was, from start to finish, highly organised, the steady, purposeful execution of a great work. Sir Walter Scott called it 'the most impressive work of art I have ever seen'. And it is still one of the wonders of Wales and a masterpiece of engineering architecture unsurpassed in its day and ours. It cost only one life, and was completed and opened just a month after Nelson's victory at Trafalgar. 'The stream in the sky' it was called. It stands – and at the same time serenely flows – today, this miracle of stone, iron, and water, cast arrow-straight across the Vale. Telford channelled the 'navigable road' of what is now known as the Llangollen Canal into a cast-iron trough some twelve feet wide, including the towing-path and the water-way, over a distance of 1,007 feet at a height of 127 feet across the Dee and the valley. Eighteen soaring piers of squared ashlar masonry, springing on the south side from an approach embankment 1,500 feet long, march across the vale, and laid on top of them with mathematical precision is 'the stream in the sky' in its cast-iron container.

Pontycysyllte aqueduct is the first major work of Telford's genius and in a long life of bridge-building and road-making he never, in the opinion of many good judges, achieved a nobler structure. In later years the Conway and Menai bridges added to his by then international renown; but it was not until he drove the Holyhead road past Lyn Ogwen through the Pass of Nant Ffrancon – a road that was opened by the flying post-horses of the Chester Mail – that he found a challenge and an arena comparable in scale and grandeur to the aqueduct bridging the 2,500 feet traverse of wood, water, and mountain in the romantic Vale of Llangollen. Today the spectacular road through the mountain pass, like all of Telford's close upon one thousand miles of roads in Scotland, Wales, and England, has come into its own again. In the lapse of the best part of two centuries the aqueduct has suffered a different vicissitude. It has long since lost its commercial importance. The rise of the railways in the early nineteenth century cast the canals into partial disuse, and now the aqueduct, which at first carried coal, iron, and slate, is used by pleasure craft chiefly from Chester, Ellesmere Port, Shrewsbury, and the midlands, and from the popular new canal marinas in between, and to convey water from Wales to the Hurleston Reservoir of the Mid-Cheshire Water Board. It is in the care of British Waterways and is, they say, in as good and watertight condition as when it was opened for traffic in 1805.

On Tuesday, November 26, 1805, thousands of people thronged the valley and the hillside, silencing the sound of the Dee's miniature cataracts with their clamour, and crowding the high canal embankment in the hope of being among 'the first' to cross in the Ellesmere Canal Company's bedecked barges. Telford and Fletcher were there, and Fletcher described the scene in two columns of the Chronicle of December 6 (number 1,587). When the junketings were over the aqueduct entered on its serious business of carrying Cheshire salt, Welsh coal, lime, slate, and iron, and Shropshire and Cheshire farm produce ferried on the Nantwich-Tilstock length of the canal contracted for by Fletcher and Simpson. In the succeeding 20 years Telford went on from Shrewsbury deep into North Wales, surveying the London-Holyhead road (the modern A5), the re-routing of which caused some hurt to Chester's civic pride, for until 1810 the highway had passed through Nantwich and Chester. Telford's new survey fixed upon Shrewsbury as the staging post from the midlands and the south, and the road was constructed between 1815 and 1830. (The coast road from Chester, improved by Telford, continued as before and as it does today, of course.) Fletcher's claim (Chapter Three) to have 'made the new road from Wrexham to Llangollen and so on to Ruthin' implies that he carried out contract work with Telford on minor links with the great mountain highway.

On Fletcher's association with the Chester Canal and its subsequent extension to the Mersey from Chester, and from Nantwich through Shropshire to Chirk, Llangollen, and so on to Llanymynech, Welshpool, and Newtown we are on firm ground. There is the evidence of the contracts, and from the records of the Chester Canal Navigation it is clear that Fletcher attended many meetings as one of the guarantors of the loan of £9,000 raised for the purchase of William Egerton's mortgage and interest on the first stage of the navigation. The Number One Chronicle reported the canal under construction to Nantwich in 1775, and the paper of August 6, 1779 (number 224) announced: 'The canal is now opened between this city and Nantwich in this county and in consequence two boats loaded with timber, iron, and other goods were navigated last week through the whole length, being eighteen miles. Passage boats will soon be fixed to ply between the above places twice or thrice a week. The utility of this canal must be evident to all persons conversant with the internal trade of this kingdom, as it will open a communication the whole distance for all articles of commerce between the ports of London, Bristol, Hull, and Chester, and the intermediate towns.' In May, 1796, the committee ordered the insertion of advertisements in the

Chronicle and the Courant for proposals for building a passage boat, the specifications to be sent to Mr. Fletcher, and Fletcher was also instructed (as engineer or contractor or both) to engage labour to 'cleanse the canal and take out the stones and bricks between Chester and Beeston Brook so as to make it navigable.' For this work he was paid £200 on account. A passage boat having been ordered from Mr. Littler, Fletcher was ordered to see that the work was satisfactorily done to specification.

Earlier (in 1791) Fletcher had published at the Chronicle Office a pamphlet by Charles Turner, architect and engineer, of Ellesmere, in which the linking of the Severn, the Dee, and the Mersey was practically advanced. This was effectively the origin of the Ellesmere Canal. The Chronicle reported a public meeting at Chester in the same year approving the project, a Bill was promoted, and an Act obtained in 1793. By 1795 the Wirral Line from the Mersey to Tower Wharf, Chester, was opened, and Fletcher was one of the leading promoters and engineers (with Telford superintending) of this communication, which transformed Whitby Locks (Netherpool), lowering the canal to the Mersey, into Ellesmere Port, so called as the terminal port of the Ellesmere Canal. In June, 1795, Fletcher launched a passage boat on this section, upwards of a hundred passengers, the paper reported, making the trip from Chester to the Mersey. 'A cheap, pleasant, swift, and easy intercourse with Liverpool . . . the boat made two trips the same day.' Thus 'Projector's' plan in the Chronicle of May 28, 1779, of a new communication by water from Chester to Liverpool, 'not subject to the present necessity of a tedious, expensive, and dangerous passage round the West Point of Wirral or the expense attending a land carriage of seven miles between Ince Boat-house and Chester', became a reality.

At the same time the fortunes of the old Chester Canal and its sunken shares were revived by the junction with the Wirral Line of the Ellesmere Canal at Chester in the basin below the spectacular staircase of the Northgate Locks, the sub-junction with the Whitchurch branch at Hurleston, near Nantwich, and so on into Wales. A steam boat, the Countess of Bridgewater, met the Chester packet at Ellesmere Port and completed the journey from Chester to Liverpool in under three hours. The development of modern Cheshire industry, salt, chemicals, textiles, and the improvement of its agriculture by the easier distribution throughout the country of cheese and other farm produce, were given a considerable impetus by the canal speculators. John Fletcher and the Chester Chronicle may justly be said to have had a large pioneering share in the remarkable expansion of Ellesmere Port, which has never looked back since Telford directed the canal to Whitby Locks and is now a multi-centre of modern industry. With the exception of Crewe, no Cheshire town has grown faster, and now 'the Port' is moving ahead of the railway town, which has not yet fully recovered after the passing of the Steam Age to which it owed its creation and its subsequent fame as the Grand Junction. Compare Ellesmere Port today with this description of it when the canal junction with Chester was first made: 'There was on the site of this commodious and flourishing little town', wrote William Mortimer, the historian of Wirral, in 1847, 'only one public house, three small cottages, a mere shed for a warehouse, and one set of locks.' The canal altered all that rapidly, warehouses went up, a floating dock was constructed fed by several locks, and in 1894, when the Manchester Ship Canal superseded the Mersey Navigation, Ellesmere Port's fortune was made.

John Fletcher was present at a meeting of the Chester Canal Navigation proprietors and mortgagees on November 26, 1804, and voted for a proposition by the Ellesmere Canal Committee that the two concerns should amalgamate since they were now effectively in business together. On July 29, 1813, he was again present at the first general assembly of the united company of which he became a shareholder. In Chapter Three I have speculated on the mystery of where Fletcher, aged 27 at the time and previously an impecunious schoolmaster, raised the money to buy the paper from John Poole. His canal earnings, as we have now seen, came years later, in the 1790s and after the turn of the century. But perhaps there is no mystery: he was always a speculator, and it is not improbable that the schoolmaster acquired the Chester Chronicle on a mortgage! Of Fletcher's other public works of which we now have any knowledge the first grandstand on the Chester Roodee Racecourse remains to be mentioned. I cannot find the fact acknowledged in such of the old records of the Race Company that have survived, but it is claimed that he carried out the work in 1816 for the subscribers in shares of £50 each at a total cost of £2,500. He was certainly a member of the first Grandstand Committee, on which also were Earl Grosvenor, General Grosvenor, Sir John Egerton, Sir W. W. Wynn, and other patricians, civic, sporting, landowning, and political. Hanshall in his *History of Cheshire* published a vignette of the stand, which he described as a neat building. That Fletcher also at the same time 'laid out the race course' (as he told his friend the traveller, Chapter Three) is probable enough in his capacity as a general contractor.

When Joseph Hemingway, who had edited the Chronicle with distinction from 1824, retired in 1830, the long, stabilising Fletcher period of the paper, as remarkable as any in newspaper history, was drawing to a close. Our first knowledge of Hemingway is as a partner with Jonas Nuttall in a Blackburn printing business from 1797 to 1800. He was in Chester in 1807 and printed a collection of controversial papers relating to the election of the 'Glorious Sixth of May' which earned a rebuke from Fletcher at the time. Registered bankrupt in 1809, Hemingway moved to Manchester, where from 1814 he published in conjunction with Martin Began 'The Manchester Magazine' or 'Chronicle of the Times'. In 1817 he was back in Chester, editing the Courant until in 1824 he moved over to the Chronicle. He was twice married and at the time of his death on December 20, 1837, was resident in the South Row, west side of Bridge-street. Hemingway's *History of Chester*, many times quoted in these pages and assessed in Chapter Three, was one of Fletcher's last publications from the Chronicle press, in 1831. After Fletcher's death, Hemingway wrote and had published elsewhere *A Panorama of the Beauties of North Wales* and *A Panorama of the City of Chester*, in 1836. All of these books are in my possession, but another larger work of his, *A History of the Spanish Revolution*, I have not seen.

The Courant and the Chronicle share equal credit in Hemingway's career; he enhanced the quality and reputation of both papers; and none of his successors in Chester journalism would challenge his precedence as editor and writer. But, had it not been for his decision to retire from the editorial chair so as to complete and publish his *History*, he would now be forgotten and there would be many gaps in the annals of Chester. I doubt if Fletcher paid this greatest of his editors as much as £300 a year, and certainly he paid his successor less, as we shall see later. It was not easy to support the character of scribe, scholar, and gentleman in the local 'Grub Street'. So it is good to know, as we learn from a letter, that Hemingway was pleased by the immediate success of the *History*, dedicated to Earl Grosvenor and handsomely and carefully printed by Fletcher. Posterity has done the rest. 'Hemingway's Chester' the book trade has called it ever since: the names are synonymous. And if you wish to meet Hemingway in fiction, read Raymond Foxall's *The Dark Forest*, published by Robert Hale in 1972.

To John David Barry fell the difficult task of succeeding Hemingway as editor of the Chester Chronicle. Not much is known about him, but he is the editorial link between the old Fletcher paper and its modern self. The six years of Barry's editorship were the first years of Parliamentary and social reform and we see the paper giving total support to the Whig statesmanship of Lord John Russell and Lord Grey. In the Whig ministry that overthrew the Tories after the election of 1830 Grey gave Robert Grosvenor a job as Comptroller of the Household. Robert had held his seat in Chester and his brother, Lord Belgrave, had been elected in the county, thus anticipating the extension of the county franchise. In 1831 and 1832 Lord John pushed his Great Reform Bill, the first new charter arising out of the Industrial Revolution, through Parliament with the loyal help of the Grosvenors and against the rearguard opposition of the Tory peers. Although they had sought to monopolise Chester for so long in the past, and although they stood to lose considerably by the Bill's thoroughgoing destruction of rotten and pocket boroughs by the redistribution of seats, the Grosvenors stuck to their traditional liberal principles which were never discarded even when, intermittently, they chose to adopt a Tory disguise. They accepted the realities of Whig politics. The world was changing fast, the aristocratic landowners, Whig and Tory alike, would have to share the power-base with the new middle class whose influence lay not in country estates and the patronage of old 'tied' towns like Chester, but in Liverpool, Manchester, Newcastle, and Birmingham, and it was necessary for the peace of the entire country to extend the franchise and liberalise the economy for the good of trade and security of employment.

The Chester Chronicle, too, supported all this wholeheartedly from the beginning, when the reforms were significant but tentative, and right through to the major Whig-Liberal political revolutions of the next 50 or 60 years. Chester's status declined with the rise of the big towns, but conversely the Chronicle's political influence was never better exercised than at this time. In 1831 Robert, second Earl Grosvenor, became the first Marquess of Westminster, his son Richard, Lord Belgrave, succeeding as Lord Grosvenor. These Eaton honours were fittingly remembered by John Fletcher in November, 1832, when, as Mayor of Chester for the second and last time, he held the grand mayoral banquet at the Exchange. He had a lot to celebrate, including the successful battle for reform and the continuing good feeling between his paper, Eaton Hall, and the now more 'open' Corporation. But he had one sad recollection, the death of his wife Mary, who had shared his troubles and triumphs. On this occasion another, unnamed, lady 'kindly officiated as Mrs. Mayoress', said the Chronicle report on November 9 (number 2,992). As he presided at the copious feast – turkeys, geese, venison, pigeon pie, sirloins of beef, pheasants, hares, woodcocks, and a plentiful supply of lobsters, mince pies, custards, tarts, whips and jellies – did he recall, I wonder, the famous Christmas pie in the King's Bench Prison? If so, he did not mention it, but did the honours of the table and praised Miss Turner, the City Cook, and 'Mrs. Mayoress', who had had the selection and arrangement of 150 dishes of dessert. Mr. Mayor, aware that after this there would probably be no more cakes and ale, sat late at the board. His editor, John David Barry, I trust was with him until they subsided on to the floor, for he reported that when most of the company had retired Alderman Fletcher continued in the midst of a few stalwart hearts and valiant flagon-holders who kept the hilarity going until the candles flickered and the City Watch called a decidedly foggy morning.

December of that year closed with the first election for the Reformed Parliament and the Chronicle supporting the Whig candidates in the city (Robert Grosvenor) and South Cheshire (the new Lord Grosvenor and Mr. Wilbraham). Sir Philip Egerton, for the Tories, gave the latter a stiff fight, but the Whigs won. In the week of the nominations the Chronicle produced a supplementary edition emphasising the importance of the election and of the historic new representative Parliament that would come out of it. Lord Grosvenor's nomination speech was described in laudatory terms the like of which would never be used today. His Lordship 'addressed the electors with extraordinary effect. Like a lion roused from his lair that rises in his might and shakes the dew drops from his mane, the noble Lord grappled with and scattered into thin air the various objections insidiously propagated against him . . .' Well, well . . . fulsome, but it worked. When the Reformed Parliament met in the spring of 1833 there on the benches were the indestructible Grosvenor brothers, as of old, supporting Lord Grey's first reforming measures with as much zeal as any of the new breed of politicians who were beginning to come up to Westminster. At the end of the

year, however, Lord Grosvenor informed the Chronicle and the electors that he would not stand again for the county. He had indeed
worked hard, engaged in many slogging contests, and attended to
much Parliamentary business, and for the time being he had had
enough.

Old John Fletcher was coming to the end of his days. His friend
and great contemporary, Thomas Telford, died in 1834, and with
that event it may be said that the useful years of the canals were passing also. The Steam Age of the railways was coming in. On January
7, 1835, John Fletcher died, in his 80th year. He had conducted the
paper for half a century and by commercial sagacity, hard work, and
good luck and good judgment in his appointment of editors raised it
to a reputation high among provincial journals. In the paper of January 9 John David Barry wrote this tribute: 'Born of humble but
reputable parents at Halton in this county, he was the architect of his
own fortune, and rose by the force of his genius and talent alone to
considerable eminence among scientific men. . . The history of his
life is curious and instructive and furnishes a practical lesson of the
value of temperance, prudence, persevering industry, unsullied probity, and uncompromising integrity in all the relations of social life
. . . His servants have lost a liberal and considerate master, his fellow
citizens an upright and intelligent magistrate, the cause of public
and private charity a munificent benefactor, and the community
among whom he lived a kind-hearted and benevolent man.' Well,
well, again. You will see that this deserving eloquence gives away
very few facts. But it is characteristic of the foundation period of the
paper: it was always reticent about its own people: a modest propen-
sity that has made my task all the harder two hundred years later.
There was another Fletcher to come, and that part of the story will be
taken up in Chapter Fourteen, when the internal history of the paper
is pursued to the present day. Now let us look at the external life and
times of the Chester Chronicle and see the reporting of two hundred
years rolling on into the actuality of today and tomorrow.

The Customs House.

Left Richard Fletcher Smith, son of William and Anne Smith, publisher of the Chester Chronicle in its centenary year. *Below right* William Smith (1817–1863), son of Richard and Peggy Smith, proprietors of a stage coach service. William Smith entered the Chester Chronicle ownership by his marriage to Anne, daughter of Thomas Fletcher, John Fletcher's nephew. *Below* Kop House, Saltney, home of William and Anne Smith, where the coach houses of the family business are still to be seen.

Above Frederick Coplestone, who served the Chronicle for over half a century. *Left* Title page of John Trevor's *Panorama of the City of Chester*, 1843. *Below* The Dee Bridge, with the Mills and St. Mary's Church, 1798.

Northgate Street West, with the White Lion Inn, the Exchange, and the markets.

Part 2

7

Cock and bull –
and other tales

'O Yez! O Yez! If any man stands within twenty yards of the bull
ring let him take – what comes!' It is the shout of the City Crier, who
is standing in the midst of a blood-lusting mob at Chester High Cross
under the very windows of the Mayor and Corporation. The annual
bull-bait is indeed a civic occasion, commanded by the outgoing
Mayor on the day of the election of the new Mayor and the two Sheriffs during the great Michaelmas Fair beginning on October 10 or
thereabouts. Leaning out from the casement of the Pentice, the
Mayor's Parlour of the old days – 'a brave place builded for the purpose, under St. Peter's Church and in the midst of the city, in such a
sort that a man may stand therein and see into the four streets' – the
Mayor and the Common Council Men have a privileged view of the
beastliness that follows the Crier's warning. The bull – or maybe the
bear, it is all one – is tied to the whipping-post in the centre of the ring
by a rope about four yards long. The bullward – or bearward – in
charge of the pitiable beast, who is much scarred and showing some
still open wounds from recent contests, reads the 'rules', such as
they are, the citizens roar in anticipation of rare sport, and the first
mastiff is let loose to the attack. As one by one the maddened dogs
go in, and maul and are mauled, and the blood flows, the citizenry
and the magistracy alike are possessed by the frenzy of this bitter
business.

Soon there is a riot at the ringside, spreading rapidly to the
crowd. The butchers and bakers are at cudgels in a dispute over the
precedence of their dogs. And so the spectacle of the bull-bait, popular with the citizens, gentle and simple, from Tudor times, closes in
disorder, as so many times before, and the bull is dragged away out
of the tumult down a back lane into Watergate-street. Bearward-
lane, so called until it became Linenhall-street at the time of the
building of the Linenhall and the 'Chester Chronicle's' first decade,
bears witness to the enduring tradition of the bear and bull-bait. It
went on clandestinely after several attempts to put it down, and as

late as 1787, in the advanced age of 'enlightenment', we hear of a particularly sadistic refinement of the sport: the bull, 'smarting under his wounds and fatigue, was very naturally induced to lie down. The argument made use of in this situation as naturally induced him to get up, his humane followers hitting upon the ingenious expedient of setting fire to some straw under his body.'

The scrupulous Henry Hardware, Mayor in 1599, who had proscribed the lewder exhibitions of the famous Chester Midsummer Show, to the anger of the guildsmen, citizens, and apprentices, was the first magistrate to order the bull-ring to be taken up. But his successor, Robert Brerewood, sensitive to public opinion and, possibly, his own indulgence and that of the body corporate, restored the custom. In 1754, in the Mayoralty of Dr. William Cowper, the Corporation, at last ashamed that 'not even the ermined cloak was security against the carcases of dead animals with which spectators without distinction were occasionally saluted', withdrew their sanction of the annual bull-bait by staying away. James Broadhurst, Mayor in 1776, made another effort to stop the bull-bait and incurred the active displeasure of the citizens. 'His utmost exertions', wrote Joseph Hemingway, historian Editor of the 'Chester Chronicle', 'proved unavailing, and the lovers of the sport returned his endeavours to deprive them of it by forcing the bull into the Row below the steps of the Feathers Inn.'

The Mayor's house was in Bridge-street Row hard by the Feathers and the mob fastened the end of the bull's rope to his Worship's door-knocker, which was wrenched away by the animal's terror in striving to get free of his tormentors. Hemingway goes on, in sorrow and in anger:

> 'It is said the worthy magistrate was so alarmed at the transaction that he made a hasty retreat down a passage into Pepper-street, from whence he precipitately fled into the country, nor made a moment's pause until he had secured a safe retreat at the distance of several miles. From this period no serious attempt seems to have been made to put an end to the bull-bait until the year 1803, when a clause was introduced into the new Police Act by which it was finally suppressed. It is, however, a subject of regret that there is still [1831], in the immediate vicinity of the city, one of these annual brutal spectacles. It is exhibited on Boughton heath, a spot just without the jurisdiction of the city magistrates, during the wakes; and it is somewhat extraordinary that the county magistracy have not efficiently interposed to put it down. Although there is no specific statute to interdict the exhibition there,

yet upon every such occurrence violent breaches of the peace are committed; and besides the Act against cruelty to animals sufficiently arms them with authority to commit the participators in these orgies to gaol.'

Bull and bear-baiting went on, in defiance of the laws, at Cheshire market town and village fairs, as in the outskirts of the city itself, until the middle of the nineteenth century. Nantwich at one time had four Town Bears, the Middlewich bear was known as Old Nell, the reputation of Congleton suffers from a couplet

Congleton rare, Congleton rare
Sold the Church Bible to buy a new bear

and at Bunbury Fair and other village wakes the bull, excited by the blowing of pepper into his eyes and nostrils, was hunted through the village street, a fiddler going in front: this was the bull-run. The bull-bait at Bunbury continued without concealment until 1848 and afterwards secretly in the depths of Delamere Forest. The 'Chester Chronicle' of June 20, 1776 (number 61) reported 'We are informed by a Correspondent at Bunbury that, at their annual feast on Monday and Tuesday next, beside the usual entertainments on such occasions, there will be horse-races and bull-baits. Much company, he says, is expected, on account of the present agreeable mode of conveyance to Beeston Brook, where genteel ordinaries will be provided on Sunday, Monday, and Tuesday.' 'Genteel ordinaries' were lunch and dinner or refreshments. 'The present agreeable mode of conveyance' was by the recently constructed canal.

Nine years later the paper is still campaigning for the total abolition of the bull-bait in an eloquent and subtle paragraph that chides the Mayor and Corporation for playing politics at the expense of the citizens' rights when they could be better employed seeking out those who continued to bring the good name of the city into disrepute. Chronicle number 488, October 15, 1784, says:

'There is not anything that reflects a greater stigma on mankind than the cruelty of bull-baiting . . . To the honour of the present age, the barbarous custom of throwing of cocks is nearly abolished . . . As professed advocates of the peace and tranquility of the city, our Police should exert themselves; for at no other time appear so great riot and disorder, and prejudice to the inhabitants, as on this mad day of uproar. To say that custom hath established the act and 'tis madness to oppose the bloody festivity is futile. Cannot that all-powerful by-law that can abrogate Charters and disfranchise the burghers crush this so violent act of inhumanity; this barbarous game of death?'

In the last quarter of the eighteenth century horse-racing was gaining in popularity over its companion sport of cock-fighting, or cocking as it was commonly called, but it was some years before the notices of the Spring and Autumn Race Meetings on the Roodee at Chester and of the August or July Races at Nantwich in the advertisement columns of the Chronicle ceased to mention a Main of Cocks as an auxiliary attraction. In Chronicle number 4, May 22, 1775, William Leche and James Tomkinson, country squire stewards for Nantwich Races, announced 'A main of cocks will be fought between the Welsh and English gentlemen for five guineas a battle and 100 the main' – and these were the customary stakes. On April 25, 1776 (number 53) the advertisement for the Chester Spring Meeting announced that on Monday, May 6, the Annual City Plate would be run, and on Tuesday and Wednesday the purses would be £50 each, 'every horse to be entered at the Pentice on Thursday, May 2.' Under the sub-heading 'Cocking' the advertisement added: 'A Main of Cocks will be fought on Monday, 6th May, and on the subsequent race-days, between Sir Hugh Williams, Bart, and John Crewe, Esq., – to weigh 31 for the main and 20 for the byes. – Feeders, Bennet for Sir Hugh and Smith for Mr. Crewe.' Patronage of the cockpit was widespread and enthusiastic among the Welsh and Cheshire squirearchy. Every gentleman kept his gamecocks scientifically groomed for battle and armed with steel or silver spurs, and to possess a champion cock was to stand high with one's neighbours, to say nothing of the esteem of lesser folk who also knew the game and laid their bets. At Chester in May, 1783, the cocking stakes were high, the gentlemen of Cheshire and Lancashire competing for 10 guineas the battle and 200 the main. The contest was drawn, each county winning 17 battles: honour was satisfied, said the Chronicle.

There was a Cockpit Hill on rising ground outside the Chester City Walls near the end of Cow-lane in early times, and in 1619 William, Earl of Derby, 'made a fine cockpit under St. John's Church in a garden by the waterside to which resorted gentlemen of all parts, and great cocking was used a long while.' A new Cockpit was put up near the same site as late as 1825 and became a place of fashionable resort, says Hemingway, adding 'I take it for granted that the sale of tickets at five shillings each day for admission to the sport, during the Race Week, sufficiently remunerates the speculators for the outlay on the building.' The baited bull and bear and the gamecock fighting to a finish were in turn victims of the 'speculator' providing vicious and bloody combats for the city and county gentlemen and the common sort who alike crowded round the bull ring and the 'little amphitheatre' of the cockpit. The Rules and Orders of Cocking devised in the reign of Charles II were still in force when the Chronicle first went to press. A main consisted of any odd number of cocks from seven to 40, and the victorious bird was he that won most battles. In the Cheshire villages cockfights were sometimes held in the churchyard, and 'shakebag' contests took place spontaneously in the inn yard – so-called because the farmer would enter the inn with a bag over his shoulder and, over his beer, would shake out the contents, a prime cock or two, and wait for a challenger similarly to arrive. (Another country 'sport' that took place in the inn yard was badger-baiting, the badger being secured by a chain to a stake and set upon by the customers' dogs.) Cock-throwing (which, as I have noted, the Chronicle in 1784 described as this 'barbarous custom nearly abolished, to the honour of the present age') was a notable piece of savagery in which all-comers could for twopence have three throws with a stick or other missile from 22 yards at the cock tied by the leg to a peg. If the thrower could knock the cock down and quickly retrieve the stick before it could recover the bird was his. The cocks were no doubt fiendishly trained in tactics of evasion.

Public exhibitions of cock-fighting were stopped by the Cruelty to Animals Act of 1849, but that the sport of centuries continues to be indulged under cover has been proved by some celebrated prosecutions, including the case heard at Broxton Magistrates' Court sitting at Chester Castle in September, 1956. On the two days of the final hearing people queued for standing room in the public gallery. The Chronicle of September 15, 1956 (number 9, 430) devoted two broadsheet pages to a report of the case against 36 defendants, including 13 farmers, on summonses alleging that they assisted as spectators or procured the fighting by providing the birds. Court told of Sunday morning raid on Cheshire farm . . . Blood-spattered cockpit found . . . People scurried about in all directions – the headlines tell the tale of cockfighters surprised by a Police raid on a farm near Chester. Here is a paragraph of the evidence. Read it aloud, and it sounds like an echo from the eighteenth century:

'The cockpit upstairs, which had apparently been dismantled in haste when the alarm was given, was a wooden structure measuring 11 feet by 11 feet by 16 inches, with green matting inside lying on a sheet of

rubber sponge. It was painted white inside, but the white was spattered with blood. Round the side of the cockpit chairs and benches
were disposed. There was a good deal of blood and feathers about the
place. There was a large number of containers of one sort or another –
crates, packages, and bags – and in those containers were found a total
of sixty-two living birds. Some of these had evidently been in battle earlier that day . . .'

The defence admitted that there could be no doubt that a cock
fight took place at Cotton Edmunds farm on Sunday, June 10, and
that the Protection of Animals Act, 1911, and the Cock Fight Act,
1952, had been contravened. But it was permissible to wonder,
argued defence counsel, why cock-fighting should be singled out as
illegal. There was no law, he said, against fox-hunting, stag-hunting,
or coursing, where the odds were hopelessly unequal. The Court decided that the evidence of organised cockfighting was overwhelming,
and fines and costs were imposed amounting to more than £1,000.
The Chairman (Col. G. Egerton Warburton) said he found it hard to
believe, as had been said, that no betting had taken place: 'if it is
true, it means that you people assembled at Cotton Edmunds farm
simply for the pleasure of seeing birds tear themselves to pieces.' So
ended the cockfighting *cause célèbre*, and no more has been heard,
although without doubt the Police continue watchful in country
places. As a footnote to that case may I recall that it was the Tarporley hunting poet, R. E. Egerton Warburton, of the same family as
the Court's Chairman, who celebrated in song the Cheshire sporting
annals of earlier days:

> Our King the first William, Hugh Lupus our Earl,
> Then poaching, I ween, was no sport for a churl;
> A noose for his neck who a snare should contrive,
> Who skinn'd a dead buck was himself flay'd alive!

Horse-racing on Chester Roodee has been carried on almost continuously since the late fourteenth century. At first silver bells were
the prizes. The Grosvenor family papers at Eaton contain a foolscap
sheet of racing rhymes, one of which begins:

> Goe on, Gray Daintie, growe thou gray with yeares
> In yearely Tryumph, thou hast borne the Bell
> From Speede itselfe . . .

The claim has been made for Chester that the first organised horse-races in Britain began on the Roodee. Whether that claim can be sustained or not – York, as you might imagine, offers a strong coun-ter-claim – Chester Races are of ancient date and are indeed the last prosperous survivors of the Roodee pageants and citizen revels. The Midsummer Show, dating from the fifteenth century, was a spec-tacular affair round about Whitsun which spread through the entire city. The Christmas custom of appointing a Lord of Misrule prob-ably had its origin in the freedom and license of the Show. That same Mayor Henry Hardware who caused the bull ring to be taken up also tried to purge the Midsummer Show of its gawdy giants and dragon, its naked boys, and 'the Devil in his feathers'. At the Restoration the Show was revived, but the glitter had gone out of it, and it was finally abolished by an order of the Corporation in 1678. Archery, wrestling, foot-racing, football, athletics, morris dancing were Roodee sports and entertainments from very early times, and football is still played there, though of a different order from the robust game for which the city shoemakers annually provided a leather ball, value 3s. 4d. Mili-tary tournaments, tattoos, and exercises have been held there: the Cheshire Regiment has received its Colours there. The Roodee has been used in many wars as a camping ground and bivouac – I recall a scene during the evacuation of Dunkirk when a company of soldiers marched wearily down Watergate-street watched with a silent sur-mise by the citizens. The Autumn Sports (a later and very well-behaved version of the Midsummer Show) made an August Bank Holiday festival in the streets and on the Roodee until recent years. The Roodee also accommodated the Cheshire Agricultural Show each year until torrential rain one June day turned the ground into a quagmire. Circuses pitch their Big Tops on this famous public com-mon.

'Race Week' dates properly from 1609, when William Lester, the Mayor, and Robert Amery, Sheriff in the previous year, gave three silver cups for competition by 'all gentlemen that would bring their horses to the Roodee on St. George's Day and there run'. John Brere-ton, Mayor in 1623, reduced the number of cups to one 'fair silver cuppe', value £8, for a race to be run five times round the Roodee. The beat of a drum from the top of the spire of St. Peter's Church was the signal for the start of the race meeting on St. George's Day (April 23). 'A fair silver cup', but still not the Chester Cup as we know it today. The establishment of the Jockey Club at Newmarket in 1750 brought some order and regulation into racing for the first time, both on the course and among the spectators, who frequently fought among themselves and invaded the track, impeding horses and riders. And jockeys crossed and jostled and impeded each other. Races of up to four miles were run in heats and laggard horses were eliminated at the 'distance post'. Victory went to the horses that won a majority of heats, so that staying-power was more valued than speed before the days of the thoroughbred.

In the Chester Chronicle's first decade the Roodee Races, held in May and September, were established as a fashionable as well as a sporting assembly, under the patronage of the Mayor and Corporation, and the Grosvenor, Stanley, Cholmondeley, Egerton, Williams Wynn, Puleston, Wilbraham, Mainwaring, Mostyn, and other Cheshire and Welsh county families. There had been racing at Doncaster since 1725, Manchester and Nottingham started in 1777, the St. Leger was first run in 1776, the Oaks in 1779, and the Derby in 1780. The Chronicle of September 4, 1775 (number 19) sets the scene for the Autumn meeting: 'We have great reason to expect that this City will be remarkably full at the ensuing races, which are to begin on Monday next, as most of the lodgings are already engaged. Several horses are come and many more expected before the day of entrance. The sweepstakes are filled by the first Noblemen and Gentlemen on the Turf, and there is no doubt that this meeting will annually vie with York, Newmarket, or any other in the kingdom.' And after the event, issue number 21 (September 18) reports: 'The meeting at our races last week was crowded with the most noble and polite company ever seen on such an occasion. The Concert for the Infirmary, and the Assemblies, were very brilliant, and we hear the Noblemen, and neighbouring Ladies and Gentlemen, are determined to continue their subscriptions and, if possible, make this meeting vie with any other in the kingdom.'

Popular race meetings were held at the county towns of Nantwich and Knutsford, and the annual meeting at Farndon Hay had been going for more than a century. It was on January 28, 1631, that Robert Viscount Cholmondeley, Sir Thomas Grosvenor, Sir Phillip Egerton, Sir Peter Warburton, Sir John Hanmer, Thomas Cholmondeley of Vale Royal, Sir John Egerton and others concluded articles for a 'free cup to be run yearly and perpetually at Farndon' in March – everything to be ordered according to the 'Rules of Horsemanship and the most probable to increase the sport and continue

Amitie and Virtue.' Gentlemen jockeys first took the field in the Flintshire Hunt meeting at Holywell, established by Earl Grosvenor in 1767. Knutsford's prudent conduct of its race meeting is seen in this notice by the stewards, Richard Wilbraham Bootle and William Bankes, in the Chronicle of May 29, 1775 (number 5): 'No horse to stand at any house but what shall subscribe half a guinea to the Town's Purse. No person will be permitted to erect any booth, or sell any liquor, etc., upon the Common without first contributing half a guinea to the Town's Purse.' Genteel, purse-proud Knutsford – Cranford-to-be nearly a century later.

In the same year the Tarporley Hunt agreeably provided hunting and racing at Crabtree Green near that country town. The Chronicle of November 13 (number 29) reported:

> 'On Saturday last the first subscription hunt for this season ended at Tarporley, when twenty-three of the members were present, among whom were the Earl of Stamford, Sir Thomas Broughton, John Crewe, Esq., member for the county, etc., besides a large number of non-subscribers. Each day was spent with the festivity peculiar to the Noblemen and Gentlemen of this Circle; and on Thursday a further addition was made to the sport of the day by two races being run on Crabtree Green . . . There was excellent diversion at the chase each day; several Foxes were killed, and the whole was supported with the true spirit of the descendants of Nimrod.'

By 1783 the number of heats in the principal races at most meetings had been reduced to a manageable three. A typical five days at the Chester Spring Meeting is reported in the Chronicle, May 9 of that year (number 418). On the Monday of that Race Week the Corporation's City Plate, value £30, with a purse of £20, was run for. The big race on Tuesday was in the £50 gift of the city's two M.P.s, Thomas Grosvenor and R. W. Bootle. On Wednesday the Maiden Plate was awarded for the best of three four-mile heats, and on Thursday Lord Grosvenor's Gold Cup was at stake over the same distance. The Cup (£50) was of the same value as the Maiden Plate and the Ladies' Plate, and the race for this last trophy concluded the meeting. Mr. Witty's Will Scarlet won the Maiden Plate, Mr. Astley's Herod colt falling within two yards of the winning chair. William Clough's bay mare Beauty won the Gold Cup.

In 1802 the Earl of Chester's Plate, of 100 guineas, to be run three times round the course, appeared on the card for the first time. And by 1821 the values reflected Chester's determination to keep its high place in the racing calendar. There were the Royal Plate, the Prince of Wales's (as Earl of Chester), worth 100 guineas; the City Plate, a silver punch-bowl, value 60 guineas; the Gold Cup given by Earl Grosvenor, value £70; a purse of 60 guineas given by the city M.PS; and the stand Subscription Cup of 100 guineas, 'besides matches and sweepstakes formed by the gentlemen of the Turf.' Writing in that year, John Broster pictured the scene: 'When the weather is favourable the views from the different parts of the course are rendered singularly interesting by the concourse of people, the various carriages and horsemen; and what adds still more to the whole appearance is the beauty, fashion, and gaiety which are ranged on the Walls and on the hill beneath them. The meetings are honoured with companies of the first rank, and the assemblies equal most in the kingdom.' This consciously picturesque prose gives way, in May, 1824, to the critical scrutiny of Nimrod, writing to the Sporting Magazine. He observed that 'as a convivial meeting' Chester was not what it had been, 'a chilling stream of refinement' having affected the habits of the Welsh and Cheshire sporting squires. Was the coming Reform of the landed interest troubling them? It would seem very unlikely. But 'as a place of sport Chester is greatly improved and as a country meeting may rank next in the list to Epsom, Ascot, York, and Doncaster, having no less than nine good sweepstakes, one King's Plate, two Gold Cups, and five other plates.'

Appropriately in that year, the Chester Chronicle reports the institution of the Chester Cup Race (not to be confused with the Grosvenors' Gold Cup), first known as the Tradesmen's Cup, value 100 guineas, to be run for on Monday, May 5, with a free handicap stakes of 15 guineas each in addition – 'to start at the Castle Pole, run twice round, and end at the Coming-in Chair.' The first Cup winner was Sir Thomas Stanley's Doge of Venice, starting a clear favourite at 6 to 4 against, with Lord Grosvenor's Etiquette second. Fortunes were won and lost that day, but not so recklessly as in the years to come to the middle of the century. Thirty-four horses started in the Chester Cup of 1848. W. E. Topham's handicapping 'gave great satisfaction' (not to all, surely) and the owner of the winner, Peep-o '-Day Boy, received the stakes of £2,500. The Cup was established as one of the leading long-distance handicaps, and men would reckon their lives by the number of Chester Cups they had seen run and treasure in the memory such evocative names as Tom Pepper, Chivalrous, Brown Jack, Heron Bridge, and Major Rose. In 1964 the 'Flat' entered a

new era with the Betting Levy Board's grant of £2.3 millions on the
first stage of a programme for the modernisation of seventeen of the
country's major courses. In a Chronicle editorial of March 21 of that
year (issue number 9,815) I commented that 'A complete modernisation of the racing facilities of Chester Roodee has been estimated
to cost £200,000. If the historic meeting is to survive in the new financial and social climate of the mid-sixties, something will have to be
done. And that something will take the form this year of seven days'
racing – the customary three days in May and two days each in July
and September, the experiment to include Saturday and evening
racing.'

The Race Company received its first direct contribution from the
Levy Board in 1973, by which time the various improvements at the
Roodee, the reduced admission prices and increased prize money, as
well as the innovation of the Saturday and evening fixtures, had
enhanced the popularity of the meetings. In July, 1973, for the first
time in all the centuries of racing on the Roodee, women jockeys
competed in the Ladies' Race. The values of the principal races
today (1974) are Chester Cup, £8,200, and Chester Vase, £6,100, and
the Ormonde Stakes, Dee Stakes, and Chester Oaks have all increased in value. The Grosvenor Stakes, the Earl of Chester, the
Prince of Wales and the City Handicaps all continue as of old but for
relatively modest rewards. Conditions for the racegoer have never
been better, but the scene in the Roodee amphitheatre is panorami-
cally the same as it has always been. Irish, Welsh, and English, and
York and Lancaster, still meet there as they have done time out of
mind. The car has replaced the carriage: costumes, conditions,
nuances alter: the essentials remain the same. The patrons of the
Turf are there, the county people, the citizens out for the day. All are
attracted by the old spectacle which constantly changes but is for
ever the same. Hotspur, Captain Heath, Robin Goodfellow, The
Scout, or the gentlemen of the Press who have inherited these celebrated names, descend upon Chester for Race Week with the regularity of migrant birds. And now there is a new dimension: the
television cameras rove over the gay and varied scene under the City
Wall, in the paddock and the stands and rings, and on the course.
There is no picture like it in the country.

Sporting relations between the 'gentlemen' and citizen and country
commoners were generally cordial in the last quarter of the eight-

eenth century, but when it came to poaching a hare, pheasant, or partridge, that was another matter. Mr. Egerton, of Oulton Park (today the site of a motor-racing circuit), inserted this notice in the Chester Chronicle of August 28, 1775 (number 18): 'The game in the manors of Egerton, Hampton and Bickerton having of late been much destroyed, Mr. Egerton requests his friends to desist from sporting there till it is restored, when he shall be glad to oblige them as usual. Poachers will be prosecuted.' Mr. Egerton was protecting the landowners' jealously-guarded privilege of preserving game for their own use and pleasure and that of their neighbours, secured for them by an Act of 1671 and reinforced by an Act of 1770. Farmers subject to increasing land enclosure were bitterly hostile to the enclosure of game; birds and beasts were to them common property; they poached to eat and incurred drastic penalties if caught. Under the Act of 1770 the penalty on conviction of poaching between sunset and sunrise was up to six months in gaol; for a second offence, up to twelve months and a public whipping. But the war between the poachers and the gamekeepers went on, and in the next century the Game Laws had become so savage that the poacher caught at night could be in danger of transportation for seven years, that is if he escaped death or mutilation by man-trap, leg-breaker, or spring-gun.

Not to be outdone by the country folk, the citizens of Chester evidently stole across the Dee Bridge by night to raid the Grosvenors' game at Eaton Park, which caused Sir Richard Grosvenor, chairman of Quarter Sessions, to give this ruthless charge in the city's Shire Hall in 1642:

> 'Poachers, such as are enemies to the sports and pleasures of gentlemen, to whom the law allows such recreations as are not held fit for persons of a meaner condition; and these are those who destroy hares by tracing them in the snow, or kill them with hare-pipes, or other engines. Likewise those who take pheasants, or partridges with nets, or any other device . . . so also stealers of deers and conies . . . and those that shoot in pieces at hares, pheasants, partridge, pigeon, heron, duck, or any other fowl prohibited, of which kind of offenders this our neighbour City affords plenty, who (by their boldness in continually offending) proclaim that they think the Charter and privilege of their City should patronise and protect them from punishment in the country. Myself have heretofore caused diverse of them to be indicted, but I never heard yet that any of them were punished. Where the fault is I know not.'

Perhaps the citizens were too cunning for Sir Richard's game-keepers, or perhaps the keepers were in their pockets. To be fair to the Baronet, he also at the same time condemned extortionate inn-keepers who preyed upon travellers.

The penal Game Law of 1816, so far from deterring the poachers, caused desperate affrays, angered the people, and aroused the criticism of the Press. The Chester Chronicle in April, 1829, reported the trial at Chester Castle of twenty poachers apprehended after an armed raid on the pheasants of Squire Edwin Corbett, of Darnhall Grange, near Winsford. First news of this affair appeared in the Chronicle of December 26, 1828 (number 2784). Twenty to thirty men with shotguns entered the wood at Darnhall shortly before midnight, fired on the keeper and coachman who surprised them, appeared openly before the Grange, and 'continued firing until they had killed almost all the pheasants within reach'. Not until February of the succeeding year were the ringleaders arrested and locked-up at Nantwich. When the prisoners were being brought out for examination by the magistrates, some four thousand of the Nantwich townspeople, including all the shoemakers, surrounded them and hustled them away from the courthouse three-quarters of a mile out of town. Led by Major W. Tomkinson, of Dorfold Hall, the magistrates pursued the mob on horseback and Tomkinson intrepidly read the Riot Act, summoning the troops from Chester. 'This city,' says the Chronicle of February 13, 1829 (number 2791), 'was thrown into great consternation by the drum beating to arms and the consequent assemblage of the 87th in the Castle yard . . . The military had been called out in aid of the civil power at Nantwich.' At the subsequent trial, to which the prisoners were brought chained together in carts and wagons, 'elegantly-dressed females' anxious to see the celebrated poachers occupied the grand jury box at Chester Castle. The sentences were fourteen years' transportation for seven of the accused and imprisonment for the rest, and the Chronicle declared uncompromisingly at the end of its otherwise objective report that the severity of the Game Laws was a matter crying aloud for reform. The sequel was curious and perhaps the beginning of a concession to outraged public opinion that eventually modified the laws. The convict hulk was about to sail for Botany Bay when a technical flaw was discovered in the indictment, and this being communicated to London the Cheshire poachers were suddenly taken out of irons, released, and sent home. Eight years later public opinion spoke again when Squire Corbett was ignominiously treated and defeated in the election to the first Parliament of Queen Victoria.

The eighteenth-century Englishman would gamble on anything, even on executions. Beneath the surface polish of the age there was a blood-lust for brutalities publicly enacted, with a wager to heighten the zest. A street quarrel, with high words leading to a swift blow, and the crowd would gather, making a ring and laying bets. That was how the bare-knuckle prize-fight 'game' began, in the streets and at town and country fairs, and continued with the utmost fero-city and the support of the aristocratic 'Corinthians' and young bloods who backed their protégés for thousands of pounds, until Jack Broughton, Champion of England from 1734 to 1750, devised a set of rules and introduced 'mufflers' or rudimentary boxing gloves. Before that the sport was described as 'downright slaughtering' in which death was not infrequently the sequel. Even Broughton's code did not prohibit butting, gouging, and biting. The 'mill' went out only with the development of real boxing science by Daniel Mendoza and John (Gentleman) Jackson in the last years of the century. Broughton lost his title eventually to Jack Slack in a famous fight and at the same time the countenance of his patron, the Duke of Cumber-land. From 1761 to 1783 the title changed hands several times, and Peter Corcoran (or Cochran) claimed it in 1771.

The defeat of Cochran in a short, savage contest is described in the first of the Chester Chronicle's prize-ring reports, June 27, 1776 (number 62). Forget the Queensberry Rules which govern boxing today and let the contemporary words recreate the scene on that day of late June nearly two centuries ago:

'A bet was made for a battle of fifty guineas a side between Cochran, the noted Irish bruiser, and Sellers, a sawyer, from the West of Eng-land. The combatants tossed up which should choose the place of fighting, and Sellers winning, chose Staines in Middlesex, where he had a number of acquaintances. Leonard was chosen as second to Cochran, and the famous Maggs was sent for from Bristol to second Sellers. Monday being the day fixed for the battle, a stage was erected at the White Lion Inn, and thousands of people assembled in coaches, landaus, post and single horse chaises, and on foot; the road from Hounslow to Staines being a perfect fair. The combatants mounted the stage at two o'clock, and it being agreed that the conqueror should have the door money, it was deposited in the hands of a gentleman, amounting to about £60. Just as the antagonists had shaken hands, and were putting themselves in a posture of defence, a barn, on which were above one hundred people, fell at once to the ground, but not one person was materially hurt. The battle now commenced; and after a severe contest of twenty minutes, victory was declared in favour of Sellers, who by one blow cut Cochran's cheek-bone from the top of the jaw-bone to the neck. Immense sums were lost by the friends of Cochran, who was never beaten before, whereas Sellers had never before mounted a public stage. One gentleman lost £1,800 and Sellers cleared about £110 by the victory. The news was brought to Whitechapel by pigeons in forty minutes after the battle ended.'

After his defeat of Cochran, Sellers the sawyer was in the money and he is reported next, in June, 1777, taking on Wood the weaver at Windsor for 500 guineas. He had a shock and a setback. One eye was beaten out, and he lost the fight. Sellers turns up again in the Chronicle columns on September 11, 1778 (number 177) in a fifty-guineas-a-head fight with 'the noted Nayler', a wily and experienced pugilist, on Hounslow-heath. The battle had been long anticipated, the 'fancy' being anxious to see how the veteran Nayler, aged 50 and labouring also under 'the disadvantage of a debauched constitution', would stand up to the one-eyed Sellers, 'not yet thirty and a remarkable abstemious man'. Thousands flocked to the heath and the betting was heavy, the odds of evens to five in favour of Sellers increasing as the ten-minutes fight went on. By comparison it seems to have been a well-ordered affair. 'The Nayler,' says the Chronicle reporter, 'had not entirely forgot the art, for he once fairly laid his antagonist at length, but in retaliation suffered the same three successive times, till at last victory was proclaimed in the favour of Sellers, who by a West-country trick disabled his antagonist from any further defence. The seconds were Peter Leonard for Sellers and Pitt for the Nayler.' What the West Country trick was is left to the imagination. It could have been a wrestling throw or worse.

To Peter Cochran's (or Corcoran's) loss of the Championship, if he ever really held it, was added the mortification of his wife's failure to sustain the domestic credit in a battle of her own – for money, of course – with another woman in Duke-street, Leicesterfields, in September, 1777. Before engaging, the combatants cut off their hair and stripped to their under-petticoats. After twenty minutes of scratching, clawing, and rolling about, Mrs. Cochran received, in the words

of the reporter, 'a blow in the mark' (the stomach) which incapaci-
tated her. The other woman got the purse. An oyster-seller and 'a
nymph of pleasure' made an exhibition of themselves in Stepney-
fields on September 13, 1776. 'A severe battle was fought,' says the
Chronicle of September 20 (number 74), 'for five guineas a side;
when after a long contest, wherein was shown much experience in
the Broughtonian art, victory was declared for the nymph of pleasure; the female oyster-seller lost an eye.' In the first decade of the
Chester Chronicle there is, curiously, no report of prize-fighting in
Cheshire, but the full rigour of the ring, miles away from the reforming rules of Jack Broughton and Gentleman Jackson, is seen in this
stark account of a drawn-out drama from the neighbour county of
Shropshire, December 17, 1784 (number 497): 'A few days ago a most
terrible battle was fought at Ludlow, consisting of 35 rounds, between one Bloody, a butcher, of Montgomery, and another noted
bruiser, for £25. It was at last won by Bloody, the other being so
much bruised that he has since died.' And they waited until 1867 for
the Marquess of Queensberry's definitive rules of boxing: there must
have been a deal of slaughter in the meantime.

Not least in the 'grand mill' to which Chester and all the country
round flocked to see, three miles out of the city at Lache Eyes, between Boscow the Butcher and Magee, an Irish stonemason, on
Tuesday, October 11, 1825. This battle went 39 rounds and each one
was 'scientifically' reported in the Chronicle of October 14 (number
2623). The Editor introduced the two-columns account thus: 'We
were fearful that our Reporter was not sufficiently accomplished to
give the detail of a Prize Fight, with all the embellishments of slang,
etc.,' but some members of the fancy being in town on Wednesday
the 'copy' was submitted to and approved by them! The city magistrates objected to the fight and sent officers to stop it, but the promoters had chosen their ground carefully, just inside Flintshire, the
Lache Eyes being described as a piece of waste ground partly in the
parish of Dodleston, but outside the city limits.

A hundred sovereigns were at stake, and from the start the betting
was on Boscow. When the fight began at 1 o'clock there were between eight and ten thousand spectators in massed ranks round the
ring. Boscow disabled his opponent in the sixth round with a blow
which lanced his right eye: 'Magee exhibited a frightful spectacle.
His mug had an appearance as if it had been scalped. His drawers
and stockings were literally bathed in blood.' In this, and a steadily

worsening condition, the Irishman went another 33 rounds before two blows, one to the ear, another to the throat, paralysed him. The victor had got in the clinchers none to soon, for after the fight he was 'taken off the ground in a gig, his face frightfully swollen; he seemed insensible to all around him.' But with the money in his pocket he was able to recuperate in the comfort of the White Lion at Chester. As for the Irishman, thousands of people were reluctant to quit the scene until they had satisfied their curiosity as to what effect 'the terrible beating he had received had had upon him. He sat in a sort of stupor . . .' It took a long time to clear the ground, the crowds withdrawing slowly and fighting among themselves on the way to the nearest alehouses. 'The appearance of the roads after the conflict might have been compared to that of a beaten army,' wrote the Chronicle reporter. 'Carriages of all sorts, horsemen and footmen – women and children – spread over the country in all directions. Charleroi, after the defeat of Bonaparte, never was more choaked up with refugees than were the adjacent villages, and especially Hawarden, with company.'

Tennis was not much played outside London and there mostly by the wealthy and leisured. But the game, like all others, attracted sharpers and hangers-on, or court-flies, and the players naturally backed their own skill. The state of the game and its social and other sidelights are admirably set forth in this Chronicle report of May 7, 1779 (number 211) of a match at the Tennis-court in St. James's-street, Haymarket, between Sir William Draper, Knight of the Bath, and M. Bellafong, 'a French marker and tennis-player at Paris, lately arrived in England'. The Frenchman was clearly what we should now call a professional, for 'tho' Sir William Draper is accounted almost as good a gentleman player as any in England, yet Bellafong gave him half the court, a fifteen and four bisks, which are reckoned most extraordinary odds to give a person who knows any thing of the game. The English Knight of the Bath and Monsieur le Marquer Francais played for 30 guineas a set, when Sir William was pidgeoned out of 180 guineas by the Frenchman (by way of being his expences to Paris next Tuesday), besides a considerable quantity of bye-betts with gentlemen and rooks of all denominations.'

Cricket about this time had discarded the crooked bat for the straight one. Hampshire, for whom played most of the famous

Hambledon Club cricketers experienced on Ha'penny Down, were the leading county, and in September, 1777, they took on and defeated All England on the Artillery Ground at Finsbury. Play lasted three days in this 'Test', each side batted twice, and Hampshire won by 130 runs or, as the scoring custom was, notches on a stick. The report says that the game finished earlier than usual because most of the players were quickly caught out. Rudimentary cricket was played in the Cheshire villages, but Cheshire, Flintshire and the neighbouring counties have never been among the foremost cricketing counties. Club cricket dates from the next century, Boughton Hall, Chester (centenary 1973), Nantwich and some others achieving a very high standard of play. Lancashire's Old Trafford has always been the real headquarters of cricket in the North-West.

8

Clear the road for the
flying mail coach

It is a January night of deep snow, the year 1776. Comfortably settled
in a corner of the tap-room of the White Lion Inn, in Northgate-
street, reading the Chester Chronicle, with his glass and pipe at
hand, is a much-weathered character of indeterminate age but none
the less very well known to the citizens. He wears short top boots
with spurs, a short coloured jacket, and a tall beaver hat. The hat is
the denomination of his trade and by force of habit he does not discard it within doors. He is the postboy (and a very mature 'boy' at
that) of the London-Chester mail. Weary of riding postillion on the
nearside horse of a pair, stage after stage, in the worst weather of late
years, he is thankful to have survived the hazards of the road, his
mails intact, and now to recruit his spirits before a blazing fire in the
great city and county coaching house. He has an audience about
him, agog for news of the road, of highwaymen and foul weather.
(Appropriately, a London newspaper of the time was called The
Postboy.) The bad weather has continued for more than a fortnight
and our postboy has the satisfaction of reading about himself in the
Chronicle. In the week of January 15, when Chronicle number 38
went to press, delayed until two o'clock in the morning, he was unable to get through at all because of the 'prodigious' fall of snow between London and Coventry and Monday, Thursday, and Saturday
nights 'expresses' of metropolitan intelligence were undelivered at
the newspaper office. Conscious of the omissions, but forbearing to
apologise for what can't be helped, the Editor hopes that readers
'will not find us totally destitute either of amusement or information'.

That had been a very trying week for the postboys, both ways between Chester and London. Communications having been inter-
rupted, the story did not come out until the end of the month, when
London reported the Chester mail 'detained at Dunstable, where the
snow was so thick that the postboy could not get through, and was
obliged to take out his horses to save their lives'. From Oxford came

news that the Chester postboy was lost in the snow between Birmingham and Wolverhampton – 'in some of the turnpike roads the
snow is drifting from six to eight feet deep, and in many of the by-
roads to a depth of eighteen feet'. The Chronicle, its expresses at last
to hand, caught up with the weather on January 22 and 29 (numbers
39 and 40) and reported also the plight of two 'poor women' caught in
a blizzard on Saltney marsh, picked up humanely by a man passing
with a cart and carried to Handbridge, where one woman died 'upon
being set down'.

Constantly on the road, the postboys carried the mail and the
news packets and were a prime source of news themselves. Before the
fast Royal Mail coaches superseded the slower stages in 1784, the
postboys were in the service of posting inn landlords who mounted
the 'boys' on relays of horses along the road and distributed the mail
in their districts. After the passing of the General Turnpike Act in
1773, stage coaches improved with the state of the roads and outstripped the postboys, who kept their name but now became drivers
as well as riders. The innkeepers' monopoly of the carriage of mail by
postboy and stage coach lasted until John Palmer, of Bath, organised
a Royal Mail Coach service, each coach having an armed guard and
carrying four inside passengers, whose fares paid for the carriage of
the mail. But the postboy, either as driver or outrider, continued in
the service of the mail into the high coaching days of the next century, immortalised by Charles Dickens in *The Pickwick Papers*.

All through the long and eventful reign of George III the life of the
road was increasingly the life of the country. People moved about as
never before, travelling on horseback, by coach and carriage on the
turnpike roads that linked and crossed the land. Turnpike Trusts
formed by Parliamentary sanction by local landowners, merchants,
and others to improve and maintain roads formerly in the somewhat
casual care of parish highway surveyors advertised in the Chronicle
for loans to be paid back out of the tolls. In the last quarter of the century the paper reported progress on turnpike contracts carried out in
Cheshire by the famous engineers John Metcalfe ('Blind Jack of
Knaresborough'), Thomas Telford (friend and coadjutor of John
Fletcher, of the Chronicle), and John Macadam. Just as they were
discussed in the paper, the American war, politics, the revival of the
Port of Chester, canal and River Dee navigation, and always the
events of the road were subjects that made up the staple of news at
the White Lion, the Yacht, the Plume of Feathers, and the other

much-frequented coaching inns of Chester. Situated at the very heart of the city, the White Lion (on the site roughly of the present Town Hall), with the Exchange (the seventeenth and eighteenth centuries Town Hall) at right-angles to it, the meat shambles, fruit and vegetable markets in the foreground, the Dublin Packet Inn near at hand and always full of travellers in transit to Parkgate for the Irish packet boats, the Exchange coffee-house round the corner, the Theatre Royal across the street, and two other coaching inns, the Pied Bull and the Golden Falcon up the street, was in constant activity night and day.

Travellers set down by the stage coach could hire an elegant, yellow-flashed, steel-springed post-chaise with a pair of horses for their forward journey off the turnpike route. For this service postboys and ostlers were at the ready, listening for the posthorn that heralded the dashing arrival of the coach-and-four or coach-and-six. Departures and arrivals were affairs of much panache, the coachman and postillions achieving a theatrical flourish and burst of speed that were only briefly sustained on the road. Food, drink, and accommodation were available at all hours for the stage passengers and for travellers in private chaises and carriages; and for long journeys the Lion maintained a hire service of post-chaises with postillions and a regular change of horses at the posting inns along the road. The Number One Chester Chronicle (May 2, 1775) publishes the daily timetables of the post-coaches to London and Holyhead from the White Lion and the Yacht Inn, the journey taking two days in each direction. A woodcut illustration of a flying coach heads this announcement by the White Lion management in the paper of April 25, 1776 (number 53):

Two Machines, in two days,
to and from London,
set out from the WHITE
LION INN on Sunday, Tuesday,
and Thursday nights at
eight o'clock,
by way of Whitchurch; and
on Monday, Wednesday,
and Friday nights at
six o'clock,
by way of Nantwich; and
arrive every day, Monday
excepted. Inside passengers

to pay £2.2s. Children
on lap and outsides
half-price.

Three years later on January 1, 1779 (number 193) the Lion advertises its full week's services, beginning with an improved post-coach to carry four passengers, plying between Northgate-street and the Golden Cross, Charing Cross, every Tuesday and Saturday mornings at four o'clock – 'performs in two days and a half', fare £3.3s and 20lb of luggage allowed, overplus 2d. per lb. At the same time two six-passenger 'machines' to and from London, one by way of Whitchurch, Newport, Castle Bromwich, and Coventry, the other through Nantwich, Stafford, Lichfield, Tamworth, Atherstone, and Northampton, performed a regular alternate service of two days and two days and a half on the latter (and longer) route. Inside passengers paid £2.5s, outsides £1.1s, 'the full fare to be paid at booking and half returned in case the party does not go. Also the post-coach to and from Holyhead, to carry four passengers, sets out from the White Lion at Chester and the Eagle and Child at Holyhead every morning (except Sunday), performs in two days, fare £2.11s.6d.'

After the introduction of the Royal Irish Mail Coaches, the White Lion adjusted its fares in competition for the Irish carriage. Its advertisement in the Chronicle of November 11, 1785 (number 543) gives the fare as £1.11s.6d. (inside) and 16s (outside), and on route to Holyhead stages of Holywell 6s., St. Asaph 10s., Kinmel 12s. 4d., Abergele 13s., Conway 16s. 8d., and Bangor £1.2s.6d. That was cheap travel by comparison with the fares charged some years earlier. For the quality custom landaus to be driven by two postillions were promised for the summer season, to 'render the conveyance more agreeable'. The rival Yacht Inn had a regular diligence travelling to and from London by arrangement with the famous metropolitan coaching house, the Swan-with-Two Necks, in Lad-lane, Gresham-street. The fare was £2.5s.6d and 'the drivers have particular orders not to solicit any gratuity from the passengers'. The outward route as given in the Chronicle of April 11, 1776 (number 51) was Tarporley, Nantwich, Woore, Stone, Onsleybridge, Lichfield, Coleshill, Coventry, Towcester, and Stoney Stratford. Appropriately, it will be seen that all the Chester-London coaches – the mileage of the Cheshire coach roads was computed from the door of the White Lion – followed the line approximately of the two arms of the Roman Watling Street, which passed (and still passes) along Foregate into Eastgate. Along the same historic route Telford early in the next century engineered his great road from London through the Welsh mountains to Holyhead, which today corresponds more or less with the A5. Along Telford's road the Holyhead mail coach, running twenty-four hours of the day, achieved a record eleven miles an hour.

Eleven miles an hour was a spanking pace. A stage coach journey before the middle of the eighteenth century and the improvement of roads and vehicles was slow, tedious, uncomfortable, and often dangerous. 'Outsides' paid less and had the worst of it, but they could at least talk to the coachman if that worthy were not in a morose and taciturn humour, which the nature of his function not infrequently induced. 'Insides' travelled first-class, so to speak, but being nearer the lumbering wheels in springless carriages suffered unspeakably from jolting and being flung about in company that was sometimes far from congenial. Dean Swift endured these trials many times passing through Chester on his way to Ireland and was moved to write:

> When soon, by ev'ry hillock, rut, and stone,
> Into each other's face by turn we're thrown . . .
> Sweet company! Next time, I do protest, Sir,
> I'd walk to Dublin ere I'd ride to Chester.

Familiar with all the hostelries on the road, the coachman and postillions made many unscheduled stops for refreshment, whether the passengers would or no, and resumed the journey foxed with liquor. Coaches were ditched or overturned, sometimes by accident, sometimes because the coachman was 'high'. An 'outside' was killed at Nantwich 'by falling headlong from the top of a coach as it was being carelessly driven past the Black Lion Inn'. As the coaching trade expanded and the computation of fares and allowances for luggage to be carried became more sophisticated, the satirists took a hand. Here is a jesting letter to the Editor of the Chronicle, October 17, 1783 (number 441):

> Sir, – I think that the rates of passengers in stage coaches might be made more equitable than they are now. I was present the other day when a slender gentleman (returning from his travels on the continent), who weighed only 8 stone, was obliged to pay for 7 lbs. of extra luggage, while a corpulent gentleman (who had never been out of England), who weighed 18 stone, was admitted at the usual fare with his 14 lbs of luggage. Now if the matter was placed upon a just foundation, by

making all people pay according to weight, the latter of these parties would have been charged for 19 stone and the traveller for only half the weight; instead of which, the home-fed passenger, of twice the burthen, was dragged more than fifty per cent cheaper than his slight-built neighbour. One inconvenience, it must be allowed, would attend this *equalization* of carriage: some sort of people might starve themselves into a less degree of ponderosity; but even this might be remedied by an Act obliging all people (previous to their undertaking a journey) to eat a certain number of days under the inspection of proper officers, and thereby prevent the proprietors of these vehicles from suffering by the abstemiousness of their passengers.

Footpads, who watched the movements of the postboys on the approaches to and exits from London, on stretches of heathland or common, stopped the Chester Mail driver on his way out of town near Highgate on the morning of Wednesday, January 24, 1782. This was a carefully-planned hold-up by three men having a get-away vehicle near at hand, as in many twentieth-century bank robberies. The Chronicle of January 25 (number 353) tells the story, which has a sequel, as we shall see, in which the Chester postboy behaved with much prudence. The footpads, having stopped the mail, 'led the horses, with the mail-cart, down a lane, and then taking out some mailbags as they chose, and setting the horses loose, tied the postboy in the cart and went off in a single-horse chaise that was there waiting for them'. Bow Street Runners, out all night on patrol, found the postboy, released him, and traced the thieves to town as far as Upper Moorfields, where they picked up some of the mailbags that had been dropped in their getaway and flight from pursuit. 'There is little doubt of their being soon taken, as they were well known.' They had not, however, been taken by March 1 of the same year, when the Chronicle (number 358) reported the sequel. Four footpads armed with pistols stopped the postboy with the incoming Chester Mail near the Queen's Head, Islington. 'They demanded if he was the same who drove the mail-cart when it was robbed last. To which the postboy replied No, for he had not been out since. They then told him it was well he was not, and bid him go on'.

That surely was the subject of a winter night's gossip at the White Lion, where also there must have been speculation, a few years earlier, about the identity of the whip of a post-chaise convicted before the Mayor of driving furiously and negligently through the city streets, endangering the life of 'an aged and deaf person who was passing; and we hear that Mr. Mayor is determined to put the law in

force against all such offenders within the city liberties.' That was in
1777. A year later, on March 27, the Chronicle (number 153) printed
a facetious account of a race between two post-chaise drivers returning from Wrexham Fair 'elevated to an uncommon pitch by the ale of
that town'. Racing neck and neck until within a mile of Chester, one
rider unexpectedly drew ahead, when the surmise entered his fud-
dled brains that he had lost the second horse of his pair and the
chaise. Turning about, 'on the spot where he had gained the
superiority he found the chaise overturned and his three passenger
still in it – they received no damage but what arose from fright. We
recollect not any thing similar to this unless the stealing of Sancho's
ass from under him may bear some resemblance to it'.

'Drivers of carts, carriages, etc., are by law compelled to give way
to the mail coach'. These warning words heralded the start on
Monday, October 3, 1785, of John Palmer's official Royal Irish Mail
from London through Chester to Holyhead. The Chronicle and the
citizens and the Mayor and Common Council Men were relieved
and delighted that the Postmaster-General had ended the contention between Shrewsbury and Chester for this fast, reliable, punc-
tual, well-conducted and well-armed service, carrying four inside
passengers besides the mails, fare from London to Chester £3. 3s and
from Chester to Holyhead £1. 11. 6d. According to the Chronicle of
September 9, 1785 (number 535) Shrewsbury had fought determi-
nedly for six months to divert the new service away from Chester's
Dee Bridge to their own Welsh Bridge, unscrupulously seeking to
'depreciate the credit of the Chester road at the expense of every degree of truth and generosity.' But the 'superiority and eligibility' of
the Chester road was not to be gainsaid. Besides, was it not at least
sixteen miles shorter? And so 'the mortified Salopians have now no
other than this consolation left, that, as they have been denied to run
with the authority of Royalty they must at last be contented to drag
on their heavy wheels *without* it.' Shrewsbury, however, had its way
after the turn of the century when Telford preferred that town as the
gateway to Wales for the passage of his highway from London to
Holyhead, Chester being obliged to drive a link road to it above
Corwen. But the coast road was still Chester's and for that Telford
constructed the Menai and Conway bridges. An eye-witness wrote of
the scene at the opening of the Conway bridge on July 1, 1826, 'between twelve and one o'clock by the Chester Mail with as many passengers as could possibly find a place about it that they could hold by.

The horses went on steadily over, which was more than I expected they would, as the people were shouting and waving by the side of them from the embankment to the pier, the passengers at the same time singing 'God Save the King' as loud as they could.'

But all this was more than a quarter of a century in the future when the Chronicle in 1785 welcomed with a flourish, 'by the authority of Parliament' and with a woodcut of the Royal arms flanked by G R, the start of the conveyance of the 'official' Irish Mail through Chester to Holyhead, 'under the protection of a Guard.' The Pied Bull, Northgate-street (also called the King's Arms and, earlier, the Bull Tenement), in the occupancy of J. Paul, had the honour and profit of the new service, receiving the coach from the Swan-with-Two Necks in London. Commodious stables at the Pied Bull extended no doubt along King-street, but they have long since been built over. Here, in 1789, the Chronicle reported a disastrous fire in which a drunken ostler was burnt to death, he having gone unsteadily into the loft, it was supposed, with a lighted candle. Thomas Hughes described the Pied Bull in the 1850s as 'a venerable hostelry serenely triumphing over the dust of centuries, and still one of the most respectable inns of the city'. It is still there, having undergone a respectful renovation in the 1970s, and Hughes's description fits today. John Paul, the landlord at the start of the Royal Mail service in 1785, afterwards moved to the White Lion. The Pied Bull has the distinction of being probably the oldest surviving inn, continuously in use as such, in the city, having a certain, recorded history in its own right going back to the sixteenth century. Two other coaching inns, the Hop-pole in Foregate-street (in the yard of which, you will remember, the Chronicle had its first printing press) and the Plume of Feathers in Bridge-street, also started new services in 1785, the first to Liverpool, Manchester, and the North, linking up with the canal boat for Manchester at Preston Brook, and the second to Neston, Parkgate, and New Ferry, both advertised in the paper. The Hop-pole lasted until this century and is remembered now only by the Hop-pole Paddock, extending to the City Wall below the Cathedral. Here formerly were the stables, now a parking place for cars and the site of recent development. Of the Feathers only the Lane of that name, which led to the stables at the rear, remains. You can see the inn, with incoming and outgoing coaches at the door (the 'outsides' are all wearing top hats) in W. Tasker's etching of Bridge-street, about 1839. A little lower down the street from the Chronicle office, it was probably a house of call for the newspaper men, and J. H. Hanshall, the paper's second Editor, knew it well, before 'the hand of innovating improvement' destroyed some of its quaintness. Writing in 1816, he recalls that the place had a kind of dim religious light which gave travellers and customers the novel impression that they were in a public-house of monastic origin. 'The hall', he says, 'always attracted the notice of the curious – lighted only by a few small transome windows at the top, which shed a gloomy ray and inspired beholders with ideas very different from those which are supposed to inhabit inns. At one end is a loft curiously ornamented in carved wood, with a variety of grotesque figures, called the Pulpit. On a shield in the centre, supported by two naked figures, is the date 1551.' Chester saw the last of the Feathers in 1863, when the first Duke of Westminster, innovating on a grand scale for the time, caused the construction of the Arcade on the site of the inn and adjacent old property, including the Commercial Inn to be seen in Tasker's drawing. The Arcade is now one of the principal entrances to the shopping precinct at the rear of the Rows, another Grosvenor development of the twentieth century.

At this time there were a remarkable number of taverns for a city and suburban population estimated at 14,713 in 1774. The Company of Innkeepers, Victuallers, and Cooks, incorporated in 1583, had the authority in earlier times – before the days of Brewster Sessions and Licensing Justices – of granting, or recommending, licences and regulating the conduct of inns. In 1540 the City Corporation felt it necessary to issue an order that no tavern or alehouse shall be kept by women between 14 and 40 years of age, the city having got a bad name by 'wantonness, brawls, frays, and other inconveniences as thereby doth and may arise among youth and lightly disposed persons'. The discrimination had clearly long been outlived by 1775, when, in Chronicle Number One, Jane Chatterton, late of the Queen's Head, Gloverstone, announced that she had taken the Star Inn, Watergate-street, 'where she hopes, by an obliging behaviour and a steady resolution to please, to give entire satisfaction to all who favour her with their company'. One January night in 1776 there was a cock-fight at the Ship Inn, Foregate-street, and in the excitement below stairs thieves stole £5 from a box under a bed upstairs, a mean and contemptible crime at the expense of 'poor people', says the censorious newspaper. A week later the members of the Gang Club are 'desired to dine' at the Talbot Inn in Newgate-street. Star and Ship are no more, but the sign of the Talbot – which disappeared in the almost total encapsulation (I can think of no better word) of New-gate-street in the shopping precinct – has been transferred to an elegant hotel in Lower Bridge-street, built in 1715 as the Albion Hotel. The Albion, with its splendid Assembly Room and its flower gardens and bowling green at the rear, declined into a seedy gentility first as Park House, then as a sort of warehouse or furniture repository until, in late years, with the growing awareness of the need to restore the dignity of the Lower street, the house was refurbished inside and out and relicensed as the Talbot. Opposite is the Old King's Head, dating from the early sixteenth century, town house of two of the family of four successive Randle Holmes, Chester Deputy Heralds, and an inn since 1717.

Throughout the eighteenth century and for the first twenty years of the nineteenth one of the sights of Chester was the Lamb or Old Lamb Row, successively town house, shops, market, inn, and lodging tenement, which stood at the junction of Bridge-street and Lower Bridge-street. It was an inn or lodging house of no great reputation in the Chester Chronicle's first decade and the paper has little to say about it until 1821, when the entire fantastic fabric literally fell down. At three o'clock in the afternoon of Friday, May 25, reported the Chronicle of June 1 (number 2395), 'this ancient pile, like all the other works of man, underwent a severe shock from the hand of Time . . . the projecting portion of the south end suddenly gave way and tumbled into the street with a loud crash. An immense volume of dust rose from the ruins, and it was some time before the bystanders could ascertain what damage was done and whether any injury had been sustained by the numerous human and *other inhabitants*'. No one, astonishingly, was injured, unlike the terrible death and desolation caused by the fall of the lofty 'land' in Edinburgh, so memorably described by Robert Louis Stevenson. An old woman, one Sarah Adams, had a lucky escape when the wall of the upper room of the Lamb in which she was sitting parted within six inches of her chair under the weight of the collapsing overhang.

Quaint, ramshackle, gabled, latticed, projecting drunkenly over the street, the Old Lamb became the epitome of ancient Chester before the changes that began in the nineteenth century and have continued ever since. Its curious construction of wood and twigs of hazel covered with clay and mortar, with massy oak beams, heavy roofs, interior panelling, and top-heavy overhang, gave the entire pile the appearance of extreme antiquity. Actually it was built after its near neighbour, the Falcon Inn which, much restored and no longer an inn, stands today at the head of Lower Bridge-street, having lost one by one most of its contemporaries. When the Lamb fell down a stone came to light with the inscription 16 – H – 55 RH. The initials are said to be those of Randle Holme (1627–1700), third of the Heralds whose family home was the Old King's Head lower down the street, noticed in a previous paragraph. Randle Holme the Third presumably started the building of the Lamb in 1655 and lived there until the end of the century. In 1688 he published the first of two folios of four books of his life's work The Academy of Armory, which may claim to be the first book printed in Chester. Where the type was set is not known, but it is possible that Randle Holme had a press in the Lamb and not only wrote the book there but also did the laborious job of printing with an assistant. This, however, is conjecture. The fourth Randle (son of this one) was the last of the Heralds to live at Lamb Row, which passed out of the family's possession in 1707. House and family went down together. In the nineteenth century a descendant worked as an occasional boots and waiter at a Liverpool hotel and Lamb Row became a tavern, then a butter market and a market-place for dealers in Welsh flannel and linseys. And so down the scale to the dubious condition of a common lodging-house. It was in one of these last declensions that George Cuitt, the most gifted of Chester portraitists, saw it in 1814 and preserved it for ever by the masterly plates in his Sketchbook. In our own time another inn, the Lamb Vaults, since removed, occupied part of the site.

The Chronicle notes the custom, from time to time, of the Company of Innkeepers, Victuallers, and Cooks – and, indeed, of the other City Companies – to hold their meetings alternately at several inns. In this way there is a record of the Lower White Bear, Black Bear, Holywell Packet, Black Dog, Boot, Swan-with-Two Necks, Crown and Mitre, and Golden Phoenix, all of which, with the exception of the Boot in Eastgate Row North, have gone. About 1855, says Thomas Hughes, the Innkeepers met at the King's Head at the corner of White Friars and Grosvenor-street, 'where they annually discuss a substantial and epicurean feast, in which a haunch of venison from Eaton regularly plays its part.' The reigning Grosvenor was traditionally free of the Company and the present Duke of Westminster was their guest at a recent observance of the 'feast' at the Bear and Billet Inn in Lower Bridge-street. The modern King's Head occupies the site of an earlier inn of the same name. The Bear and Billet, much altered inside, still presents to the street the famous timbered gable of many window-panes that coach passengers of the eighteenth century saw on their way in and out of the Bridge Gate.

The sacrifice of the Old Lamb to the passing of time has been told. The slow decline of the Yacht Inn from the end of the stage coach days to its disappearance in this last decade is an even sadder story. As the Chronicle advertisements show, the London and Irish stage coaches appeared regularly in Watergate-street at the door of the Yacht, then a house of princely accommodation and famous for its entertainments. Dean Swift stayed there, and Sir Watkin Williams Wynn and his friends from the great house of Wynnstay in Denbighshire. This Sir Watkin – there is a long descent of them – was the friend of David Garrick, had a taste for theatricals, and a private little theatre at the family mansion. Visiting or passing through Chester, he put up at the Yacht, where the innkeeper shared his delight in theatrical costume by playing a part himself. (The presence of Garrick one night probably cast a spell on the inn.) At all events, Chronicle readers were informed on July 24, 1775 (number 13) that

> On Wednesday last Sir Watkin Williams Wynn, Bart., and Lady, accompanied by Mr and Mrs Boycott and several other ladies of the first distinction in Wales, came in a covered wagon from Sir Watkin's seat at Wynnstay to the Yacht Inn in this city, dressed in the characteristic dresses of the Merry Wives of Windsor, which play they had lately performed, and were received by Mr. Carter, the landlord, in the character of Sir John Falstaff. A most elegant entertainment was provided for their reception, and the evening concluded with that magnificence and hospitality which always abounds in the worthy families of that neighbourhood.

In which chamber of the inn that 'most elegant entertainment' was set forth would be difficult to conceive by those who remember the Yacht as no more than a corner tavern. When I went through the inn before its removal about 1965 to make way for the passage of the inner ring road there were no upper rooms of any size or distinction. J. Romney, the topographical draughtsman who published a notable set of engravings of Chester as he saw it in 1853, did not trouble to depict the Yacht, 'now reduced', he said, 'to very humble pretensions compared with its former character.' And a print of about the same period, by another hand, shows the Yacht very

much as it was at the end of its days. There is no doubt, however,
that in the eighteenth century the Yacht was a place of much consequence in the life of the city and sufficiently spacious as to be able to
accommodate all the passengers of the coaches, flying machines and
diligences, the relays of horses, postillions, and all, and to put on
feasts and entertainments to the satisfaction of the Squire of
Wynnstay, if not to that of Dean Swift, who sometimes carried his ill-
humour with him. A passenger to Dublin, as he frequently was, the
author of Gulliver's Travels passed a night at the Yacht and is said to
have left his mark on the inn in the form of a waspish couplet

> Rotten without and mouldering within,
> This place and its clergy are all near akin

scratched by him with the diamond of his ring on one of the windows.
His invitation to the Cathedral dignitaries to dine with him had been
inhospitably refused, the story goes – or they had neglected to invite
him to dine with them. The window pane thus vicariously scratched
has never come to light or it would have found its way to Sothebys
long since. But that the Dean was capable of the couplet is not in
doubt, and he appears to have had a habit of writing on inn windows,
as had Robert Burns after him. The Cathedral's cold shoulder still
rankling, Swift scribbled this also

> The Walls of this town
> Are full of renown
> And strangers delight to walk round 'em;
> But as for the dwellers,
> Both buyers and sellers,
> For me, you may hang 'em or drown 'em.

Possibly a clue to one cause of the decayed fortunes of the Yacht
may be found in the writings of Thomas Pennant, who made annually a journey from Chester to London. One morning in March, 1780,
he said farewell to his neighbours at Whitford, Holywell, and the
Mostyns at Mostyn Hall, saddled his horse, and set out. Arrived in
Chester, he noticed that a very commodious building had, since his
last visit, been erected in the Yacht Field near the Watergate-street
'for the sale of the Irish linen at the two Fairs. It surrounds a large
square area, on each side of which are piazzas with numbers of shops
well adapted for the purpose.' This was the Linenhall, still in use but
as stables and loose-boxes for horses engaged in the Roodee race

meetings. Whether or not he passed the night at the Yacht Pennant does not say, but in this account of his journey to London he certainly followed the route of the stage coach. On the Yacht Field, perhaps, were the inn's original coaching quarters and the place of its grand entertainments, and it may be surmised that when the site was lost to the Linenhall custom began to fall away. Today not a vestige remains of the Yacht, sacrificed, like many another old haunt of men, to the demands of twentieth-century traffic, for now almost every family has its own private stage coach or motor carriage; and you would be hard put to it to hear even in the imagination the ghostly sound of the post-horn in the roar of the ring road cars and lorries. Two old-time near neighbours of the Yacht, the Axe and Custom House Taverns, continue in business.

Not every traveller found ease and comfort at the inn. There were (as today) rapacious landlords and customers difficult to please. If we take Thomas Hughes, historian of the city snugs over a hundred and twenty years ago, on trust, all the Chester innkeepers were beaming Bonifaces serving refreshment and home-brewed ale of the best quality. But it cannot always have been so. George Borrow records in *Wild Wales* that, staying very comfortably at an old-fashioned inn kept by a nice old-fashioned gentlewoman, he found the Chester ale undrinkable and the Cheshire cheese ('in the capital of the cheese country') uneatable. For their part, the innkeepers at this time of the war with America had a grouse against the Government order commanding them to provide food, drink, and quarters for the militia. The Chronicle of March 30, 1781, (number 310) has a report on the economic unfairness and dubious social consequences of this obligation: 'There never was a juster petition than that which has been lately presented to Parliament by the innkeepers in the several counties of England, for a redress of the various grievances they sustain from the mode which exists of distributing and quartering the militia, which is replete not only with injustice, but cruelty. Many country innkeepers are at this time compelled to submit to the enormous inconvenience of feeding twenty men each, for the trifling and inadequate pittance of four pence per day, by every individual of whom they must invariably lose, at the lowest estimate, sixpence per diem, which in one week constitutes no less than £3. 10s. The misfortune, however, does not terminate here, for these gentry generally contribute so abundantly to the increase of population that, what with discarded wives, and the plentiful produce of their promiscuous amours, the poor rates are obliged to be raised to an immense height; insomuch that thirteen shillings in the pound are actually paid for this rate only in some counties of England.' That was not, of course, the first or last complaint about the licentious soldiery.

'Fast' turnpike travel was also beginning to depopulate the Cheshire countryside, already suffering from enclosure. Arthur Young, in his *Farmers' Letters* of 1771, lamented that 'young men and women in the country villages fix their eyes on London as the last stage of their hope. They enter into service in the country for little else but to raise money enough to go to London . . . Besides rendering the going up and down so easy, the numbers who have seen London are increased tenfold, and of course ten times the boasts are sounded in the ears of country fools to induce them to quit their healthy, clean fields for a region of dust, stink, and noise.' To which it may be added that for years after this, the first cry of 'Back to the land', the Chester Chronicle, as the county paper, sustained the cause of agriculture against Government neglect and exactions and forwarded the formation of the Agricultural Workers' Union to safeguard better wages and conditions of service on the land. Today, in spite of the inroads of industry and many changes in land usage, the Cheshire acres are still among the fairest and most productive in the country, and probably the most scientifically managed.

We opened this chapter, if you remember, with the postboy complaisantly reading about himself in the Chester Chronicle at the White Lion Inn on a winter's night of 1776. And for the end of the chapter to the Lion we shall return, some 42 years later. At this time the Lion was at the top of its reputation as the great coaching house of all this part of the country. The Grosvenor (or its precursor, the Royal) and the Blossoms (formerly a coaching house of some note) were there then and are the city's leading hotels today, but the White Lion was the foremost place of resort right through the eighteenth century and into the first quarter of the nineteenth, when the civic character of Northgate-street underwent a change. For many years the proximity of the Exchange (the old Town Hall) and the Lion contributed to a constant press of business and pleasure, the like of which probably has not been seen since, coaches and travellers and town councillors and citizens and market people all mingling. Across the way from the fish market at the end of Shoemakers' Row was the Theatre Royal, where the leading players of the time performed, travelling up from London on the coach and putting up at the White

Lion or the Feathers or the Golden Lion in Foregate-street (adjoining the Blossoms until the Second World War). The London actors at the Theatre Royal no doubt held court also at the White Lion, and when the Theatre became a Music Hall Charles Dickens gave a reading there from his novels (the Chronicle's account of which will be found in the chapter on the Theatre). Dickens was probably a guest at the Lion on one of his journeys into Cheshire, and it is possible that he heard a tale or two of the turnpikes there. Certainly the inn lives for us in the pages of the *Memoirs of Joseph Grimaldi*, in which Dickens relates with gusto the story of the clown's encounter in Chester with his fellow harlequin Bologna. Both were billed to appear (as the Chronicle's advertisement attests) in the pantomime *Mother Goose* at the Theatre and both stayed at the White Lion in October, 1817.

The White Lion has gone, from what date I cannot precisely determine. Thomas Hughes described the house as he knew it in 1855, after 250 years as an inn. William Pue, I find, was mine host in 1605. One George Smith was the landlord at the beginning of the eighteenth century, and he and his family made the fortunes of the house in the high coaching days. William and Daniel Smith, both of the Lion, were Sheriffs of Chester in 1740 and 1765 respectively. Picture the scene on September 22, 1761, when for the coronation of George III and Queen Charlotte the conduit at the Cross ran with wine, bonfires blazed in the streets, and all the city and county notables dined at the White Lion. From this time the house, says Thomas Hughes, was

> 'always full of the right sort of visitors, and seldom a vacant stall in the immense stabling at the rear. Then the happy joke went merrily round at the door of the hotel, as some jovial whip stood playing with the ribbons or familiarly patting the necks of his noble team. . . Times are changed now. Every dog has his day and doubtless every Lion, too: at all events, our White Lion is neither so brisk nor so vigorous as he was of yore. The present worthy landlord is himself a retired whip, and as he rambles up and down through those noble rooms, once swarming with company, must often, we fear, look back gloomily upon the past.'

Turning from that sentimental evocation, I discovered that the landlord in 1851 was Peter Hilton and he was advertising in the Chronicle 'cars to and from the railway station.' Horse cars, of course. But the Lion's days were indeed done. I have the impression that Peter Hilton was the last of the 'retired whips'. The White Lion, as you recall, first appeared in the Chronicle Number One in May, 1775, and he had already then entertained company for nearly a century and three-quarters.

9

Port of Chester, sunk in Sands o' Dee

It is the first week of May, 1775. There are rumours of war but otherwise there is qualified optimism in the air, and the citizens are talking about the revival of trade in the Port of Chester, which, because of the silting of the Dee navigation, has been losing some of its custom to the upstart Liverpool on the Mersey. But, with the New Cut and the deepening and containing of the channel, things have been looking up of late years. Besides, if the Americans – mostly our own kin, at that – have no better sense than to go to war, is there not money to be made out of that, too? Chronicle Number One this week has published a manifest of ships sailing in and out, with cargoes of pig-iron, copper, slates, lead ore, oats, cloth, wine, coal, timber, and earthenware, in transit between Chester and Cardiff, Conway, Caernarvon, Aberystwyth, Aberdovey, Beaumaris, Pwlhelli, Barmouth, Holyhead, Dublin, Belfast, London, Liverpool, Bristol, Greenock, Barcelona and Malaga. Evan Roberts, master of The Betty, clears a passage for himself in sailor style through the press of carts, carriages, coaches, traders and travellers crowding the narrow defile of Watergate-street between its high gables, past the bonding cellars, the ships' chandlers and marine store dealers, the coopers and ropemakers, and the cavernous storage vaults beneath the Rows, to the Customs House. Here he has business with the Comptroller of the Port, which being transacted the Captain continues through the Watergate to the Old Crane Wharf. There The Betty, a cheese ship with berths for passengers, is loading for London. Her papers in order at the Customs House, she will be cleared to sail in six days, and on board the master and Hugh Jones the broker discuss the applications for freight and passage. At the neighbouring New Crane there is rumour of a ship for sale later in the year, The Elizabeth, Captain Hubbert, of 240 tons burthen, known to be extremely well found and of good dimensions for any trade. A private contract of sale possibly around September, thinks Hugh Jones: it is worth thinking about. At Parkgate, lower down the river on the Wirral shore, where the passages are social and fashionable as well as mercantile and the packet-boat services ply four times a week to and from Dublin, weather permitting, much company has arrived on The Dorset packet for the good air and sea-bathing. Among others, Mr. McCartney and family, Major Brereton, and the Hon. Mr. Rowley have put up at the Mostyn Arms Hotel.

The fair prospects continue. On July 3 (issue number 10) the Chronicle reporter is at Parkgate observing that 'the great resort of people of rank, at this season of the year, for the purpose of bathing in the sea, has made this place vie with Brighthelmstone [Brighton], Southampton, etc., and it is imagined it will still improve, as its situation, as well as for prospect and serenity of air, as its conveniency for bathing, is much more eligible than any other public place of resort for that purpose.' At this time Parkgate (astonishing as it may now seem to those who have never known it other than as a Dee village overlooking a vast reach of mudflats, weeds, and grass) was one of only two ports of embarkation for Ireland – the other was Bristol – and to the relative regularity and security of its packet-boat service it was adding the reputation of a salubrious seaside resort, which lasted for some forty years after the packet service stopped about 1830. Week by week the Chronicle lists the arrivals and departures of the Parkgate packets Trevor, Nonpareil, and King George (for each of which a dreadful misfortune was in store), Kildare, Prince of Wales, Princess Royal, and Dorset. Parkgate had its Custom House, Quay House, Ferry House (where the packets berthed and merchant ships discharged and took on cargo), hotels (the Mostyn Arms is now a school), inns, theatre, and assembly rooms. Milton's Lycidas sailed to a watery grave from Parkgate, Handel awaited wind and tide here, and Dean Swift (inevitably), Lady Hamilton, afterwards Nelson's love, and the Rev. John Wesley, who records in his diary the several crossings he made between here and Dublin, on some of which he had his horse as fellow-passenger.

On his way to Ireland in 1762 Wesley embarked at Parkgate and had the best and worst of the weather. Upon setting out 'the sun shone bright, the wind was moderate, the sea smooth, and we wanted nothing but room to stir ourselves; the cabin being filled with hops, so that we could not get into it but by climbing over them on our hands and knees. In the afternoon we were abreast of Holyhead, but the scene was quickly changed. The wind rose higher and higher and by seven o'clock blew a storm. The sea broke over us continually and sometimes covered the ship, which pitched and rolled in an uncommon manner.' This account accords with the sentiments of the Dublin ditty then current:

> I gave the captain seven thirteen
> To carry us over to Parkgate;
> But before we got the half of the way
> It blew at a furious hard rate.

Lady Hamilton (born Amy Lyon in 1765 at Ness) was a native of the Dee shore and to a convenient lodging in Parkgate she was sent more than once by her protectors to be out of the way. She was there in 1784, ostensibly so that the sea bathing would cure a skin rash that blemished her beauty. She complained about the expense: 'I am obliged to give a shilling a day for the bathing horse and woman and twopence a day for the dress.' The price evidently had gone up since 1782, when the Chronicle, May 10 (number 368) inserted this advertisement:

> Joseph Manlove,
> of the George Inn, Parkgate,
> informs the Ladies, Gentlemen,
> and others that, for their
> better accommodation
> during the bathing
> season, he has purchased an
> additional BATHING MACHINE on
> an entire modern construction,
> in which Ladies may bathe
> with the utmost ease
> and SECRECY.
> Price for a single bathing, 8d.,
> and every Lady will (if desired)
> be attended with a female servant.

Back in the summer of 1775 the Chronicle had high hopes for the increasing prosperity of Parkgate and for the maintenance of good trading in the Port of Chester, which in the first week of August reverberated to the sixteen-gun salutes of The Juno, Captain Eagles, sailing for Africa, and The Adventure, Captain Smallwood, sailing for Newfoundland. At the same time The Diligence, Captain Massey, left for London, and several other coasters for other home ports – all indicative, said the paper (August 14, number 16) of 'an agreeable prospect of the extension of the city's commerce'. Would it last this time? That was the question in discussion at the inns and coffee houses and down at the two Cranes below the Watergate. The Port authorities, the Mayor and the City Common Council, the merchant gild, and the more knowledgeable citizens were cautiously sanguine. They knew the long and wayward story of the vicissitudes of their river since Roman times, when the invaders made use of the rude harbour which afterwards developed into the Watergate Quay below Nuns-road until the making up of the Roodee in the sixteenth century. Until then also ships sailed up river to Chester Bridge, discharging their cargoes below the causeway or weir first built by Hugh Lupus, nephew of the Conqueror and the first substantial Norman Earl of Chester. This weir was suspected by some to be the principal cause of the subsequent silting of the channel by reducing the river's natural scour. From the Bridge merchandise was taken ashore through the Shipgate or 'Hole in the Wall' (which was removed in 1838 and re-erected in 1923 in the Grosvenor Park, where it stands today).

In the fourteenth century the Watergate Quay had an accession by the construction of the Water Tower, at a cost of £100, extending out from the City Wall to the river. But the silting of the estuary went on, and although the Port of Chester held jurisdiction over the entire coast from Barmouth to Solway, the navigation, civil and military – armies and navies as well as merchandise moved in and out – was being steadily impeded by the shifting sand, the 'loose, light, white, skittering sand' constantly drifted by wind and tide into the channel. Presently ships could not reach Chester at all and the merchandise of the Port, including the valuable import of Gascony wines, had to be landed lower down at anchorages at Shotwick, Neston, Dawpool, the Redbank at Caldy, and rowed ashore from the Hyle Lake at Hoylake. The Merchant Venturers of Chester obtained an Act of Parliament in 1733 authorising a 'New Cut' under the supervision of the marine engineer Nathaniel Kinderley. There were doubts from the start whether this project of narrowing, deepening and confining the channel within artificial boundaries over a length of some ten miles from Chester down to Connah's Quay on the Welsh side was the right solution to the silting. There were particular fears that the 'natural flow' at Hoylake would be irreparably obstructed rather than improved. But the work went ahead and was completed in 1737 and the River Dee Company incorporated.

For thirty years or more all went well, or so it seemed. Thomas

Pennant, observing the busy scene at the Watergate on his annual visits to the city from his home near Holywell, collected details of the commerce of Chester in exports and imports. The best year was 1771 when he recorded 297 coasters coming into the Port and 562 going out, carrying lead, iron cannon, two thousand tons of cheese, and other goods. From foreign ports 95 vessels came in, and 216 went out for Ireland, Portugal, Spain, Italy, and America. Flax, tallow, hemp, and iron were imported from Norway and the Baltic; from Leghorn came kid and lambskins, dressed in Chester for manufacture by the glovers. Spain and Portugal sent fruit, nuts, and wine. And Chester's exports in that flourishing year included 6,000 chaldrons of coal from Cheshire and Flintshire collieries, 1,000 tons of lead and 300 of lead ore. So that, four years later, when the Chronicle went to press for the first time, and Captain Evan Roberts was making his way down Watergate-street in the opening scene of this chapter, people were thinking about the war with the American colonists that appeared now to be inevitable and its effect upon the city's foreign sea trade and its domestic trade with Wales and Ireland, likely to be disturbed by the activities of armed privateers. In 1778 the Chronicle was to report the sailing of three of our own privateers out of the Port of Chester – The Empress of Russia, 24 guns and 120 men, The Hero, 16 guns and 80 men, and The Spy, 10 four-pounders and 12 swivels, and 50 men.

But before that there was a running story in the paper which took precedence of the fortunes of war: the Dee estuary reasserted its treachery in a hurricane-force storm on Thursday, October 19, 1775, in which the Parkgate packet brigs Trevor, William Totty master, and Nonpareil, Samuel Davies master, were ruthlessly destroyed. The warnings of some years back about the danger of interfering with the natural flow of West Hoyle Bank, extending from Hilbre Swatch to the Chester and Rhyl Flats, were brought to mind. This was the Davy Jones's locker of the Dee in all the days of sail, and evidently the New Cut had done nothing to lessen its perils when the north-westerly gales were blowing. Trevor and Nonpareil were two-masted schooners or brigs on the regular Parkgate-Howth (Dublin) run and it was Nonpareil that foundered on Hoyle Bank. They set sail from Parkgate about eight o'clock on the evening of October 19, and what happened is vividly told in the Chronicles of October 23 and 30 (numbers 26 and 27):

'The vessels being near Holyhead, the wind came about from s.s.w. to the westward, and so violent a hurricane rose that they could not carry any sail but were obliged to lie to and drive before the wind. In this situation Totty's ship drove upon the banks near the Lancashire shore and is totally lost. Every person on board perished, except one Samuel Fairclough, a mariner, who miraculously saved his life by leaping on board another vessel called the Charming Molly, Holloway master, which by accident ran foul of the Trevor, and at the instant the two vessels struck together Fairclough made his leap. The Nonpareil, it is supposed, stranded upon Hoyle-sands and is lost. Not one person is saved. Her boat and a coach belonging to one of the passengers have been since taken up. The Trevor and the Nonpareil had on board near two hundred passengers . . . also £6,000 in spices, besides silks, woollen cloths, jewels, and other things, to the amount of between £30,000 and £40,000 . . . This gale of wind continued near thirty hours, and is supposed to have been the most violent storm that has happened in these parts within the memory of the oldest men living.'

Bodies cast upon the sands below Talacre and Gronant on the Flintshire shore were robbed and nineteen beach ghouls, said the Chronicle of November 13 (number 29), had been apprehended. In the succeeding week's paper the Chester Port authorities advised jewellers, goldsmiths, silversmiths, and particularly travelling chapmen, to be cautious 'in purchasing any part of the rich cargoes which, there is reason to apprehend, have been taken from the wrecks and detained or concealed'.

Two advertisements and an item of news tell the last of this tragic tale in the Chronicle of December 11 (number 33). Advertisement one:

A WRECK TO BE RAISED

Whereas the wreck of the Trevor, William
Totty, late Master, now lies in seven
fathom water, about ten miles west of
Blackpool in Lancashire, notice is hereby
given to all persons willing to engage in
raising the said wreck to send in
their proposals to Mr. Robert Hincks,
Mr. James Folliott, or Mr. William
Griffiths, Merchants in Chester, who
will immediately treat for the purpose.

Advertisement two:

ANN DAVIES,
of Parkgate, Widow

of Samuel Davies,
late Master of the Nonpareil,
begs leave to inform the Nobility
and Gentry travelling between
England and Ireland by way of
Parkgate, and the Public in
general, that she continues the
business of an Inn, at her house,
the sign of THE KING'S ARMS,
in Parkgate.

The news item notes the support given by 'public-spirited and humane persons' for an application to Parliament to erect a lighthouse on the Point of Ayr and to fix buoys, a measure 'of considerable commercial utility and probably the means of saving many lives.' Christmas, 1775, was a sad time for many bereaved families and many a merchant casting up his losses of another sort.

By Christmas of the next year, however, 619 coasters passed in and out of the Port of Chester and 297 sailed to and from foreign ports, and there was an increase in the imports of Irish linen sold at the Chester Midsummer and Michaelmas Fairs. Then, just before Christmas two years later, the Dee river furies sank a rich prize in the American war, the East Indiaman, Les Deux Amis, bound from China and Pondicherry to Port l'Orient in France, with a cargo of fine tea, silks, calico, nankeen, muslin, cotton, china, arrack, and barrels of wine, valued at £150,000. Taken by the Knight privateer of Liverpool on December 23, 1778, off Cape Finisterre, the East Indiaman was caught in a furious gale in the Dee estuary and wrecked off Mostyn. In the storm the privateer parted from her prize off Beaumaris and came to grief near Abergele. The Chronicle of January 8, 1779 (number 194) pieced together the confused story of the double wreck. 'On board Les Deux Amis were 24 English and 24 Frenchmen, out of which number only ten English and three French were saved . . . A great part of her cargo was lodged in our Custom-house, Parkgate, and we are sorry to say much damaged.' No doubt with the looting of the Parkgate packet-boats fresh in mind, the Mostyn family at their ancestral Mostyn Hall, then as now commanding a broad front of the estuary, took instant action. 'The spirited conduct of Sir Roger Mostyn, Sir Piers Mostyn, Mr. Pennant of Downing, and others', says the Chronicle, 'cannot be sufficiently commended. They armed their tenants and prevented the country people who assembled in great numbers from plundering the wreck; but notwithstanding all their vigilance and activity, property to the amount of several thousand pounds was carried away.' The Mostyn family's watch on the Dee shore was traditionally vigilant: they had extensive riparian and other interests.

Shipwreck and plunder and the moods of the river notwithstanding, the 'merchant adventurers' of the Port of Chester continued confident in the security of the New Cut, and with the American war over and the peace treaty signed, the Chronicle of September 2, 1785 (number 534) reported the launching at Parkgate of the first of two packet-boats to replace the lost Trevor and Nonpareil. She was The King, Richard Hammond master, burthen about a hundred tons, 'fitted up with every elegant accommodation.' A companion ship, The Queen, then building, was to be launched within two or three months. 'These two packets, we hear, are to be one joint concern with a packet called The Prince of Wales, commanded by Captain Heird, who has been for some months past in the passage trade between Dublin, Holyhead, and Parkgate . . . It is not doubted that the passage trade will regain what it has for some years back (for want of such packets) been deprived of by a neighbouring port', said the newspaper. Trade with Ireland prospered, particularly in fine linen, and the Linenhall was built in 1788 to accommodate it. But the competition of Liverpool was growing, side by side with a rapid rise in population there, as we shall see. Broster's Guide to Chester in 1795 describes Crane-street as 'lately built' below the Watergate and there 'at a small distance are the quays, port, and crane, where vessels of 350 tons load and unload, carried by the tides along the New River. On the wharf are large warehouses, and here vessels are built of 300 and 400 tons burthen.' The Port was still busy, exporting cheese, coal, and lead, and importing Irish linen chiefly. At the same time the River Dee Company was reclaiming Sealand from the Dee – a measure to be looked upon later with suspicion and recrimination as the real object of the New Cut. 'Several thousand acres of fine land have already been enclosed,' says Broster, 'and good farm houses now stand where the tides flowed a few years ago.' And there were two ferries, about which there were complaints in the Chronicle. A correspondent of the paper said they were so carelessly served that he waited at each of them upwards of half an hour and called till he was hoarse, 'and all to no purpose, although the boatmen came out and saw me'.

The challenge of Liverpool, erstwhile creek in the Port of Chester, was seen in the census taken in the first year of the nineteenth century: Liverpool inhabitants 78,000, Chester 15,142. The Liverpool slave trade, allied to cotton, was prospering – Chester never soiled its hands with slavery – and the evolution of a great town on the Mersey was in progress, an evolution by which Chester was left high and dry to preserve the mediaeval form and character of its streets, houses, Rows, walls, gates, churches and cathedral alongside a failed river and port. Then, on a September Sunday in 1806, the Dee struck another blow at the old city Port, the dreaded West Hoyle Bank claiming the best-known of the Parkgate packets, King George, Captain Walker master. Again there is a running story in the paper week by week as news came in from all along the coast. 'With the deepest regret,' wrote the Chronicle, September 19 (number 1628) 'we record the loss of the King George off Hoylake on Sunday last, and all the passengers, only four sailors and the steward being saved. It is not accurately known how many were on board, but they are generally believed to amount to about 170. They were principally labourers who had come from Ireland to assist in getting in the harvest, and were returning to their native country with the fruits of their industry. The Captain might have saved himself, but generously preferred to perish with his vessel and passengers.' (With what decent reticence that last sentence is composed.) Next week it was learned that the survivors were Henry Walker, mate of the vessel and brother of the Captain; Williams and Roberts, two of the crew; and an unidentified blacksmith. Of the four cabin passengers, all lost, one was William Benson, a farmer, who had in the hold six Leicestershire rams. In the second week of October seven bodies were reported thrown on to the coast near Lancaster, and the Chronicle printed a moving catalogue of personal effects and details.

> 'They all appeared to be broad-set, middle-aged men, and dressed like labourers in husbandry. One had two guineas, a 7s piece, and 1s. 6d. in silver in his pocket, and also a Catholic prayer-book, with Robert Collins written in it. Another had only a knife and tobacco-box, and some other trifles . . . In the pocket of another was a letter dated Dublin, from a daughter to her father, the direction of which was lost, giving an account of her mother and family since he left home, and her improvement at school. Also part of another letter, scarcely legible, an advertisement of the fare of the King George packet, 12 guineas and a half, a silver watch, several pieces of thread, silk, twist, thimble and needles. The body had on it three pairs of breeches, three waistcoats, a gown-

piece of printed calico wrapped round, and a greatcoat. Two had their hats on . . .'

In the week of October 24 two more bodies were washed up by the tide, one at Lytham and the other at Layton-Hays, near Blackpool. 'By their dress they appear to be gentlemen. One had 20 guineas and a half in his pocket and a pocket-book which contained a great quantity of bank-notes. There was only one half-penny found in the pockets of the other. But there was also an empty purse, which it is supposed has been robbed upon the sands after the wreck. There were also several bodies thrown up at North Meols on the Dee Wirral shore.' The fate of John Molloy and John Farlow Flannagan (whose bodies these might have been), returning from London to Ireland 'with the earnings of some years', was presumably never known. One, according to their legal agent in Ireland, had a thousand pounds with him and the other £1,500. A letter to the Editor from Dublin appealing for news of the men and their money was the end of the Chronicle's humanely-told tale of the wreck of the King George.

As the years go by it is clear from the newspaper and other records that the trade of the Port of Chester is drifting desultorily but inexorably into the silting sand. But if the bigger ships of the day can no longer reach her, the history of former times repeating itself, the old Port can at least build ships for others. And so, from the pen of J. H. Hanshall, second Editor of the Chronicle, we have a contemporary picture of the Crane boat-yards about 1816. 'Beyond the Watergate are Crane-street, Back Crane-street, and Paradise Row, the whole of which lead to the wharfs on the river. For a number of years Chester has carried on a considerable business in shipbuilding. Within the last ten years the trade has wonderfully increased, and even now it is not unusual to see ten or a dozen vessels on the stocks at a time. In fact, there are nearly as many ships built in Chester as in Liverpool, and the former have always a decided preference from the merchants. Indeed, Chester lies particularly convenient for the trade, as by the approximation of the Dee, timber is every season floated down from the almost exhaustless woods of Wales, at a trifling expense and without the least risk. The principal shipwright in Chester is Mr. Cortney, but Mr. Troughton's is the oldest establishment. There were lately nearly 250 hands employed in the business, two-thirds of whom were in Mr. Cortney's yard, but the trade is at present flat. Six vessels of war have been built by him, and within the last two years

(1814–15) two corvettes and two sloops of war, The Cyrus, The Mersey, The Eden, and The Levant, from twenty to thirty guns each. The firm of Mulvey and Co., formerly of Frodsham, have established a yard near the Crane.' Cortney's yard launched a brig in 1804, an East Indiaman of 580 tons in 1810, and in 1813 a West Indiaman of 800 tons, in addition to the corvettes and war sloops mentioned by Hanshall. Shipbuilding was the last positive activity of the Port of Chester and continued into the second half of the nineteenth century. The Gitana, a barque of 1,367 tons, was built at Chester in 1861; and until the 1920s Crichton's yard at Saltney was building ferry boats, river craft, and tugs.

The history of the Dee and its ships reached a tragic climax on the night of October 26, 1859, when the Royal Charter was dashed aground by a hurricane of unexampled ferocity off Moelfre on the coast of Anglesey. She was returning from Melbourne with 388 passengers, a crew of 112, and a cargo of gold valued at £300,000. Only twenty passengers and eighteen crew survived. The same night many other smaller ships were lost and a factory at Flint was destroyed by the gale. Pages of the Chronicle of October 29 (number 4487) were filled with the first detailed news of the wreck and for weeks and months afterwards the paper devoted many columns to the recovery and burial of bodies – many of them totally unidentifiable – the salvage of gold, and the verbatim reporting of official inquiries into the cause of the disaster. The hurricane, the gold, the temptation of plunder, the evidence as bodies were washed ashore that they had been battered to death, not drowned – all combined to create a legend that the wrecking of the Royal Charter was a judgment of the sea. Sustained by the credulous, of whom there are always many, the legend died hard.

Although the Royal Charter was not wrecked in the Dee estuary – which ends at the Point of Ayr – the river perhaps had something to do with her subsequent undoing. For the great iron ship, or auxiliary steamer, 2,719 tons, was built on the Dee and had an unlucky start in life. Her misfortunes began straightaway on the slipway of Sandycroft Ironworks, where she was commissioned for the Australian gold rush trade and launched in 1855. The Chronicle reported that the narrowness of the river required the ship to be launched sideways and the channel had to be artificially deepened because at first there was not enough water to float her. Then, on her way down river to Flint, she grounded on a sandbank and was for some weeks under repair at Liverpool. These circumstances were the subject of questions to expert witnesses at the official inquiries subsequent to the wreck, but not much came out of them.

From the 1820s to the middle of the century the New Cut proved powerless to resist the silting of the channel at the Port of Chester. A reading of the Chronicle at this time reflects the disenchantment of the citizens with the River Dee 'adventurers', suspected of being more concerned for the profitable land-grab of the sands o' Dee than for the reclamation of the river itself. The experience of thirty years or so caused John Broster in 1821 to blame the speculators of the River Dee Company whose title to the reclaimed acres induced them to 'conduct the river in a circuitous course, which has now nearly choked our navigation.' As the century wore on the effect of silting became disastrous. In 1850 the Hoyle Bank was described as cut in two, the Hoyle Lake choked with sand, and Parkgate and Dawpool deserted: the packet-boats had not sailed for twenty years: it was the end of Brighton-on-the-Dee. Frank Simpson, F.S.A., who contributed much to the Chronicle in the 1920s, wrote in 1907: 'From 1743 to 1899 the original company of undertakers founded by Kinderley did little to improve the navigation of the river . . . During the eighteenth century families of nobility were brought to the verge of ruin by investing in Dee stock; many sold their shares at 90 per cent loss . . . Millions of money have been spent, and today the river is in a worse state than when the so-called improvements commenced.' By 1910 few vessels were able to reach Chester and such sea trade as continued was lower down on the Welsh shore at Hawarden Bridge, Connah's Quay, Flint, Bagillt, and Mostyn. The colliery at Talacre, Mostyn ironworks and colliery, and Halkyn lead mines kept these harbours in business for small steamers and coasting schooners, and Connah's Quay, developed by the River Dee Company as a harbour in 1793, went on to build a tradition of hardy and resourceful seafarers. For some time from 1817 the paddle steamer Regulator ran a regular crossing service for goods and passengers between Parkgate and Bagillt. At Flint vessels discharged into lighters up to about 1876. Shotton Steelworks came to the Dee in 1895–6, when Henry Hall Summers bought ten thousand acres of marshland and started the plant which became a household word as the family firm of 'Summers's' and today, after employing generations of local people, faces partial shut-down in the reorganisation plans of the British Steel Corporation. Until 1917 ships of up to 300 tons could reach

Connah's Quay, but the trade gradually withered away and now the last surviving arm of the Port of Chester is Mostyn Dock.

Mostyn Deep is the true old name, and ships of a maximum tonnage of 700 are still able to go in and out of the dock on the full tide. The wheel of history comes full circle, and the Chronicle of May 11, 1973 (number 10,291) commented on the irony and the nonsense of little Mostyn's modest profits being levied, under the proposals of an official report on dock workings, to subsidise, say, the uneconomic activities of the Port of Liverpool. The paper said: 'Mostyn may only be a minnow in the docks business, but it is profitable. The idea of some of these profits being channelled off to help much bigger fish does not appeal to either the Flintshire County Council or the firm which runs the docks, Mostyn Docks and Trading Ltd. There is something faintly ludicrous about Mostyn's being asked to support a port like Liverpool, which handles a bigger tonnage in two or three days than Mostyn handles in a year . . . Mostyn is big enough to stand on its own feet, but not big enough to help others stand on theirs.' The Mostyn Docks company provides work for eighty dockers and clerical staff, and the port handled 259 ships, a total of about 200,000 tons of cargo, in 1972. Imports include wood pulp, timber, sulphur phosphates, hardboard, tinned milk, PVC plastics, ferromanganese, and marble chippings, mainly from the Continent. Among exports are steel turnings to Spain, steel rails to France, waste paper to Spain and Italy, and aluminium.

While Mostyn continues to move Continental trade in and out of the channel the Port of Chester will still be in independent business – and Liverpool must look to itself and the Government in its present difficulties. Go back, reader, to the beginning of this chapter and consider the flux of time and tide. On the Wirral shore of the Dee today Cheshire County Council is creating a conservation area and country park. Hilbre Island is the haunt of seabirds. Hoylake has still a seaside presence, and Parkgate has its memories, its wildfowlers, its seabed gone to seed, and a fugitive, deceptive flush of water on the high bore tides. On the farther shore

> As you see the grey river mist
> Hold shapes on the yonder bank

rise plumes of industrial smoke which wreathe into an enigmatic question mark over Shotton Steelworks. At the Port of Chester itself below the Watergate all that remains, apart from canal communications, is Crane Bank. The Crane streets and Paradise Row, described in 1795 as 'lately built', as we have read, declined into tenements and slums and were cleared away earlier this century. At Crane Bank, on the margin of the river, the craft of T.S. Deva are moored, for here, in a converted Shropshire Union Canal warehouse, is the local Sea Cadets' shore base, 'launched' by the Duke of Edinburgh in April, 1953, with the then Mayor present also in his capacity as Admiral of the Dee.

For centuries the challenge of the estuary has exercised the imaginations and the ingenuity of men, sailors, poets, marine engineers. The challenge and the dangers of this wide waterway gone to waste continue. The shifting sands and the rapid flow of the tides are traps for the unwary and the venturesome, whether children, bathers, fishermen, or wildfowlers. As for experienced navigators, they know the reputation of this lost world only too well. The frequent cries for help from people surrounded by quicksands and the sudden onset of wild weather and swirling mist caused the townspeople of Flint to man their own Rescue Boat, which saved many lives in conditions treacherous in the extreme. The Chronicle in 1965 invited its readers to contribute to a fund to assist in the maintenance of the boat, and the issue of December 10 (number 9,905) reported the presentation of a cheque for £262 to the Flint Rescue Boat Committee. It was a public-spirited response, but a drop in the ocean compared with the millions of money sunk and lost in past plans for the restoration of the Dee navigation. In 1966 the Royal National Lifeboat Institution stationed an Inshore Rescue Boat at Flint as part of the lifeboat service along the entire North Wales coast from Mostyn and Point of Ayr to Cemaes, Bull Bay and Moelfre in Anglesey.

As for the challenge of the Dee, it grows more imperative with the passing of the years. In the second half of the twentieth century new engineering skills, resources, and knowledge have made feasible the idea of a bridge or barrage linking Merseyside and North Wales as part of a comprehensive plan of regional renewal and development. The history of the Dee 'crossings' begins in the first quarter of the century, when there were about six projects, among them Point of Ayr–West Kirby, Greenfield–West Kirby, and Greenfield–Gayton. In that same issue of December 10, 1965, the Chronicle commented in an editorial on the practical notion of a Dutch expert to convert the Dee marshes at Flint into a yacht harbour for some four to five hundred boats of up to ten tons. In the same week the paper published a panoramic photograph of the estuary with a bridge drawn in, crossing from Gayton to Greenfield. Another planner's dream of about this time was fascinating but impracticable: a Hanseatic or Hamburg-like city with a lake centre in the middle of a reclaimed estuary, linked by motorway to either shore and to Liverpool, Chester, and the airports. The opening of the Severn Suspension Bridge in 1966, and the constantly increasing pressure of road traffic through Chester to the North Wales coast resorts, gave renewed impetus to demands for some final solution of the age-old problem of the Dee. On November 3, 1967 (number 10,003) the Chronicle published a study by Mr. T. M. Haydn Rees, Clerk of the Flintshire County Council, in which he wrote 'Flintshire's future is manifest in what was once only a theory, the Dee estuary crossing . . . The broad conclusions of the consultants are that it would be a feasible engineering task to construct a road crossing anywhere in the estuary and to combine with this other purposes, such as water reservoirs, land reclamation, and amenity projects. They confirmed the need, on traffic grounds, for an estuary crossing, and there is a clear case for a multi-purpose scheme to be carried out in the middle or inner part of the estuary.'

And so, on April 30, 1971, there was a detailed examination in the paper (number 10,185) of the consulting engineers' report in which the linking of the Cheshire and Flintshire banks of the estuary by a marine motorway on an embankment between Flint and Burton was finally projected. I have recalled the millions of money invested and sunk in the Dee in the past. Millions of money come into the story again. This road and water conservation scheme, with a water sports playground and some form of New Town based on Flint was at first estimated to cost between £65 and £78 millions, and now it will be very much higher. Fifty years ago the first tentative and modest proposals started at £50,000. Today's engineers were frank, stating that a large part of the estuary's 40 square miles of saltmarsh and intertidal sands and mudflats would undergo severe physical alteration, and for many people it would mean 'facing the prospect of looking on a treasured scene for the last time.' From which you will see that, in the 1970s as in the 1770s and much earlier, the Dee keeps its mysterious capacity to controvert as well as to inspire the ambitions of men. A plan compounded of progress, paradoxes, and politics, the Chronicle called this the greatest Dee ambition yet and went on to comment: 'The crossing would relieve the traffic pressure on Chester but perhaps affect its trade; open up new horizons for Flintshire and the Welsh coast with a direct influx from Merseyside and the North-West of England but maybe destroy the Welsh way of life as many patriots see it; create a marine pleasure ground which could, how-ever, eliminate for ever the nature reserve of the estuary and its wild life, and change for the worse the character of Burton, one of the most beautiful villages in Cheshire.' The county authorities on both sides of the estuary are for the development, but, with the uncertain future of Hawarden Bridge Steelworks, Flintshire looks at the Dee scheme in relation to new opportunities of industrial expansion and di-version. Cheshire looks to the Dee plan principally as an auxiliary in the relief of the traffic problems of Chester. The decision rests with the government of the day and in these times of raging inflation may be deferred for years.

The eighteenth-century river works described at the beginning of this chapter, canalising the channel between Chester and Connah's Quay and the raising of the first 'Kop' or bank, created a habitat for wildfowl where samphire and grass began to cover the sand and mud and the sea walls kept out the worst of the weather. Construction of the second 'Kop' from Burton Point to Connah's Quay and the recla-mation of Sealand as corn-growing land in the nineteenth century, brought the heyday of the 'gentleman fowlers', succeeding the tough fraternity of professionals who sold their game bag advantageously at Chester Market. Among these sporting gentlemen were the Gren-fell brothers, Algernon and Wilfred, the last-named afterwards to become famous as Grenfell of Labrador. As the grey river mist closes over the present generation of Dee wildfowlers, shrouding their fu-ture in a time of great change, it closes too over the vanished Port of Chester, sunk for ever in the silting sand.

10

On Gallows Hill and Tyburn Tree

It is Saturday, May 9, 1801. The citizens are out in force, lining the muddy kennels and the rocky road from the new County Gaol at the Castle, past Gloverstone into Castle-street, Lower Bridge-street, Pepper-street, through the Wall at the Newgate, and so to Gallows Hill in Boughton, where the last execution is to be seen after two hundred years of public hanging, burning and whipping. A sight not to be missed. Who knows, after this – what with this new-fangled drop and platform with curtains round it – justice may no more be seen to be done and the sensational spectacle of a fellow creature suspended, convulsed in a dreadful last agony, be denied for ever? At the Gloverstone the 'free' citizens of that privileged parish extraterritorial to the city precincts and enjoying the 'protection' of the Castle, which stands within the county, press clamorously upon the cart as the three condemned men, tied and weighted with irons, are handed over by the Constable of the Castle to the City Sheriffs, who do not scruple to disguise their contempt of the office. Is it not enough for them to hang the city criminals? The county should do its own dirty work. Such are the bitter thoughts of the City Sheriffs, who must discharge their office even as the prisoners must meet their fate. The trundling of the execution cart through the town begins. The crowds along the route are swelled by people running from the Cross, where they have been waiting, having been misinformed about the line of procession. They are mostly silent, intently scanning the faces of the three men in the cart to see with what emotion, if any, they approach their violent death – rage, repentance, indifference, or just dumb misery. For Samuel Thompson and John Morgan, convicted of uttering counterfeit banknotes, there is not much compassion – after all, they are professionals and knew what to expect. As for the third man, John Clare, sentenced for petty burglary, he is a bold-looking young fellow and says he won't hang, come what may, doesn't he? But how can he escape it? Better hurry on to Gallows Hill.

The Editor of the Chronicle is a close observer of the slow progress of the cart. He has seen many executions at Gallows Hill and since this is to be the last there, he must be present to record it, though he is sick of the sight and has long since lost all belief in its power to deter others from crime. Men and women – and children – just stand there, he thinks, gaping at the horror and the thrill of the thing. Besides, God help them, there are criminals who glory in the drama and notoriety of their taking off before a sea of upturned faces and at the last moment bid the hangman make a good job. How could good and great men like Dr. Samuel Johnson and Sir Joshua Reynolds condone such obscenities? What was it that Johnson had said: 'executions are intended to draw spectators; if they do not they don't answer their purpose; the public is gratified by a procession and the criminal is supported by it"? And Reynolds, how could he, a great artist, think that executions in public are ennobling rather than degrading? So thinks the Chronicle Editor, a sensitive man, as he observes the demeanour of John Clare, noting that he 'appeared extremely undaunted the whole of the way'. Arrived at Boughton, the cart stops between the two gallows, the old one which has had its fill of human life and, at last disused, still rears its dismal frame on the hill overlooking the river, and the temporary instrument of dissolution erected in 1791 on the opposite side of the road. (It has been in 'temporary' use for ten years, pending the tardy reform of the execution laws.) Here the crowd presses closely upon the cart and in that moment of distraction for the officers of the scaffold, Clare pulls the cord from his arms and makes a desperate leap for it, the astonished mob falling back so that, hampered by the irons on his legs, he staggers and tumbles across the road, rolls down a steep gutter-way and plunges into the river. The spectators share a single surmise: can he get away over the meadows on the other side? He makes only a few yards from the Boughton shore when he sinks like a stone, dragged down by the weight of the leg irons.

Appalled, the Editor watches the fishing out of the body, which takes twenty minutes. Meanwhile, his sympathies have switched to the two other felons, tied up in the cart and waiting to die, with the fearful miscarriage of their companion enacted under their eyes. What happened next moved the Editor to write in the Chronicle of a few days later, May 15 (number 1, 352);

'shocking to relate, their execution was stayed till the lifeless body of

John Clare was suspended on one side of them in the most brutal manner. Common decency should have dictated another line of conduct. Why disturb the few moments they had then to live? Would it not have been better, and more consistent with humanity, to have let these men meet their fate than to distract their attention by such a horrid sight, and afterwards, if it were necessary to put in force the execution of the law, to have suspended his body? But so it is. We never heard any execution more universally execrated by all ranks than this, nor one that more deeply affected the feelings of the spectators. To complete this melancholy account, on bringing their bodies from the place of execution (without any covering) the cart was thrown over in Pepper-street by the unwarrantable negligence of the driver running it against a post.'

Whatever the justiciary and the city Sheriffs might think, the Editor went on grimly with the catalogue of the sufferings of John Clare, who

'consistently declared "he was not born to be hanged", on which account every care was taken at the Castle to prevent any scheme he might have invented in order to destroy himself. He persisted in the same declaration even on the morning of Saturday last and requested one of the turnkeys to inquire at the Post Office whether a reprieve was not arrived for him. On receiving a negative answer he seemed not to be dismayed and still asserted he was not to be hanged. It would surely be more safe for the future were a drop erected in the front of the Castle or some convenient spot in the yard, without dragging the unfortunate sufferers through the streets of the city, which experience tells us daily is productive of no good as an example, and thus prevent the confusion and misery naturally attendant on such lamentable occasions.'

So the Chronicle, rebuking the city magistracy for their inhumanity, the county for not providing for the seemly execution of its own felons, and the mighty Johnson and Reynolds for what today would be called their bloody-mindedness. This execution left a long memory. Joseph Hemingway, third Editor of the Chronicle, writing his *History* of the city some thirty years later, left posterity in no doubt that he shared the abhorrence of the entire business expressed by his predecessor. 'Though Clare,' wrote Hemingway, 'evaded the letter of his sentence in escaping being hanged by the neck till he was dead, yet the finisher of the law was unwilling to forego his official duty, and the dead body was tied up after the breath had departed. The most afflictive part of the tragedy was that the two poor men who were in a like condemnation were kept in a state of awful suspense until the dead carcase of the drowned man was tied up beside them.' Note the mordancy of those words, 'the finisher of the law'.

The county authorities were unwilling to give up their chartered privilege granted centuries before of handing over their condemned prisoners for execution by the city. They took no notice of the Chronicle's suggestion that a drop should be erected in the Castle yard so as to do away with the carting of criminals through the city. As late as 1821 John Broster was writing about the continuing grisly ceremony at Gloverstone, followed by 'this disgraceful and useless exhibition of a fellow creature dragged through an unfeeling gazing multitude . . . Is there any place at this day in the kingdom where this ancient barbarous custom is not abolished?' But after 1801 the condemned were dragged first to the Northgate Gaol, then to the new City Gaol, for the city magistrates in that year heeded the Chronicle and the better part of public opinion, and took down the Boughton gallows for good. 'In the course of this week,' reported the paper on October 2 (number 1372), 'a new drop has been erected in front of the Northgate Gaol, upon which, we are sorry to add, Aaron Gee, for stealing thirty pieces of calico, and Thomas Gibson, for a burglary, are to be executed tomorrow.' The model for the new drop was set up in 1783 in the centre of London's Old Bailey, opposite the door of Newgate Gaol. On November 21 of that year (number 446) the Chronicle's London reporter describes the 'new method of execution shortly to be put in practice'. A scaffold, eight feet high from the pavement, was to have a platform upon which the condemned were to be brought out, haltered and bound. 'They will then be tied up, and on a signal given by the Sheriff, the place on which they stand is so contrived as to fall down and leave them suspended. Only six will be executed at one time, and the hour to be seven in the morning in summer and nine in winter.' This device, or something like it, did not reach Chester until 1801, and it was clumsily installed at the infamous Northgate Gaol.

Aaron Gee and Thomas Gibson were the first unhappy victims of this instrument, which from the brutally bungled manner of their execution on October 3 became known as 'the drag'. The Chronicle reporter says they were carted from the Castle in the usual way to the Northgate and propelled about five feet from a window in the attics of the Gaol on the south side. They dropped nearly forty inches, their bodies beating against the windows below and smashing the glass. A black curtain concealing the grisly preparations was 'drawn up at the dreadful moment when they were launched into eternity'. (This 'launched into eternity' is a well-worn journalistic cliché to be found in nearly all the contemporary London and Chester accounts of executions.) The frequent failure of the mechanism of the drop, as we shall see, caused the malefactors more gratuitous agony than had formerly been inflicted by the executioner performing his office at Gallows Hill unaided by innovations. But first a valedictory word about the old Northgate Gaol where the drop or drag had a brief trial before the Gate and the Gaol were taken down in 1808, and the city prisoners incarcerated there transferred to the new City Gaol and House of Correction completed in 1807. Until the gallows at Boughton were dispensed with and the old Northgate and its gaol taken down, two of the principal approaches to Chester were disfigured by these lugubrious and unsightly erections dedicated to noisome confinement, torture and death in the name of the law. Writing to the Editor of the Chronicle in March, 1782 (number 361), a correspondent struck a blow for the civic pride and against the civic disinterest in the good name of what was then still one of the foremost cities in the country. 'Chester,' he wrote, 'is a city which with all its boasted advantages of situation cannot appear in a very favourable light to strangers of discernment . . . From the North the scenery is terrific and alarming – iron grates, tenfold wickets, Herculean bolts, arrest the eye at once. But, worse, at the East end stands our gallows, proclaiming with tremendous eloquence

> Stop, Traveller, stop,
> I will despatch thee in an instant:
> This is the confine of Pluto's gloomy region,
> From hence no mortal can retreat.

Surely, these are remains of Gothic, or, if you please, of Saxon barbarism, and as long as they are suffered to exist, strangers will be apt to suspect that the manners of the city's inhabitants, the ruling part, I mean, must be Gothic likewise.'

The old Northgate Gaol, the common gaol of the city from mediaeval times, has been memorably described for us by Hemingway in his *History*:

> 'The ancient gate, over which was a mean and ruinous gaol, was an inconvenient and unseemly pile of buildings. It consisted of a dark,

narrow passage under a pointed arch, with a postern on the east and the entrance to the gaol on the west. Immediately under the gateway, at the depth of some thirty feet, was a horrible dungeon to which the only access of air was through pipes which communicated with the street. In this frightful hole prisoners under sentence of death were confined – itself a living death.'

In this dungeon was immured the Rev. George Marsh, the Protestant martyr, until he was taken out and carted through the streets to be burnt at the stake at Boughton on April 24, 1555. A memorial marks the site, which is also that of the original gallows. Here Barrelwell Hill lane runs down to the river and it was about at this point that John Clare made his bid for freedom.

Pressure from the newspapers and public opinion, and the advocacy of John Howard and James Neild (a Cheshire man), who travelled the country towards the end of the eighteenth century reporting on antiquated prisons, led to the erection of new penitentiaries and a partial improvement in the conditions of custody, though very little in the methods of execution and the rigour of the law. Although the debate about public and privately executed justice (or vengeance) went on, 'throughout the century' (in the words of G. M. Trevelyan's *English Social History*), 'Parliament went on adding statute after statute to the "bloody code" of English law, enlarging perpetually the long list of offences punishable by death: finally they numbered two hundred. Not only were horse and sheep stealing capital crimes, but stealing in a shop to the value of five shillings, and stealing anything privily from the person, were it only a handkerchief.' Chester, as the execution centre for the entire county, continued to see the full effects of all this, and the scaffold, the drag and the drop figure constantly in the columns of the Chronicle until well into the nineteenth century.

After the turn of the century both city and county felons awaiting execution at least had better quarters, better food and more humane treatment at the new City and County Gaols than at the old ones, which were among the worst in the country. The City Gaol and House of Correction was immediately adjacent to the Walls between the Watergate and the Water Tower. The 'improved drop' was installed to begin with, over the front door and then at the back of the gaol, and the crowds drawn irresistibly to the slaughter were at first able to see nothing, for the drop was covered with a black curtain completely concealing the principal actors – the malefactor and the hangman. The Chronicle tells us that afterwards the Assize Judges directed 'that these fatal expiations of guilt should be public'.

The spectacle was in public view on May 6, 1809, when George Glover and William Proudlove, convicted of wounding an Excise officer, were turned off, but only at the second attempt. 'Heartrending', wrote the Chronicle reporter on May 12 (number 1766). 'They embraced and took leave of each other in the most affectionate manner, and on being tied up and the fatal signal given, the platform sank and, shocking to relate, both the ropes broke, and the poor wretches were precipitated to the bottom of the scaffold, half strangled. They were then taken into the chapel till other ropes could be procured. Requesting the Rev. Mr. Fish to be again sent for, they took a little refreshment and then joined him most fervently in prayer near two hours. When, ropes being prepared, they met their fate with the most manly fortitude and resignation, amidst the commiseration of the crowd.' It will be seen, from this and former examples, that the malfunction of the 'improved' engine of death could double the torments of the condemned, but on the old gallows also – if the hangman were drunk or past his job – there could be a most horrifying mess.

Until the ancient Chester Castle buildings began to be taken down in 1789, the Judges had lodgings there and held the Assize in Hugh Lupus's Hall, with the Court of Exchequer of the county adjoining. The City Sheriffs furnished the lodgings and the County Sheriffs took care of the Judges' coaches and horses. The Constable of the Castle held his place for life. The condition of the prisoners – and debtors – confined in the foul gaol below, was pitiable in the extreme. Howard, the prison reformer, said it was like the black hole at Calcutta and the Chronicle scribes condemned it time and again. But the most fearsome description is by Thomas Pennant, writing in 1784.

> 'Their day confinement is in a little yard surrounded on all sides by lofty buildings, impervious to the air, excepting from above, and ever unvisited by the purifying rays of the sun. Their nocturnal apartments are in cells seven feet and a half by three and a half, ranged on one side of a subterraneous dungeon, in each of which are often lodged three or four persons. The scanty air of the prison yard is to travel through three passages to arrive at them: the window of an adjacent room, a grate into the dungeon, and finally from the dungeon through a little grate

above the door of each kennel. In such places are the innocent and the guilty permitted to be lodged till the law decides their fate.'

The 'innocent' presumably meant those awaiting trial and non-malefactors such as political prisoners who (as after the Civil War and the Stuart risings) languished there until they died or were transported or found friends at court.

For the penniless 'honest' debtors there was no hope except to pay up. Revengeful creditors could keep them in duress for life, for a mere forty shillings owing, and if they could not discharge the debt and costs, only Parliament could deliver them by an Act of insolvency which would strip them of all they possessed, and since that was nothing they were suffered to linger in prison. The sharper, on the other hand, could get away with fraud and false pretences at no more risk than perhaps a year's imprisonment and no confiscation of his ill-gotten gains. No wonder, then, that the motley company in the old Castle Gaol sometimes made a break for it. Security was not very strict. Old soldiers – pensioners or invalids, as they were called – made up the Constable's guard. Bolts and bars were formidable enough, but the only way out was over the wall and the wall was high. The Chronicle (number 88) reported that on Christmas Day, 1776, the prisoners took advantage of relaxed vigilance by the 'invalids' and locked them in their own guard-house, where they had retired 'in order to regale themselves'. Eight prisoners then 'stole away over the wall of the upper ward. Two broke their legs in the fall. Another was taken about a mile from the Castle. The other five got clear off'. Ten felons, one of whom was under sentence of death and the rest of transportation, got clear away from the gaol in November, 1775, but the paper does not, for once, tell us how they did it: the Constable was evidently keeping close guard on his tongue if not on his prisoners. In going over the wall escapers took the risk of broken limbs, and, apart from that, to fail in the attempt incurred savage and ingenious punishments. James Neild, the Cheshire prison visitor, found a man who, having attempted to escape, had been compelled to wear for two months, 'in addition to the heavy double irons on his legs, a strong belt round his waist, and a long collar round his neck, with a prong that went down his back'. In even more barbarous times, pressing to death was said to be one of the specialities of Chester Castle dungeon.

Security in the Castle and City Gaols did not trouble the citizens over-much, but they were concerned for the safety of the streets and of their own houses and property. In the country districts, vigilantes formed their own protection associations, and let everybody round about know, as in this announcement, signed by many of the parishioners of Tarvin and published in the paper in March, 1777, that 'we have raised a proper fund and entered into articles of agreement, under the penalty of a hundred pounds each', to pursue and prosecute thieves, and particularly horse, cattle, and sheep stealers. Offenders, they said, too frequently escaped justice through 'tenderness' or other cause, and so they must look to themselves. Law and order in the city were the responsibility of the Mayor as Chief Magistrate, the Aldermen, the Recorder, and the City Commissioners, and their officers were the Beadle and the Watch. These, like the invalids and pensioners, were mostly antiquated characters and so ill-paid that they could be either bought or beaten off. The Watch had power to apprehend all disorderly persons, night-walkers and reputed whores, and to detain them in custody till they were brought before the Mayor and the magistrates, who could order prostitutes to be publicly whipped at the High Cross and peace-breakers such as public-house brawlers to thirty days' hard labour in the House of Correction. High-spirited apprentice boys who could elude the vigilance of their masters, the city merchants and shopkeepers, frightened the Watch after dark in the guise of hobgoblins. In February, 1776, there is a report of late-night disturbance in the neighbourhood of the Two Churches – St. Michael's and St. Bridget's in Bridge-street: 'a party of apprentice boys wantonly (among other martial exploits) fired a gun, loaded with gunpowder, against the shop window of Mrs. Whittell, hosier.' The Watch were plagued also by the less fortunate apprentice boys who, wearying of the confinement, the parish food and the drudgery at the House of Industry (near the riverbank on the north-west angle of the Roodee), eloped into the city for a bit of fun, with a reward on their heads for any person who should bring them back to the custody of the Guardians of the Poor – and a flogging. Thomas Hope, aged 17, John Rowland, 16, and Charles Whitehead, 15, made such a bid for freedom.

The Rows, so convenient by day, were ill-lit by night and became the haunt of footpads and whores. The Chronicle of July 10, 1775 (number 11), reports the waylaying of two country dealers who had come to the Midsummer Fair. About one o'clock in the morning they were returning to their lodgings when they were set upon near the

Feathers Row in Bridge-street by four men, 'one of whom clapt a pistol to their heads and with the vilest imprecations and threats robbed them of 35 guineas and their watches; then, by the advantage of the night, they made their escape, and have not yet been taken'. Nor were likely to be. In the same month there was complaint of the 'impostures practised upon the credulous public by strolling auctioneers' and other mountebanks at the City Fair, whose 'moving orations' angered the local fair traders and caused tumult in the streets. Such people, said the paper, were no more than strolling vagabonds and should be cast out of the city. The Mayor was invited to do his duty, but there wasn't much public confidence in the Watch.

To accompany the execution cart was one of the duties of the Beadle, and so unpopular and discredited was this functionary – like Mr. Bumble after him – that on one occasion he was the subject of a contemptuous remark flung at him by a condemned man on his way to the drop. It was ill time for jesting, but William Wilson, an old sailor upwards of 70, executed at the City Gaol for arson on May 28, 1814, went to his death with a bold front, as if facing enemy fire. On his way through the streets he chewed a piece of bread which at one point he spat out at the Beadle and turning to the crowd shouted: 'He's the Peeping Tom of Coventry!' And on the platform at the Gaol the old salt, according to the Chronicle reporter, reserved his last defiance for the spectators and the trappings of justice. 'What a many people are here to see an old man hung,' he said. 'There's as much fuss as if there were a hundred to be hung.'

The consequential Beadle, the forcible-feeble Watch, and the partiality (real or suspected) of the magistrates did not go uncensured by the newspaper and the public. In October, 1783, when the citizens, emulating their country neighbours of Tarvin, organised a night patrol of volunteers to 'protect the inhabitants in the tranquil enjoyment of their property', the paper made this significant comment: 'The business they undertake is generally performed with a diligence and circumspection that produce effects widely differing from those of a drowsy, mercenary, or a clamorous, ill-appointed police.' That the city volunteers were not deterred by danger, superstition, or thoughts of personal comfort is evidenced by their riding out through the Eastgate in very bad winter weather, on an all-night search of Delamere Forest for highwaymen reported to be lurking there. They found none, but in those days to venture into the Forest after dark was a courageous thing to do, for Delamere was not merely the lair of desperadoes but of witches, spectres, and the Devil himself. But within the city limits the Watch did have their uses: in June, 1775, they discovered a gang of coiners in a house in Upper Northgate-street, and dug up their tools and moulds buried in the garden; and in May, 1777, they apprehended 'many disorderly persons of both sexes in some suspected public-houses', who were committed by the Mayor to the statutory month's hard labour at the House of Correction. The innkeepers were twice warned in that month about the conduct of their houses and renewal of licences was refused to some who had permitted tippling on Sundays, entertained disorderly customers, or countenanced unlawful games on their premises.

Although the citizens of Chester might hold the city law officers in small respect, preferring to police themselves for their own better peace and security, they could not ignore the exactions of the 'bloody code' of licensed public slaughter which continued to the end of the eighteenth century and well into the next at Boughton, and afterwards at the Northgate and then at the City Gaol – a provincial city and county replica of the more extensive and bizarre transactions conducted at the same time at Newgate and Tyburn in London. These they could not ignore, either, since they were graphically reported by the Chronicle's London correspondents. But more of all this presently, after a final look at the local calendar of capitally expiated crime.

The paper's second Editor, James Hanshall, in his *History of Cheshire*, listed twenty executions at Boughton from 1776 to the end of the century. The third Editor, Joseph Hemingway, in his *History of Chester*, continued the catalogue with twenty-seven at the City Gaol to 1823, and later compilations detailed six more up to 1829. 'Rage, rage, against the dying of the light' – the words of a poet of our time, Dylan Thomas, express the pitiable, futile reaction of many a young man who found himself unbelievably at Gallows Hill to have his neck stretched for stealing a few shillings from a house, or some trumpery goods from a shop; and a crowd there to see the shame and the folly and the unfairness of it. For one gross crime deserving of the capital sentence, the files of the paper from 1775 onwards report many lives, young and old, violently ended for what we should now call misdemeanours. For stealing corn from a Chester merchant's warehouse two men were transported for seven years in 1775, but after that year

Chester Cathedral.

Right The 14th-century choir stalls are among the glories of the Cathedral. This carved pilgrim to the shrine of St. Werburgh sits on the elbow rest of the Dean's Stall.
Far right Chester Castle, Agricola's Tower and the Chapel of St. Mary-de-Castro, all that remains of the original structure.
Below The old Eastgate, taken down in 1768.

Above left South-east façade of the Exchange, the Chester Town Hall for nearly two hundred years, destroyed by fire on December 31, 1862 (Vignette from Hanshall's History of Cheshire.) *Above right* Gamul House in Lower Bridge Street, where King Charles I found a brief refuge in a city surrounded by Parliamentary troops. The house has been restored. *Above* Bishop Lloyd's Palace in Watergate Street Romney's sketch.

Top Bishop Lloyd's Palace – a contemporary close-up photograph of the richly ornamented façade showing the carved panels of religious subjects much scrutinised by visitors from all parts of the world *Bottom* The 16th-century Dutch Houses in Bridge Street, Chester, a splendid example of conservation for European Architectural Heritage Year, 1975.

the war with the Americans put a stop to transportation and instead, the Thames hulks were used as prison ships until 1787, when the transports were resumed – this time to Australia. That was one of the 'benefits' of Captain Cook's discovery of that land; we sent our felons there, and many of them never survived the long and fearful sea voyage in the foulest duress below decks.

Names long forgotten of those who suffered in one way or another stare out at us from the contemporary page of the provincial paper; it is their only memorial. Elizabeth Hunt, a Chester night-walker, was 'privately whipped' for stealing a guinea from her customer. James Knight was hung at Boughton for stealing clothes from a private house. On the scaffold he 'acknowledged the justice of his sentence and died very penitently'. Christopher Lawless, Isaac Hutchinson, Alexander Solomon and Isaac Josephs paid the penalty for robbing the shop of Mr. Pemberton, jeweller. A madman, Samuel Thorley, was hung in chains for the insensate murder of Anne Smith, a ballad singer: he cut up the body and ate part of it. William Ellis, aged 21, caught in a burglary, 'resigned himself to God', while his companion on the gallows, William Loom, aged 20, convicted of discharging a loaded pistol with intent to wound, behaved as if 'the thoughts of his approaching dissolution had deprived him of his reason'. Sarah Jones was hung for stealing twenty-eight yards of chintz from a shop, Elizabeth Wood for poisoning, and John Oakes for coining. Strung up together for burglary were Resolution Heap, aged 70, and Martha Brown, aged 28. Heap, wrote the reporter, 'exhibited a melancholy instance of human depravity at so advanced a period of life, having been twice condemned and publicly whipped prior to this. And what is very extraordinary, he solemnly declared that the first of his offences was committed after his 60th year.' The Assize Judge in April, 1781, showed clemency before his departure, reprieving Alice Hopley and Joseph Hulme, upon whom he had earlier passed sentence of death, the one for burglary, the other for stealing a mare. Charles Fowles, John Johnson, and Thomas Windsor, caught killing rabbits on the warren of Philip Egerton, Esq., at Oulton, got off with fourteen days' imprisonment, having enlisted in the 22nd Regiment of Foot, then serving against the Americans.

The Chronicle has a special word for the execution of highwaymen, who were gibbeted near the scene of their crime and the bodies left hanging until they made old bones or were secretly made away with in the night-time. This happened in the case of one Lowndes, who, for robbing the Warrington mail coach, was hung in chains on Helsby Hill in April, 1791. A short time afterwards the local people, disgusted by the sight of the swinging corpse, cut down the gibbet pole and carried it away. The law's writ continued to run many a year, however, after the hanging in chains at Trafford Green of Thomas Brown and James Price in April, 1796, also convicted of robbing the Warrington mail. Their skeletons hung on the gibbet until 1820, and when the pole was taken down, 'in Price's skull,' says the Chronicle in a final touch, 'a robin's nest was found.' For Thomas Mate, executed at Boughton in 1789 for the murder of John Parry – an officer of the peace – while attempting to serve a warrant on him, there was little public sympathy. 'From the moment of his condemnation,' says the paper, 'to that of his dissolution he betrayed a rooted, fixed, and almost savage obduracy. He declared he would not forgive his prosecutors, nor his wife, whom, though near 70 years old, he charged with infidelity.' Two burglars, Smith and Clarke, caught in the shop of Mr. Fletcher, jeweller in Eastgate, were executed on the drop in 1810. 'The conduct of Smith was exceedingly unbending and audacious, and the night before his execution he played at cards with his companions.' Our last local chronicle of wasted lives shall be the hanging of William Wilkinson and two others for rape. Wilkinson treated the scaffold as a theatre, exclaiming to his companions: 'Keep up your spirits. Never mind, my lads – we are all murdered men. I'm just as happy as if I was going to a play.' Undaunted to the end, he said as the halter was placed round his neck, 'My new handkerchief fits me nice and tight'.

Another grisly chapter could be written from the Chronicle files about crime and execution in London and the daily rolling of the death cart from Newgate the length of Holborn to Tyburn Tree just north of Hyde Park, the windows crowded with spectators all along the route and likewise the stands overlooking Tyburn Gallows. Execution days were free street dramas in which the better sort, as well as the spectacle-loving London mob, found inexhaustible tragicomedy. Tyburn was the finest theatre on earth wherein to study human nature in extremis. No play, after all, could hope to rival the formal, stylised presentation put on regularly by the hangman (the reigning Jack Ketch of his day), Mr. Leapinwell, the Sheriff's Officer, Mr. Gates, the City Marshal, the Rev. Mr. Villette, the Ordinary (or padre) of Newgate Gaol and Mr. Akerman, the Keeper of Newgate. For years their names appeared in the Chronicle's cast

of characters and local readers were as familiar with them as with the
names of the London actors. Many of the convicts, in the grim
knowledge that they were the principal performers making positively
their last appearance, wore their best clothes, travelled the death
route by mourning coach (if they could afford it) instead of going in
the common cart, and sometimes were permitted to stop for refreshment at taverns on the way. 'Dressed like a bride on the wedding
morn, in a gay suit of scarlet,' wrote the Chronicle reporter of one
Peter Scipio, an Italian, condemned for shooting at his mistress.

To bring the London part of this bloody chapter to a close, a touch
of comedy is needed, and we find it in the paper of January 10, 1783
(number 401). Lord Mansfield, Chief Justice from 1756 to 1788, is
presiding in the Court of King's Bench over a trial of crim. con.
(criminal conversation or illicit love). A handsome young woman
steps into the witness-box, to be interrogated by Counsellor Dunning,

> 'who, thinking to confuse the woman, made her take off her bonnet
> that he might have a view of her countenance and see whether the truth
> came from her lips. After he had put many ridiculous questions to her,
> he asked her whether her mistress had ever communicated the import-
> ant secret to her?
>
> 'No, sir,' said the woman, 'she never did.'
>
> 'And how can you swear to her infidelity?'
>
> 'Because I saw another gentleman besides my master in bed with
> her.'
>
> 'And pray, my good woman,' said the modest Counsellor (thinking
> to silence her at once), 'did your master (for I see you are very hand-
> some), in return for his wife's infidelity, go to bed to you?'
>
> 'That trial,' said the spirited woman, 'does not come on the day, Mr.
> Slabberchops.'
>
> Lord Mansfield (continues the report) was tickled to the soul, and
> asked Dunning if he had any more interrogatories to put?
>
> 'No, my Lord, I have none,' said the chop-fallen orator, settling his
> wig and sitting down.

At Chester the City and County Gaols continued in business until
1884. But long before that time the Gloverstone had disappeared –
nobody seems to know where, perhaps into the Castle ditch in
Thomas Harrison's massive reconstruction of the military, civil and
judicial buildings – and the custom of handing over felons and carting them through the streets to public execution was at length discontinued. Chester continued as an Assize seat of the Circuit Judges

– or Itinerant Justices – from Westminster until 1971, when the Courts Act brought in the new dispensation of the Crown Courts. The system changes, some ceremony has been foregone, but the legal tradition of centuries goes on, with the Crown Court sitting now continuously at the Castle and the Circuit Judge presiding there on occasion in the more searching cases of criminal jurisprudence.

On November 10, 1972, (number 10,265) the Chronicle published a review by the Deputy Editor, J. Ormsby Jones, of a book, *Farewell to the Assizes*, written by Sir Basil Nield, a Judge of the High Court, Queen's Bench division, since 1960, and M.P. for Chester from 1940 to 1956. Having presided at each of the sixty-one assize towns in England and Wales, Mr. Justice Nield was persuaded by his twin sister, Miss Beryl Nield, Mayor of Chester in 1961, to 'write something about these towns in particular and the assize system in general, especially in view of the proposal – now a decision – to abandon that system'. The book is a coda on the last stages of a grand judicial pilgrimage which began with the Assize of Clarendon in 1166, and Chester has a distinguished place in it. In addition to many anecdotes and sidelights on the life of a Judge on circuit, Sir Basil reflects on the nature of the judicial function. He has been guided, he writes, by these words of a great Scottish Judge, Lord Macmillan: 'Few minds are as neutral as a sheet of plate glass, and indeed a mind of that quality may actually fail in judicial efficiency, for the warmer tints of imagination and sympathy are needed to temper the cold light of reason, if human justice is to be done.'

In the two hundred years partially and episodically covered by this chapter, was human justice always done? The reader must judge for himself in the light of the times, manners, civilisation and condition of the people of which it treats. I may add, however, that nothing chronicled here from the late eighteenth and early nineteenth centuries equalled in depravity the case that was heard at Chester Assize from April 19 to May 6, 1966. This was the trial of Ian Brady and Myra Hindley for three murders. The Moors Murders, they were called – and the crime the crime of the century. This is not the place to recall the evidence. Some of it was unfit to print in any newspaper, even today. Students of psychology, a Judge and a novelist have written books about the case, variously interpreting it as a study in fiendish murder as a substitute for sex, as a reflection of the state of society and the overthrow of moral sanctions, and as a justification for the urgent reform of criminal proceedings. On October 6, 1972, I wrote an editorial comment in the Chronicle on the removal from an exhibition of Police work at Cheshire Police Headquarters at Chester, of two photographs of the Moors murders, at the request of the mother of the child victim. My comment ended (and with it I end the chapter): 'The mother's feelings are understandable, to say the least. The photographs and tape-recordings were the most terrible features of the evidence given in Court. But the Police cannot sleep, nor the responsibility of society be abrogated in a century of unparalleled crime such as this . . . We have to learn more about the complexities of evil in a supposedly civilised society, and the echoes of the Moors murders may help us.'

11
The real rich stuff
of human nature

The scene is Hyde Park in London, the time between six and seven o'clock on the morning of Monday, November 29, 1779. The town is a late riser and no interfering persons are to be expected at this hour. Four cloaked figures emerge from the mist into an open space near the Ring. A fifth personage, with a bag at his feet, stands retired but watchful among the trees. Two of the four produce pistols, examine them, hand them to the duellists, and retire also. The Hon. Charles James Fox, leader of the Opposition, and William Adam, Esq., M.P., a supporter of Lord North's discredited ministry, face each other to settle a Parliamentary affair of honour. It is not surprising to see the famous Mr. Fox in such a situation – or not improbable to suspect that with the dawn he had left one of the gaming clubs after an all-night faro session to keep the appointment. He appears, or affects to appear, unconcerned. This is not the first time he has been called out, for he has a scarifying tongue. Adam is cool but revengeful. He cannot forget the insult in the House on the previous Thursday. His first shot wounds Fox slightly in the stomach. Blood flows. The doctor makes to step forward out of the trees. Fitzpatrick, Fox's second, intervenes. 'Are you satisfied?' 'No,' says Adam, 'unless he will sign a paper retracting what he has said.' Refusing pointblank, Fox scornfully urges his antagnoist to fire again. The shot misses and Fox ends the affair disdainfully with an action full of character, first pointing his pistol at Adam, then discharging it into the air. Only then is the doctor permitted to look at the wound. Reporting this affair, as proof of the great man's 'magnanimity' in a life-and-death matter, the Whig Chester Chronicle (December 3, number 241) comments: 'The public will make their own comments on such an attack, at such a time, on so distinguished a member of Opposition.' This refers to the increasing contempt into which Lord North's (and the King's) Government was falling because of its bungling of the American war. Naturally, the Government was blamed impartially for the lewdness of the times, the extravagance of the Court (such as

it was), the dissoluteness of society, the scandals, gambling, drinking, and wenching that went on. With such examples before them,
what could be hoped for from the lower orders? But the lower orders
loved to read all about it, or have it read to them – for the newspapers
still had a residual illiteracy as well as the stamp duty to contend
with in their laudable wish to enlighten (and titillate) the nation.

As the historians describe England in the last quarter of the eighteenth century we see a picture of a fair and busy land, with a fruitful
agriculture of trim fields freshly enclosed out of the former waste-
lands, a gracious domestic architecture in town, village, and manor
house (its gardens grandly formalised by the genius of Capability
Brown), fast coaches enabling the natives, gentle and simple, to dis-
cover their own country for the first time with frequent trips to
London, Bath, and the new delights of the seaside, a settled literature dictated by Dr. Johnson, the principles of art laid down by Sir
Joshua Reynolds, political economy by Adam Smith, and political
philosophy by Edmund Burke, all within the framework of order and
freedom, urban development (Birmingham, Liverpool, Manchester), and the Industrial Revolution – and eventually at the helm the
young Mr. Pitt, 'Master Billy', a master of stop-go, reforming, tem-
porising, taxing, mending (and paying for) the break with the
American colonies, and with Napoleon ahead of him. It's all true, of
course, but the details that make up the picture look different in the
contemporary papers – more like the real rich stuff of human nature,
though no doubt some of what follows is hearsay or journalistic
apocrypha. But it's all there in the files between 1775–1785, and how
relevant much of it is to 1975 you will see.

Duels were fought over women, real or imagined insults, debts and
losses at cards, cheating at cards, political differences – 'an officer
of the Marines and a gentleman of the Temple fought a duel after a
political conversation in a coffee-house the night before respecting
the Americans' – the settlement of an estate, or just out of bravado.
Your fine gentleman would pick a quarrel on the flick of a laced cuff
or the set of a cravat, and the commonalty emulated him by brawl-
ing and fighting with fists or clubs in the street. A wager was the
usual accompaniment of every challenge. St. John's Churchyard in
Chester, then occupied by houses like a small cathedral close (St.
John's was the cathedral before St. Werburgh's), witnessed a

singular combat one morning at the end of December, 1782. A 'multitude' turned out to see the fun. Here is the Chronicle's simple, derisory tale:

> 'Last Monday evening an inhabitant of this city, about forty years of age, and, though of some eminence, is much better fed than taught, took upon him to insult, in a public kitchen, a person of a temper naturally peaceable and convivial, aged upwards of seventy. By repeated illiberal attacks, the old gentleman was so highly irritated as to dare his quarrelous opponent to single combat; but the company, fully sensible of the unmerited abuse he had received, and fearing he was by no means a proper match for such a brow-beating antagonist, prudently prevented the combatants meeting at that time. Stung, however, with resentment, the old man challenged the younger to cudgel him the next morning in St. John's Churchyard, for a considerable sum, which the other was imprudent enough to accept. The champions accordingly met, and to the no small satisfaction of many spectators, the hoary Alexander brandished his Crabtree-sapling so manfully that his hectoring adversary was happy to decamp precipitately.'

The bargaining or wagering instinct also entered into a curious country custom, which those who had recourse to it mistakenly supposed had the sanction of law; at any rate, it solved many a marriage problem. Readers of Thomas Hardy's *The Mayor of Casterbridge* will remember the public sale of a wife in the opening chapter. The Chronicle reports three such incidents, in 1775 at Wath in Yorkshire, in 1781 at Chesterfield, and in 1799 at Macclesfield in Cheshire. This was a method by which a husband could get rid of an unfaithful wife at a profit by selling her to the man who had cuckolded him. Or, wishful to discard a nagging or otherwise unwanted wife, he could offer to pay the first man who would take her. A lot depended, of course, upon the acceptability of the woman for her personal charms or as a household drudge. In the Yorkshire story William Taylor paid twenty-one guineas to Jonathan Jowett in exchange for Jowett's wife – eleven guineas paid down and a note for the remainder payable in two months. By agreement Jowett delivered his wife in a halter to the common, where, all the village looking on, he handed her over to Taylor, returning him a guinea for luck of the bargain. Good-naturedly to show that he had been cuckolded, Jowett had a board tied to his forehead with two gilt horns and the words 'Cornuted by William Taylor'. Nothing is said about the lady's side of the transaction. In the affair at Chesterfield the wife was just as willing to be rid of her husband as he of her. He therefore:

> ... made a proposal of selling her, by which method he thought not
> only of getting rid of a great plague but also of reaping the advantage of
> some money into pocket. A purchaser being accordingly found (with
> the consent of all parties), a writing was drawn up, and the husband
> agreed for the sum of 15 guineas to resign all right and pretensions of
> his wife whatever. To make the transaction (as the parties supposed)
> more firm and valid, she was formally delivered up by the husband to
> the purchaser, with a halter about her neck, in the public market place.
> The husband said upon delivery he did it as his act and deed, and the
> purchaser replied he received her as such. After this ceremony was
> over, the loving couple marched away arm in arm, the man seemingly
> much pleased with his bargain and the husband more highly delighted
> he had quit of the plague of his life and a handsome gratuity into the
> bargain.

The Cheshire account is of one Twigg, who bought two wives in
Macclesfield market from his neighbours, one for half a crown, the
other for a shilling. He, too, led them home with a halter round their
necks. Arrived there, they found that they were indeed third parties,
since Twigg's legal wife was already in possession. Christina Hole, in
Traditions and Customs in Cheshire, mentions a Mobberley woman, sold
in Altrincham market for one and sixpence, who objected and had to
be urged to sale by the husband and his friend, armed with a stick.

Not all men, however, treated their wives so cavalierly. There was,
for example, Mr. Van Butcher, 'a celebrated dentist' in London, who
was so much attached to his wife that when she died in 1775 he had
her embalmed. When the Chronicle's London correspondent called
on Mr. Van Butcher for professional treatment he was taken aback
to find (May 15, number 3) the late Mrs. Van Butcher 'in the parlour where he sits. He shows her to all her friends when they visit
him. Upon the whole, he seems pleased with his sweet, handsome,
and silent wife'. Reflecting on this remarkable oddity, the correspondent adds: 'Supposing this whim should strike those leaders of
decorum that govern the world of fashions. . . .'

Women, though far from liberated, were not without redress in
the courts when they could plead sufficient reason. In March, 1776,
the wife of Mr. Tenducci, a famous Italian singer at Covent Garden
and many provincial music festivals (including Chester), moved at
Doctors Commons for nullity of marriage on the ground that her
husband was a eunuch, and 'that he had been made such when a
boy in Italy'. The facts being 'clearly proved', the Judge dissolved

the marriage, Mr. Tenducci to pay the costs. Elopement was another way out for spirited wives and daughters under governance, and here the stories come thick and fast. Again, the women prudently took care for the money in addition to making sure of the deliverer, but they were never sure of keeping both. There was a gamble in this as in every other aspect of life at this time. Elopements reached such a pitch in 1776 that the 'great world' was reported to be seriously alarmed, rather more for its money than its morals. Women were taking matters into their own hands. 'A few days ago,' (Chronicle, August 1, number 67), 'the wife and daughter of a Baronet fled from the family mansion, but whether on affairs of gallantry or other domestic uneasiness the gossip Scandal has not yet determined.' One eloping lady of spirit and fashion took care to obtain first from her lover a promise of marriage, and then set about preparing evidence for a divorce from her deserted husband. The practical sex was refining the thing to a social system in their favour, and in this comment in the same paper, affronted masculine pride is scarcely concealed: 'Matrimonial shackles seem ill-suited to the genius of the present age – it is an old-fashioned institution, calculated for simple times. Nothing can be more incongruous than the idea of metamorphosing a modern fine lady into a wife. Girls who work samplers and are educated at home may seek happiness in domestic life; a woman of spirit lives in publick, and for the publick.'

Content to seek happiness in domestic life were the ladies of Chester, I am glad to say, as evidenced by a report of their activities in December, 1775. At a Christmas Court of Honour in the city they sought to rescue the polite game of quadrille from those who would 'prostitute it to the mean and mercenary purposes of gaming'. The Court of Honour (which I suspect had the power of social exclusion in reserve) directed that all money won at quadrille in the city assemblies and private parties should be equally divided – half to be laid out in the occasional expense of cards and half to be applied to the Ladies' Fund for rewarding good and faithful servants. The ladies of Chester must have been scandalised to read in the Chester Chronicle a few months later the reproduction of this advertisement which had appeared in the London Public Advertiser:

> A gentleman who hath filled two seats in successive Parliaments, is near 60 years of age, lives in great splendour and hospitality, and from whom a considerable estate must pass if he dies without issue, hath no objection to marry a widow or single lady, provided the party be of

genteel birth, polite manners, and is five, six, seven, or eight months gone in her pregnancy. Letters directed to – Brecknock, Esq., at Will's Coffee House, will be honoured with due attention, secrecy, and every mark of respect.

If we are to credit an anecdote published in the Chronicle in December, 1783, determined elopers frequently ended their pilgrimage (if not overtaken and brought back by relatives in a fast relay of carriages) on the consummation bed at Gretna Green, at the inn or in the house of the blacksmith parson. 'By the law of Scotland,' we read, 'it is well known that any person whatever under sixteen years of age may perform the sacerdotal rights of marriage, which stands valid only if they be consummated, that is, if the couple be seen in bed by two witnesses. If a couple be married at the inn, Vulcan, when he has finished his part, sees them to bed and calls in his principal Cyclops as witnesses, when they sign their certificate. If the pair wait on him at his own house, the ceremony of consummation is then performed in the allotted bed, which he keeps in a corner of his house and which has borne many hundred couples.' This account is capped by the bawdy story of an Irish officer eloping with a lady from Cheshire. The blacksmith told them that, as usual, they must consummate before he could sign the certificate. To which the Irishman replied: 'By my faith, parson, if that stops your signing, sign away, honey, for that part of the ceremony was over ere I reached York!'

Look now at a Hogarth-like scene of 1785: search-night among the prostitutes of London, rounded up, dragged away to the watchhouse, confined in a cellar and next morning committed to Bridewell. The ladies of pleasure in high society were one thing, the women of the town, the 'walking ladies', were another. Unless a woman had a husband or protector or a job by which to support herself she was, as we should say, entirely without social security. Jobs were hard to get, even in linen-drapery, perfumery and haberdashery, the shopkeepers preferring to employ men – because it was better for trade – in these duties that might have been reserved for women and girls. All that was left for them was servitude and kitchen drudgery, and 'Master Billy' was screwing the taxes on employers of female servants so that many of them were being instantly dismissed and thrown upon the streets. 'Is prostitution to be wondered at?' asks the Chronicle (November 25, number 545). 'Inquire into the

connection of a woman of the town and nine times in ten she will
appear to be the daughter of a poor officer or clergyman: a description of characters who, by their rank as gentlemen, could not commit
their offspring to servile labour, and yet whose poverty denies them
the power of making the necessary provision for their common support.'

Mr. Pitt proposed to raise £140,000 by his tax on female servants,
2s.6d. for one, 5s. for two in one family, 10s. for three or more in the
same family. Injudicious and oppressive, said the Chronicle, the tax
falling as it would mostly on poor families who could least afford it.
'It is true that half-a-crown a year may be looked upon by the Minister as a trifling object, but to those who are obliged to live from hand
to mouth it is an object of importance.' What, after all, did the Minister, a well-employed bachelor with all found, know about it? And
there was clinching criticism of Mr. Pitt's disinclination to tax the
theatres and the actors and actresses and other houses of 'public diversion and genteel resort'. The Chronicle published this lampoon:

> What now, Master Pitt,
> Has become of your wit,
> Thus to tax honest women for working,
> When such numbers appear
> Every day, ev'rywhere
> In pride and in idleness lurking?
>
> Since this is the case
> You must take the disgrace,
> And this must henceforth be the saying,
> Pitt tax'd all the fair
> Who industrious were,
> But he took spec'l care
> Not to tax Whores and Rogues for their playing.

Here enters the celebrated Mrs. Sarah Siddons, about whom more
will be found in the chapter on the theatre. In the present chapter we
are concerned less with the quality of her art than with her capacity
to make money in the practice of it. The fabulous earnings of Mrs.
Siddons were the talk of the town and the country. Of all the women
of the age, it could truthfully be said of Mrs. Siddons that she 'lived in
publick and for the publick'. A rogue' of the theatre, a 'player', as the
lampoon said, she won and kept the respect and admiration of all
ranks throughout a long career – and made money at a famous rate.
Mrs. Siddons appeared first at Drury-lane in 1775, without much

success. After six years playing in the provinces, she returned, full of renown, to Drury-lane in 1782. In the following year the Chronicle began to compute her earnings. Her initial agreement was for three years, at £10, £11 and £12 per week for each year. The maximum of £12 was paid after only one month, and she had a benefit worth £830, with an annual benefit to follow. 'And to crown all,' said the paper (April 4, 1783, number 413), 'we hear that within a few days past they have entirely given up her first articles, desiring her to fix her own terms in future, which are said to be mutually settled for the next season at the rate of £20 per week – or a thousand guineas for the season, gross, with a clear benefit.' In July we read of her on tour, earning 250 guineas for two nights' performance in Liverpool, after which she is expected for twelve nights in Dublin, one night in Cork, taking in Liverpool again and probably Birmingham on her way back to the capital. 'About £2,500 will, in all probability, be the amount of this lady's summer earnings.' By June, 1785, there is an even more complicated calculation. Drury-lane is then paying her 25 guineas a week, with: 'a benefit clear of the nightly charge, which, being one hundred guineas, is divisible into weekly distributions of more than three guineas more, and a second benefit subject to the payment of the charges. The profits on the two benefits, without presents, may be computed at £500; the salary produces near £900. Her profits this summer are to be clear, one night at Manchester, one at Liverpool. If she clears out of Edinburgh with as good a lading as last year, there will be a thousand guineas more. And the Belfast expedition may be laid at 500 more; in all, no less than £3,200, exclusive of presents at her benefits.' Everywhere Mrs. Siddons filled the theatres from pit to boxes. She was the first actress of the age – perhaps the most accomplished English actress of any age – and the public were pleased to pay to see her. It was otherwise with poor Queen Charlotte, whose birthday celebrations the newspapers annually criticised for extravagance.

Nowhere, however, was extravagance more to be seen than in the ludicrous fashions of dress and ornament adopted by both sexes after the mid-century. These reached their height – in female head-dressing, literally – in the 1770–80 decade. Paris, then as now, dictated the trend, London and the rising new towns copied it, often turning out the superior article at second hand, and the lower orders wore the cast-off finery of their betters. In Chester the glove-makers made a small contribution to the national rag-trade. The more bizarre styles, colours and accoutrements of dress were flaunted at the London pleasure gardens of Vauxhall and Ranelagh, at the theatres, prize fights, and race meetings, at the water carnivals on the Thames, and at Bath, Cheltenham, Tunbridge Wells, Harrogate, Buxton, Brighton and Scarborough. (Chester had not then become a season or tourist city, but was much visited and described by writers and travellers in search of antiquities – 'to this day, the buildings are very old', wrote Daniel Defoe in 1724.) Young bloods and elderly apes, Corinthians and Macaronis, and their grossly bedizened ladies set the 'bon ton' and ran up unpayable bills with tailors and milliners. In 1750, says a Chronicle note, fashions did not reach any place fifty miles from London till they were nearly run out. In 1783, such were the social changes brought about by fast coaches, diligences, and private carriages, that the fashions travelled down to all parts of the country in a day. And it was possible to cut as fine a figure in Eastgate, Chester – or nearly so – as in the capital, if you could afford it. Manifestly, observed the local scribe, 'a good many of our city apprentices are dressing beyond their means, and, indeed, of their masters'.

The town wits and newspaper scribblers affected to despise the ladies for their towering head-dresses which covered a plentiful lack of brains. 'The present most fashionable disposition of the features is a vacant stare, with the mouth wide open,' says a note of January 4, 1783 (number 403). 'Our correspondent has observed it often of late, particularly in coaches and chariots. It is deemed pretty to look foolish, which must be the case while it is unfashionable for a fine lady to possess an idea.' Fine and foolish, and very high, wide and empty in the head – that was the picture of the fashionable belle of the 1770s. Sedan chairs will have to be enlarged to contain these high heads of the bon ton, quipped the gossips. And have you heard of the ludicrous exposure of a lady viewing pictures in Cheapside Friday se'nnight? By some accident the whole mass of her capital ornaments fell to the ground and all that was left to be seen was a head clean shaved except a small circle of hair. Gad, what a sight! Lady Grosvenor, wife of the seventh baronet who had been created Baron Grosvenor of Eaton in 1761, is credited with inventing a life-saving device in the event of a ducking at water regattas which the designers took up and transformed into the new back panniers or 'cork rump'. This caught on and soon became part of the fashionable female equipment, with the perfumes, paint, cosmetic washes, artificial teeth, false hair, Spanish wool, iron stays, hoops, high-heeled shoes and bolstered hips. Treble-caped belted greatcoats and half-boots, with black slouched hats, were the next affectation, so that: 'we may shortly expect to see the parading fair in jack-boots, brandishing the club-sticks which our pretty fellows have just laid aside as too heavy for their delicate frames.'

When the Chronicle's women readers saw this verse satire in the issue of June 8, 1781 (number 320), were they mortified or seized with a determination to take places on the next fast coach to Town from the White Lion or the Yacht?

The MODERN BELLE
Muse begin the comic lay,
Sing the female of to-day;
Yet to person be confin'd,
Do not meddle with her mind,
Lest the strange investigation
Cause thee trouble and vexation.
'Twere to seek, alas-a-day!
Needles in a stack of hay.
Void of talents, sense, and art,
Dress is now her better part.
Sing her daubed with white and red;
Sing her large terrific head;
Nor the many things disguise
That produce its mighty size;
And let nothing be forgot,
Carrots, turnips, and what not;
Curls and cushions for imprimis,
Wood and powder for the finis;
Lace and lappets, many a flag,
Many a party-colour'd rag,
Pendent from the head behind,
Floats and wantons in the wind;
Many a gem and many a feather,
A fine farrago altogether!
By whose wood and wire assistance,
Formidable at a distance,
(As the elephants of yore
A fam'd Queen to battle bore),
They with terror and surprize
Strike the poor beholder's eyes.
What a quantity of brain
Must he think such heads contain?
Tho' it proves a false alarm —

Feather brains can do no harm!
Hats that only shew the chin
And the mouth's bewitching grin,
As intended for a shield
To the caput thus conceal'd:
Surely 'tis an useful art
Well to guard the weakest part:
Shoes that buckle at the toe,
Gowns that o'er the pavement flow,
Or festoon'd on either side,
With two yellow ribbons ty'd;
While a peak like pigeon's rump
Shows behind she's not too plump:
Heels to bear the precious charge,
More diminutive than large,
Slight and brittle, apt to break,
Of the true Italian make:
For women of Bon Ton, observe ye,
Like sugar-loaves turn'd topsy-turvy
(As their heaviest part's o'top),
Rest upon a feeble prop:
And that all mankind may know it,
Toss about their heads to shew it.

                                        E.F.

The men could write and talk despisingly, but what about themselves? Uni-sex was around long before the 1970s. In May, 1776, young men's fancies took a curious turn. Observing the scene from the edge of 'the gay circle at Ranelagh on Thursday se'nnight', the Chronicle correspondent picked out several fops 'exhibiting their sweet persons in coats a la Polonaise. A smart youth, with a cockade, was a striking figure indeed; his head was a pyramid of curls; the cape of his coat, which was lined with yellow, edged with silver, and without buttons, was fastened at the breast with two large silver tassels; the garment which supplied the place of a waistcoat having neither pockets, flaps, nor buttons, gave his body the appearance of a bale of yellow silk. His breeches were black, his feet covered with plates of silver of an enormous size, adorned with silken roses. And from his whole person, but from the white silken gloves in particular, exhaled perfumes that scented the ambient air.'

It is time now to treat of less exotic matters, after this last look at 'Portrait of a Modern Beau', painted in the paper of August 30, 1782 (number 383):

Here comes Hack Buck, the famous fop,
With his high friz'd Alpean top.
See, round each ear his num'rous curls,
And with what art his switch he twirls.
Behold his queue, how nicely ty'd,
Three pounds of powder in th'inside.
Look at his cheeks, with rouge well clad,
And at his plastered white forehead.
His eyes, how sweet and languishing,
How nicely formed for ogleing.
His cloaths, how smartly shap'd and cut,
Observe his Grampian buckled hat.
His shoe buckles – how curious!
How large – how long – how monstrous!
But sad to tell – not e'en a grain
Of common sense is in his head.

The new industrial towns of Liverpool, Manchester, and Birmingham were growing apace, and for the first time old-established cities
such as Chester and York (though still both larger in population
than Leeds at this time) were losing place as provincial capitals. But
they continued to be cities of consequence, publishing their own
newspapers, serving as market centres for richly productive rural
areas, and pioneering social improvement, as did Chester notably in
the hospital and educational services. The King's School had been a
seat of learning, originally for 'poor friendless boys', since 1541; the
Blue Coat School, also for poor boys, was founded in 1700 (and continued until 1949); charity schools were established in Chester in advance of most other towns, and Robert Raikes's idea for Sunday
schools was actively propagated. Advertised in the Chronicle were
several private schools of various pretension. Mrs. Franks, in Watergate-street, Mr. Franks assisting, taught young ladies French,
music, dancing, geography, writing and accounts. Monsieur Thil-
lays taught his native language at his lodgings at Mr. Wilcoxon's,
linen-draper, adjoining the Eastgate. An anonymous 'native of
France, of liberal education, who has met with some recent dis-
appointment', solicited pupils for instruction in the French language
– 'the salary no object'. Mr. Durack, dancing master, had schools at
Wrexham and Oswestry, terms half a guinea entrance and 15s per
quarter, and he assured parents that 'the report of a dreadful fever
raging in Wrexham is groundless'. In 1766 the Grammar School at

Weaverham, Northwich, advertised for a master, salary £37 per annum.

A regular feature of the Chronicle from its first publication was a detail of the number of patients admitted to the General Infirmary, established in the nucleus of the present buildings in 1761. Widely acknowledged in the medical world were the anti-plague measures introduced by Dr. John Haygarth (1740–1827), a physician at the Infirmary, and, in the light of history, Chester's most distinguished citizen in the eighteenth century. He countered contagion and reduced deaths from smallpox and typhus infection by the isolation of fever patients, with proper attention to cleanliness and ventilation – a notable advance in medical practice which later spread to hospitals throughout the country (154 hospitals were founded between 1700 and 1825). The good work of the Infirmary and the Chester Smallpox Society is reflected in the return of christenings, marriages and burials in the city parishes, published in the paper of January 11, 1782 (number 351). That christenings outnumbered burials is attributed to inoculation against the smallpox, 'the great destroyer'. In September of the same year a long report reviews four years' work by the Smallpox Society during which parental opposition to the inoculation of their children has been gradually overcome. The Society, voluntary, of course, appeals for funds; there were, as yet, no official funds for any social provision – if you couldn't look after yourself, you lived and died by charity. Institutional provision was, however, improving with the slow advance of medical knowledge, and, in Chester, with more humane consideration than in some of the new fast-growing communities. At the same time there was another, more dubious and equivocal, side of medical care and practice dating from the previous century and still in being. Dr. Stephen Hyde kept a house for lunatics in Foregate-street from which in October, 1775, a patient escaped and ran through the streets 'covered only by his shirt'. He was secured in Castle-lane and brought back to bondage. Dr. Hyde advertised regularly in the paper; and Robert Skerrett, surgeon, 'humbly solicited' the favour of the public upon the removal of his practice from Malpas to High Town, Nantwich. Teeth were savagely drawn in the market place by itinerant 'dentists', and quacks advertised side by side with those who claimed to be physicians and doctors so that it is difficult to distinguish among them. John Truman, from an address at Mr. Bingley's yard, a grocer, in Forest-street, declares: 'I will lay a guinea I will sweat a man in the middle of the market place, and give him nothing nor rub him with nothing', and claims that he can, 'with the blessing of God', infallibly cure the venereal disorder, piles, fistula, scurvy, gout, rheumatism and King's Evil, and 'break the stone'.

The Chronicle catalogued the principal causes of death in the city and district in 1775 as apoplexy and suddenly, bloody flux, colic, gripes, twisting of the guts, evil, grief, lethargy, St. Anthony's Fire, stoppage in the stomach and tympany. Extraordinary claims were made week after week in standing advertisements for nostrums and patent medicines (patent in the sense of brand-name) for almost everything. The paper made a steady revenue out of:

> Henry's calcinal magnesia – 'operates without griping.'
> The balsam of liquorice root – 'for all disorders of
>   the breast and lungs, colds, coughs, catarrhs,
>   consumptions, asthmas, hoarseness, and the chin-cough.'
> Spilsbury's improved anti-scorbutic drops – 'purify the
>   blood, promote digestion, and strengthen the nerves.'
> Dr. Bateman's original pectoral drops – for 'acute
>   rheumatic pains, fluxes, agues, and fevers.'
> The true genuine Daffy's elixir, Dr. Radcliffe's
>   purging elixir, Dr. Harper's female pills, Dr. Rye's
>   tincture antipodagrica, 'or great relieving tincture
>   for the gout', Dr. Stoughton's great stomachic elixir,
>   Dr. Bateman's patent ointment for the itch, and
>   Godfrey's general cordial.

In addition to consuming all this stuff, the public listened to old wives' tales from the country, especially in the winter, when they were recommended to keep the cold out with honey spread on toast or boiled buttermilk with treacle, with a sprig of rosemary. After all this, it is a relief to read of the discovery in 1785 of a styptic solution to relieve haemorrhage – it sounds less empirical.

James Boswell arrived in Chester at midnight on Monday, October 18, 1779, and was entertained by the clergy and the military. He wrote off to Dr. Johnson to tell the great man that 'Chester pleases my fancy more than any town I ever saw', and, in a second letter, 'I was quite enchanted at Chester, so that I could with difficulty quit it'. Whether he meant the place or the company is not certain, but that he was enchanted by a young woman, 'niece to one of the Prebendaries', is clear enough. Johnson had advised him to look around, for 'in the place where you now are there is much to be observed', meaning no doubt the Rows and the Walls and all that. The Autumn Fair was on at this time, and one of the sights that Bozzy could have seen, but probably did not, was the exhibition of the Ethiopian Savage at the Elephant and Castle near the Eastgate. At sixpence a head, servants threepence, the citizens and country people flocked to see this 'amazing animal, very like a man', presumably an ape or gorilla, exhibited by Mr. Heppenstall.

But the wonders of nature were surpassed by the marvels of science when Mr. Vincent Lunardi, the handsome young Neapolitan, who had already had London in thrall with his balloon ascents, put up at the White Lion on Wednesday, August 10, 1785, and the citizens besieged the great inn to see 'this intrepid aeronaut'. Mr. Lunardi immediately placed an advertisement in the paper inviting subscriptions for a possible ascent. There was a delay until August 26, when the aeronaut put another advertisement in the Chronicle, presenting his respectful compliments to the public and apologising for the mishap that had prevented his getting off the ground sooner – something had gone wrong with his inflation arrangements. On the following Wednesday, if the weather proved favourable, he promised to rise from the Castle-yard at four o'clock. 'N.B. Mr. Lunardi proposes to inflate his balloon in little more than an hour. At the firing of the first gun the balloon begins to be inflated – the second, when the inflation is completed – and the third, at the time of ascent.' It was Thursday, September 1, before the balloon actually went up after some further delay caused by the escape of 'inflammable air'. The day was serene and a great crowd collected in the Castle-yard. Lieutenant French, of the Royal Cheshire Militia, took the balloon up on his own after Mr. Lunardi had inflated it. Ascending 'majestically, with the greatest coolness and collected courage', he flung down a basket of refreshments, whereupon the balloon rose rapidly to a great height and after twenty minutes disappeared from sight. Two hours later the lieutenant came down safely near Macclesfield and his military friends set out with a band of music to escort him back to Chester.

Mr. Lunardi continued another week at the White Lion, filling that establishment with custom and excitement. Of engaging manners and acute business sense – the stages of inflating the balloon directed by cannon fire were pure showmanship – he talked far into the night about aerial navigation, and among his listeners was one

Tom Baldwin, a Cestrian who took the thing very seriously, having constructed an aerostatic globe of his own and studied the subject with the aid of instruments for observation and measurement. Lunardi was delighted; he had another eager customer. Accordingly, on Thursday, September 8, Tom Baldwin climbed into the balloon's car on the Castle-yard, first liberating his precious aerostatic globe, ornamented with mottoes and devices, which, wrote the Chronicle reporter: 'formed a beautiful spectacle, turning round its own axis in the calm atmosphere, and serving as a sort of pioneer to delineate the track of the large balloon.' Into the car went 50lbs of ballast and the instruments of observation and measurement and on the firing of the third cannon the balloon went up, the spectators cheering 'with terror and delight'. Mr. Lunardi on the ground shared the crowd's misgivings when it was seen that the balloon was heading out to sea. But Tom Baldwin knew enough to change course, came down ten miles away at Kingsley (he was fortunate to keep clear of Delamere Forest), got off again (by whose aid we are not told), and finally descended five miles from Warrington. The militia band met him on his return to Chester the next day. The Chronicle, of course, talked to the amateur aeronaut, who had some curious things to say.

> 'The apparent diminution of objects immediately below him seems to take our adventurer with wonder and surprise: and he continues to assert, what is perhaps beyond belief, that the objects, such as towns, enclosures, public roads, etc., which lay immediately beneath him, were less at the height of a mile and a half than they would appear at seven or eight miles distance if seen in an horizontal direction. Hence he argues that the falling of the quicksilver is no true test of the height and therefore balloons rise much higher in the atmosphere than is imagined, or that objects immediately below are an exception to the common rules of perspective.'

What Mr. Lunardi thought upon reading this we shall never know. And it doesn't matter now. But Tom Baldwin had his moment of fame, and John Fletcher, proprietor of the Chronicle, cashed in on it a year later with the publication of *Airopaidia*, an account of the Chester balloon voyages illustrated with copper-plate engravings.

In Chester, where the citizens gambled on the State lottery – for which bookseller George Bulkeley in Bridge-street was the principal advertised agent – the race meetings and foot races on the Roodee,

and on such casual challenges as that thrown out by the City Huntsman to ride his horse round the Walls in 15 minutes, (which he accomplished comfortably in 9 minutes and a half), the Chronicle
entertained its readers with stories of the deep play of the gamblers in
the London clubs and many other absorbing follies committed on
the turn of a card or the throw of a dice, including the forfeiture of
nine estates worth £170,000 a year. In the issue of November 29, 1776
(number 84), the Editor tacitly invited readers to draw their own
conclusions from this:'INTELLIGENCE EXTRAORDINARY – This morning a very great man from the St. James's end of town was at the
Bank in order to discount a bill, signed G.R., for two millions of
money, which was immediately done, though it had twelve months
to run.' Reading all this, thoughtful people in Chester, Cheshire and
Flintshire could not fail to contrast the reckless gambling fever of
some owners of great estates with the prudent and business-like conduct of their own lords of the manor, the Grosvenors of Eaton, for
whom Richard, the seventh baronet (Baron Grosvenor in 1761, Viscount Belgrave and Earl Grosvenor in 1784) was engaged at this time
in consolidating the Westminster lands which were Chester's closest
link with London. In the first decade of the century Sir Richard
Grosvenor, fourth baronet, obtained an Act of Parliament to enable
him to grant building leases on the fields and swamps of the Manor
of Ebury, which came into the family when Sir Thomas Grosvenor,
third baronet, married Mary Davies, the London heiress. Of the 570
acres of the manor, seventy were south of the Oxford-street of today
between Marble Arch and Bond-street and the rest between
Knightsbridge and the Thames. This Sir Richard developed Grosvenor and Eaton Squares, and the fifth, sixth and seventh baronets
increased the family's wealth and power as metropolitan ground
landlords to the end of the century. They looked to their affairs in
Chester also, holding on to the city representation in all the Parliaments through the reigns of the four Georges and bestowing their
patronage liberally at election times – too liberally, as the Chronicle candidly said in 1784. (See the chapter on that memorable election for the new Parliament of young 'Master Billy'.)

The fortunes of the house of Grosvenor have been in good hands
always and to this day, but if they were ever in danger it was in the
Civil War, when the city fought for the King and a good part of the
county for the Parliament, and afterwards during the 1715 Stuart
rebellion for the Old Pretender. The Grosvenors received their

baronetcy from King James I in 1621, and they fought for King
Charles in the Civil War until after the surrender of Chester, when
they pursued a more prudent path. After the defeat of the Old Pretender at Sheriffmuir in 1715, the Council of Ten Cheshire gentlemen, among them Sir Richard Grosvenor, held their fateful meeting
to decide which side to lean to: King George I or the Stuarts. The
votes were equal, and a casting vote being required it was given by
Thomas Assheton, Constable of Chester Castle, at whose house the
council was held. He decided for the House of Hanover. It was a near
thing, and the security of some great Cheshire estates may well have
been saved that day. In 1745, when Prince Charles Edward made his
gallant last throw for the Stuart succession and lay at Macclesfield
with the Scots Highland army, little or no support came from Cheshire and Lancashire; the Old Cause was dead in the old loyal pala-
tinate counties – loyalty now was of a different colour. The '45 ended
on Culloden moor, but Bonnie Prince Charlie lived on until 1788, and
on May 15, 1775, the Chronicle (number three) contained news of
him which must have awakened uneasily sleeping memories in the
minds of those readers who recalled the '45: 'By a letter from Italy we
learn that the condition of the Pretender is truly deplorable. His finances are limited almost to poverty . . . He is exceedingly corpulent,
owing to a total disuse of exercise; and his face is remarkably carbun-
cled from an excessive indulgence of the bottle, to which he constantly flies as a refuge from reflection.' So this was the sad latter-day
of Charlie is my darling, the King Charles the Third of intention
only –

> As he cam' marchin' up the street
> The pipes play'd loud and clear,
> And a' the folk cam' rinnin' out
> To meet the Chevalier.

In the Chronicle's first decade three great men were borne to
Westminster Abbey: the statesman, William Pitt the Elder, the
Great Commoner; the actor, David Garrick; and the man of letters,
Dr. Samuel Johnson. Pitt's last speech in the House occupied the entire back page of the paper; Garrick acted in Chester and after his retirement (see the chapter on the theatre), revisited the city as the
guest of his friend, Sir Watkin Williams Wynn, who was a pall-
bearer at his funeral; and Johnson passed through Chester on his
way to and from North Wales, of which fleeting visits the citizens

knew little, but they were often able to read about him leading the literary conversation in London at the famous club of which Burke, Reynolds, Garrick and Goldsmith were members. With the year drawing to a close, the Chronicle of December 17, 1784 (number 497), printed a London report of Tuesday, December 14:

> 'With the truest concern we inform our readers that at seven o'clock yesterday evening the great and good Dr. Samuel Johnson breathed his last . . . We know not whether he has expressed any desire respecting the place of his interment. If not, it is natural to suppose that it will be in Westminster Abbey; or at least that a noble monument will there be erected to the memory of a man who certainly has not left an equal behind him.'

I began this chapter with a duel and end it with the death of Johnson, who, if any one person did – or could be said to do – epitomised the greatness and eccentricity of the eighteenth century.

12

Two hundred years of theatre

It is the evening of Monday, November 7, 1785, the last night but one of Mr. Cooke's second season with Their Majesties' Servants at Chester's Theatre Royal in Northgate-street. The theatre is crowded from pit to gallery, and although the audience is not perhaps as fashionable as in the spring season of the Race Week, the new Royal Mail coaches, operating together with local 'flyers', have brought to town many more people, some of whom have never seen a play or a theatrical entertainment before. In the narrow, murky passageway at the side of the theatre there has been the usual rush for the gallery doors. The weakest have gone to the wall and the veterans of the City Watch have been swept away in the stampede. Outside, the theatre looks mean enough. A matter of policy and prudence, this, for in its former vagabond, unlicensed days the less obtrusive it was, the better. So the building has none of the splendour of the new theatre in Liverpool or of the great metropolitan houses. Inside, it is sufficiently well appointed, with all the appurtenances of boxes, pit and front stalls (or benches), and a fairly deep stage having doors at the wings and a drop-cloth just within the proscenium. At the back of the stage are steps to vary the level and these, when the dropcloth is presently lifted, will serve as entrance to the battlements and courtyard of the rudely painted presentment of the Castle of Elsinore. For the play of the night is *Hamlet* as written by William Shakespeare and, for once, no other author has been permitted a hand in it, unless, of course, this production is going to follow David Garrick's 'improved' version.

There have been many changes in the house since Mr. John S. Townshend obtained in 1777 a Crown patent converting the New Theatre, as it was then called, into the Theatre Royal, officially licensed so that the city magistrates can no longer break open the doors and stop the performance. Tonight the Mayor, aldermen and council-men and their wives are in the house. It may not be 'respectable' for such dignitaries to be seen in a common playhouse. Indeed, a few years ago it would have been unthinkable, but now the county notables are patrons of the players and even invite them to their mansions, and what is good enough for them is good enough for the magistrates. Besides, Mr. Mayor reflects complacently, did not Sir Watkin Williams Wynn sit in this same box with the great Garrick beside him? And Mr. Cooke, who has brought renown to the city by making one of his first appearances on the boards here last year, is now among the leading tragedians in the provinces and surely destined for Covent Garden. That performance of *Macbeth*, about the same time last year, has been the talk of Chester ever since and many other towns have acclaimed the rising actor. Tonight he comes again in the greatest part of all, and, in the lustrous sheen of the candle-clusters and the acrid smoke of the oil-lamps, the house is invested with mystery, expectation and excitement. The theatre has cast its age-old spell.

Up front are the amateur critics and the local cognoscenti, among them the newly-appointed Editor of the Chester Chronicle, Mr. Cowdroy. As we know, Mr. Cowdroy is a man of the theatre himself as well as a journalist. He has a local reputation as a wit and versifier, exemplified in the columns of the Chronicle and earlier the Courant, where he first displayed his talents. Tonight he proudly shares the bill with Shakespeare himself, for it is the custom of the time to round off the play and send the audience happily home with some locally-allusive song, sketch or absurdity. After the rigours of the tragedy – and Mr. Cooke, it is well known, plays Hamlet to the top of his powers – the house expects such after-pieces to dispel the calamitous wonder and soul-searching of the drama and indeed will not disperse without them. For this night Mr. Cowdroy has written a comic song called *The Learned Pig's Levee* or *A Peep into the Sty of the Eloquent Grunter*, which is to be performed by Mr. Munden (after divesting himself of the character of Polonius), with a grunting chorus. And since Mr. Platt (who first brought Cooke to Chester) is taking a benefit, Cowdroy has written for him to recite a piece called *The Wonders of 1785*, in which he has satirised the recent balloon flights from Chester Castle Yard as 'the fashionable rage of dancing in the clouds'. Nothing can be more diverting or topical, for the populace admires the aeronauts' courage and laughs at their folly.

Cowdroy looks about him and wonders if, after all, there will be any trouble tonight from the apprentices in the gallery and the town gallants in the pit. The company's performance of Murphy's *The*

Grecian Daughter, a popular play given in the first week, has not been well received and a waspishly critical letter has been delivered at the Chronicle office. This the Editor has summarily dismissed with a note in the paper: 'The critique on several of the members of our Chester theatre is totally inadmissible. The gentleman has our thanks for the very flattering opinion he is pleased to express of our paper – but it is not consistent with our present plan to enter into any criticisms that can injure the feelings of individuals. And we think it an act of unpardonable cruelty to make attacks upon persons in their profession, more especially as they depend upon the profession for a livelihood.' There speaks the master of puff and true friend of the players – a theatrical writer rather than a critic of the drama, for that art is as yet seldom practised in the provinces and not with much authority even in London. But on with the play. The cast is set forth in the bill:

Hamlet	Mr. Cooke
The King	Mr. Gloster
Horatio	Mr. Kemble
Polonius	Mr. Munden
The Ghost	Mr. Platt
Laertes	Mr. Whitlock
The Queen	Mrs. Taplin
Player Queen	Mrs. Munden
Ophelia	Mrs. Kemble

Joseph Munden, 27 at this time, is a favourite on the Chester boards. His inimitably droll performance as Launce in *The Two Gentlemen of Verona* is well remembered, as also his *Budget for the Year 1784*, written for him by Mr. Cowdroy, then a printer at the Courant. This text of *The Two Gentlemen* had been, according to the Chronicle, 'altered by a Lady of Chester' who, alas, while 'carefully preserving the master-strokes of its great author, has most judiciously grubbed up some of the weeds without cutting the thread of a single flower' – a wanton act of theatrical vandalism, but, after all, the intrepid lady had done nothing worse than take her cue from David Garrick himself, a great spoliator of the Poet. Munden, of course, is expected to take farcical liberties with Polonius, and this he does to the uproarious delight of the Chester audience. He makes a mock of the old man's doting sententiousness and the house is too diverted to notice that much of the pathos has gone out of the part. John Philip Kemble, aged 28, is an engagingly handsome figure as Horatio. No prince could have a truer friend. The women in the audience cannot take their eyes off him. Besides, he brings with him the magic of a London reputation, having played Hamlet at Drury-lane only two years before – and is he not the brother of Sarah Siddons?

Can George Frederick Cooke match Kemble's Hamlet and earn at Chester a London season? That is the question, although few if any in the house this night have any means of judging. It is sufficient to say that they will, all of them, remember Cooke's performance for the rest of their lives, even though, as they drift away into the dark city lanes and alleys and towards the coaches waiting at the White Lion and the Yacht, ringing in their ears is the anti-climax of the grunting chorus! Cowdroy goes home to the Nine Houses and, late as it is, sits down to compose his notice for Friday's Chronicle. Dare he offer a small criticism? He writes: 'Universal satisfaction . . . Mr. Cooke's intrinsic ability is here . . . The pathetic situations he played to the heart, and in the 'very whirlwind of passion', in our opinion, 'his actions were suited to his words and his words to his actions'. . . His instructions to the Players (which ought never to be omitted) were recited with a degree of energy and ease that very sensibly impressed every part of the theatre. As we would wish, however, 'not to extenuate or set down aught in malice', we cannot forbear mentioning a single speech, and indeed the only one throughout this arduous part, which with deference to Mr. Cooke's judgment, he seems to have mistaken; and that is the one to his mother in the closet scene –

> Once more good night,
> And when you are desirous to be blest,
> I'll blessing beg of you –

which, by accenting the preposition of, instead of the pronoun you that immediately follows, the meaning of the author was not only destroyed but the harmony of the verse materially injured. The most finished performance is not, however, without a blemish; and here the beauties are so many that ill-nature and envy must stand up and say to all the world, 'This is an actor!' Mrs Kemble, in Ophelia, answered every expectation that has been formed of her. The eye that does not weep at her mad scenes must be dry indeed. . .' Oh, scrupulous William Cowdroy! And not a word of the London star, John Philip Kemble. Still, it was Cooke's night and George Frederick is looked upon as Chester's own, having first made his name here. The rest of the notice is a determined puff for the last night of the season, when a new comedy by Mrs Inchbald, *I'll Tell you What*, and a farce, *Peeping Tom*, are to be performed.

With some license, pardonable I trust, I have tried to recall that single night of theatre out of the past – a night that was possibly not equalled until September 13, 1815, when Edmund Kean played Richard the Third, of which more in its place later on. The story of the living theatre in Chester begins with the mediaeval mysteries or miracles and after many transitions, sacred and profane, continues at the civic Gateway of today. From May 2, 1775, until now, very few editions of the Chronicle have gone to press without a theatrical or musical advertisement of some kind. Indeed, the advertisements are a study in themselves, epitomising as they do the evolution of the stage over two centuries. In the late eighteenth century and for many years afterwards the players came to town for spring and autumn seasons, coinciding with the Races or the sitting of the Assize or the twice-yearly City Fairs. Or a play could be specially performed for an occasion, such as the illumination of the city to celebrate Rodney's and Nelson's victories and the final defeat of Bonaparte. The Number One Chronicle, appearing in the week before the Races, advertised a new tragedy, *Matilda*, and a farce, *The Virgin Unmask'd* or *Old Man Taught Wisdom*, for performance at the New Theatre in Race Week. The New Theatre – the same Theatre Royal of our opening scene in this chapter – started clandestinely in 1773 under the management of Messrs. Austin and Heaton, who converted the ancient St. Nicholas's Chapel in Northgate-street for the purpose, and braved the displeasure of the City Common Council and a Mayoral edict against the continuance of unlicensed playacting in a building, moreover, of sacred origin belonging by perpetual lease to the Abbey and the Dean and Chapter. St. Nicholas's Chapel dated from the fourteenth century and there are several allusions in this book to its changeful history as church and adjunct of the Abbey of St. Werburgh, common hall and seat of justice, warehouse, theatre, music hall, cinema, and now supermarket.

When Austin and Heaton took it over as a playhouse they built up the ecclesiastical and Tudor windows with brick, took off the high-pitched oak roof (afterwards partly restored), raised the walls by fifteen feet, and shaped the theatre within the case of the old chapel

structure. The religious atmosphere, though powerfully counter-
acted in the years to come, was never finally dispelled. Even as the
Music Hall cinema – where as a boy I saw Charles Chaplin, the
serial of *The Lost City* and other films of the silent screen, the action
accompanied by a pianist of astonishing dexterity – the interior
looked remarkably like a church. In 1773 and onwards the Common
Council blustered and occasionally exerted a show of authority, pha-
risaically puritan, against the uncovenanted goings-on before and
behind the curtain at the New Theatre. For the most part, however,
the authorities must have turned a blind eye. It was difficult to pro-
scribe the drama in Chester, whose citizens had show business in
their blood, having inherited the tradition of the Whitsun plays, the
Midsummer Show, pageants and pastorals, and the visits of the Elizabethan strolling players, of whom Shakespeare himself might have
been one in William Stanley's company. Of the first Chester indoors
theatre earlier in the eighteenth century little is now known. It was in
a small court on the south side of Foregate-street approached
through a long, narrow lane opposite the Nag's Head Inn. In this
humble temple of the arts the theatrical mysteries were celebrated,
behind the veil, so to say, by Garrick and Samuel Foote, according to
tradition, for I have seen no actual record. When St. Nicholas's
Chapel became the New Theatre and the magic ground shifted to
Northgate-street the old theatre declined into a tennis court – there is
record of its use as such in 1778.

In October, 1777, we read of Garrick (as noted in Chapter Eight)
accompanying Sir Watkin Williams Wynn and his house party from
Wynnstay to the Theatre Royal in Chester, a few months after it had
received its Crown patent. Sir Watkin, a genial and popular patron
of the players, has bespoke a performance of the play *The Busy-Body*.
The Welsh knight's passion for theatricals, the Christmas present-
ations at his private theatre to which three hundred guests were
invited each evening, and the flying visit in 1775 of a coach-load of
Wynnstay house guests, dressed in the costumes of characters in *The
Merry Wives of Windsor*, to the Yacht Inn, Watergate-street, have
been mentioned earlier. Sir Watkin was stage-struck and Garrick
was his good and famous friend who now had the leisure to taste the
pleasures of country house hospitality and sit back and watch others
perform. In October, 1777, as the Chronicle reported, he was enjoying himself (with Mrs. Garrick) at the ancestral home of the Watkin
Wynns, and no doubt he obliged his host by taking part in a play

there. What he thought of the Chester company's performance of *The Busy-Body* we are not told, but we may be sure of his indulgence for Messrs. Austin and Heaton. Last scene of all: in the issue of January 29, 1779, the Chronicle reported Garrick's death on Thursday, the 20th – 'the first of actors, the best of friends, and the most sociable companion' – and on February 5 the funeral at Westminster Abbey. Sir Watkin was one of the pall-bearers and Dr. Johnson was among those who followed the hearse.

Garrick and Kemble widened the range of Shakespearian acting, but they altered and added to, or curtailed the text of the plays to suit themselves, and this practice spread to the provinces. Chester saw many a doctored version of *Hamlet* and *Macbeth* in which inferior actors mouthed the extravagent 'improvements' of prentice hands. We have seen how a *Lady of Chester* had been given the opportunity to play about with *The Two Gentlemen of Verona*. In September, 1779, *Coriolanus* was got up at the Theatre Royal for a local masonic benefit: 'before the play,' ran the Chronicle advertisement, 'a prologue on masonry by Brother Whitlock, end of the play, an epilogue in character of a Free Mason's Wife, by Mrs. McGeorge.' You can imagine what happened to the play in between. Samuel Foote, the comedian, was not much less celebrated than Garrick and the farces that each turned out helped, after their London run, to round off the bill at the Chester and many other provincial theatres. Two very popular pieces at Chester's Theatre Royal, judging by the frequency with which they were played by the Austin-Heaton company, were Garrick's *High Life Below Stairs* and Foote's *Devil Upon Two Sticks*.

In August, 1775, Mr. and Mrs. King came from York to play in *The Grecian Daughter* for one night only, a limited engagement 'because they are obliged to be at London for the opening of Drury-lane Theatre'. In the same month, Austin and Heaton's company put on *The Inconstant* or *The Way to Win Him* and a farce, *Cross Purposes*. Boxes were priced 2s.6d., pit 2s., and gallery 1s. The presentation in September of *As You Like It* was somewhat diminished in public esteem by the after-piece, *A Trip to Portsmouth*, designed to show off a spectacular new transparent scene representing the Fleet at Spithead as reviewed by his Majesty. And on October 2, Mr. and Mrs. Austin proudly announced *Hamlet* for positively their last benefit but three! – Mr. Austin to play the Prince, Mr. Heaton the Ghost, and Miss Hurst, Ophelia – supported by a farce, yes, the perennially popular *High Life Below Stairs* as acted at Drury-lane. Theatre tickets were to be had at Mr. Carter's, the Yacht Inn, Watergate-street; Mr. Leech's, the Black Dog, Bridge-street; Mr. Leet's, the Pied Bull, Northgate-street; Mr. Poole's, bookseller, Eastgate-street; and of the two performers, Mrs. Bogle and Mrs. Booth, at their lodgings opposite the theatre. Members of the company were expected to act as box-office agents. The current production was *The Wonder: A Woman Keeps a Secret*. Sheridan's *The Rivals*, first produced at Covent Garden in the previous February, and *The Deserter* were the last plays of the season. By the time of the next May Races the price of the boxes had been increased by sixpence and Mr. and Mrs. Austin were temporarily missing from the company. But Mr. Heaton was still there and with him were Mrs. Reddish, Mr. and Mrs. McGeorge, and Messrs. Johnson, Emery, Marston, Mills, Whitlock, Comerford and Hamilton. With the possible exception of Mr. and Mrs. Whitlock, it was an ordinarily competent company without distinction.

Their first play, *Edward and Eleanora*, fell flat, but was rescued by the accompanying farce, *Miss in Her Teens*. Performances were now beginning at seven o'clock 'or as soon as the Race is over'. A Wrexham lady who went to the Theatre Royal in Chester in the May Race Week of 1777, afterwards wrote a letter to an old friend in the city describing the experience. *Sir Thomas Overbury* was the well-known play, but it was the farce, *The Romp, or Love in the City*, that drew the spectators and especially the younger sort. So that the Wrexham lady found herself in the midst of a voluble, spirited, ill-mannered, provincially fashionable audience, the women affecting the 'absurd and ridiculous' style of artificial high head-dressing criticised by our London correspondent in a foregoing paragraph. Luckily for us, part of the visitor's letter got into the paper by some means, and we have this contemporary account of a typical night at the theatre: 'My old friend – I promised to let you know how we got home from the Races; the poor Tim had much ado to draw us up Marford-hill, but for all that my grand-daughter and I got home safe. On Thursday, after I drank tea with you, I went to the play and got a seat in the middle of the front box – the house is very pretty indeed. Just before the play began, in bounced six ladies, with such heads (Lord have mercy upon us!) that I could not tell what to make of them. Down they sat, and there was an end of my seeing any thing. I did not mind that much, as you know that my ears are better than my eyes; but, alack a day!, no sooner had the play begun than the young men behind and young women before set a-talking and laughing at such a rate that,

Top Eastgate Street as Cowdroy and the early Editors of the Chester Chronicle would see it. *Bottom* Lower Bridge Street, in the late 18th-century, with the mass of the Dee Mills beyond the Bridge Gate at the bottom of the hill.

Left 1851: section, of the city, now much changed, the junction of Bridge Street and Lower Bridge Street, with St. Michael's Church before its restoration, and the opening of Pepper Row and part of the Inner Ring Road. *Below* The Chester Chronicle has asked the City authorities to restore the High Cross, at present in the Roman Garden at the Newgate, to its original site in front of St. Peter's Church. Here, by superimposing one picture upon another, the photographers have anticipated the restoration.

Above Partial destruction of the mediaeval
City Wall to make way for the Inner
Ring Road. *Right* The 20th-century Police
Headquarters framed in the 18th-century
entrance of Thomas Harrison's Chester
Castle, with Field Marshal Viscount
Combermere on his cavalry horse in the
middle of the road. *Below* Eastgate Street
today, looking towards the Cross from the
City Walls.

Above The Roman amphitheatre outside the south-east angle of the City Walls was discovered almost by accident. Here is the entrance to the area in the first stage of excavation. *Below* An early print of Bridge Street, when St. Peter's Church had its spire.

as I hope to be saved, I might as well have been at my fire-side at Wrexham as there, for any thing I could hear or see. It was not so in our days, my friend, and I wish you would tell them so. I am, your sincere friend, of forty years' standing . . .'

Two years later, in the same month which saw the presentation of *Coriolanus* for the Ancient and Honourable Society of Free and Accepted Masons, the Editor of the Chronicle rejected with contumely a letter from a critic. 'Had he expected his strictures to appear in the paper,' wrote the Editor, 'the postage should have been paid, but this, as well as the letter, shows the author is not only possessed of a narrow mind but also of an evil spirit. We therefore decline to foster his brat and recommend him to nurse, with care, the offspring of his disappointed malevolence.' I have a certain sympathy for that unpublished critic so brutally rejected. He might have deserved such treatment. On the other hand, it is possible he was defending Shakespeare from the wilful depredations of the Free and Ancient Masons! In 1780 Mr. Austin had returned to the company, Mr. Heaton had dropped out, and Austin and Whitlock concluded an arrangement with Mr. Younger, manager of the Theatre Royal in Manchester, for the Manchester company to perform in Chester's Race Week. Since the one-night appearance of Mrs. King there had been only minor celebrities on the local boards, and now the management were looking for talent and perhaps wistfully remembering the former glory of Garrick and Foote at the superseded theatre in Foregate-street.

Cooke's Hamlet in 1785 (as we have seen at the beginning of the chapter) rang up the curtain on our Theatre Royal's most glittering period, running from the late eighteenth century to the first quarter of the next. It is not less than the truth to say that there has never been anything like it in Chester since that time. The great players numbered the city in their country circuit, often pausing here on their way back to London from Ireland, and the classic Shakespearian parts, presented in a highly flavoured, individualistic style, an extraordinary blend of sentiment and realism, alternated with the latest plays of Sheridan and others, and a copious flow of farces. Mrs. Siddons, Cooke, Mrs. Jordan, Munden, Bannister, Kean, Mrs. Glover, Miss O'Neill, Master Betty (the Young Roscius), Bologna and Grimaldi, the celebrated clowns, all acted in the Northgate-street theatre. George Frederick Cooke was back again in September, 1786, to begin with in support of the queen of the stage, Mrs. Sarah Siddons, who accepted this one engagement to add lustre to a grand festival of the music of Handel held at this time in 'the broad aisle' of the Cathedral and at the Shire Hall. In the mornings and afternoons for a week there were oratorios in the Cathedral and in the evenings dancing assemblies and the rare opportunity to see Mrs. Siddons at the theatre.

The Chronicle of September 8 contained an advertisement that Mrs. Siddons would play the part of Belvedira in Otway's *Venice Preserved* – a famous role – on the following Monday. In the cast also were Cooke and Platt. Mrs. Siddons (as we have read in the previous chapter) commanded a fabulous salary and at this time she was in her early thirties and at the height of her fame and powers. Perhaps on this occasion (since the music festival, which had influential city and county and ecclesiastical backing, was for public charities) she waived her customary demands on the box-office. If so, it did not deter the management from putting up the price of boxes to five shillings, the pit to three shillings, the gallery to two shillings, and adding the three upper seats of the pit to the profitable boxes. The news columns of the paper gave the information that Mrs. Siddons's engagement 'is positively for three nights only'. And so, for the sake of the record, let it be set down here that the divine Sarah acted in Chester on the nights of Monday, September 11, Saturday, September 16, and Monday, September 18, 1786. The Chronicle of the following week made the point that Chester had now had the pleasure and distinction of seeing three members of a famous theatrical family on the local boards – Mrs. Siddons, her brother, John Philip Kemble, and her sister, Mrs. Whitlock, wife of the Theatre Royal's actor-manager who had succeeded to the Austin-Heaton partnership. Acknowledging that the great actress's performance in *Venice Preserved* demonstrated beyond all question that 'she is now the leading tragic actress in the kingdom', the paper went on to express its local pride in that 'rising player' Mrs. Whitlock for her performance in Colman's *The Jealous Wife*, the farce that rounded off the evening.

And that was all – disappointingly, no studied critical notice of Mrs. Siddons's acting from the pen of Mr. Cowdroy, but a great deal of well-intentioned puff for the arrival of Mr. Munden. Sarah had come and gone, and Cooke was in command of the theatre. In the succeeding two months he undertook a prodigious task, playing Hamlet, Macbeth, Lear, Richard the Third, Shylock, and Charles Surface in Sheridan's *The School for Scandal*, besides many minor comic and farcical parts in which, with Munden, he displayed the variety of his genius and delighted the city. For Munden, the Editor of the Chronicle turned his hand to another comic song, *Life's a Farce and Every Man's a Player*, and for the rest of the company a sketch based on *Venice Preserved* – 'to be attempted in the manner of Mrs. Siddons'. But, regrettably, he wrote no original dramatic criticism in the paper – a modest reticence on his part but a lost opportunity all the same. In this famous season it is possible that Cooke sought relief from the toil and stress of all that acting in the indulgence of his weakness, drink. In his cups he would defy the public, the management and his fellow players, sending all to the devil in a fearful display of temper and temperament. And this might explain why he felt obliged to inform the Chronicle that: 'whereas the injurious report has been propagated of his intention to quit the company immediately on the night after his benefit, he assures them that it is an invidious falsehood, as he never entertained an idea of leaving Chester until the season finally ends.' He was as good as his word.

Cooke came to Chester again, for the last time, in 1803, when he was an established star at the Theatre Royal, Covent Garden, where recently he had been hissed off the stage for being palpably drunk. He appears to have continued sober enough at Chester to play in *The Man of the World*, *John Bull* and *The Stranger*, winding up with Iago and King John. The Chronicle this time took little notice of him, devoting most of its space that week to the threat of invasion by Bonaparte's army. Cooke went to America in 1810 and died in New York a year later. With all due allowance for his weakness for the bottle – much was forgiven the great players for the pleasure and excitement they gave – he was acknowledged, with Kemble, as one of the most compelling of English actors, and Chester had the luck to see the best of him. Mrs. Jordan played twice in the city, in September, 1789, when she was 27 and as a Drury-lane draw only some way behind Mrs. Siddons, and in December, 1813. On the first occasion she played the Country Girl in the play of that name, Lady Bell in *Know Your Own Mind*, and her most famous part of The Romp.

By this time William Cowdroy had left the Chronicle for Manchester, and it was a less knowledgeable and appreciative quill that wrote thus somewhat slightingly of Mrs. Jordan:

'She has reaped no small share of golden grain during her short theatrical harvest in this city, her four nights producing £130 simply to her

own purse. This winning little favourite is no doubt entitled to approbation in every part she undertakes; tho' we cannot help thinking that
we have seen her equals, if not her superiors, in some on these boards.
However, this lady is at present the fashion, and 'tis enough.'

It was enough; the town flocked to see the delightful and vivacious
Romp. There was at the same time a rival attraction at Eaton Hall,
where the Grosvenors put on a 'season' of their own, Lord Belgrave,
Mr. T., Mr. R., and Miss Grosvenor performing in *Othello* and other
plays. Before Mrs. Jordan's second appearance in her maturity,
Chester theatregoers' curiosity was titillated by a week of the child
prodigy, Master Betty, billed universally as the Young Roscius, in
November, 1804. Anticipating a rush, the management announced:
'No person to take places for more than one family. In order to secure
the places taken, servants must attend at the back door of the theatre
by a quarter past five o'clock at farthest' for doors opening at six
o'clock and the performance beginning early at seven. Like the juv-
enile pop stars of today, Master Betty was something of a public
show and in London and on tour he had been mobbed at the stage
door. Chester prudently decided that 'on no pretence whatever will
there be admittance behind the scenes'.

In addition to his usual repertoire, sentimental tragedy and farce,
Master Betty actually appeared briefly as Hamlet and Richard the
Third, aping the grand manners of his seniors to the excessive delight of the uncritical. The Chronicle was not less impressed than the
audiences:

> 'As this wonderful phenomenon has made such a noise, the curiosity to
> witness his debut was so great that the avenue leading to the theatre
> was crowded by five o'clock and such has been the satisfaction of those
> who have had the pleasure of seeing him that it has been the case ever
> since. We never witnessed such a display of rank, beauty, and fashion
> as graced the boxes every evening to behold this infantile genius. He is
> about four foot and a half high, slender made, possessing a handsome
> countenance, his eyes full of fire – treads the stage with grace and dig-
> nity, has all the action of a veteran performer, and quite unembar-
> rassed before the curtain. Who knows but we may soon have a
> Lilliputian Theatre.'

One can forgive the rest for that last sentence. Very famous indeed
was Mrs. Jordan, and nearing the end of her career, when she came
for her second and last season in Chester in 1813. 'The Admired Mrs.
Jordan' said a respectful advertisement and this time the paper was

unreserved in its praise of her performance in *The Soldier's Daughter*
and *The Belle's Strategem*. Truly a wonderful woman, they said, 'and
her appearance is still interesting, although she is loaded with the
weight of above 50 winters'.

According to the Chronicle Editor John Hickson Hanshall, writing in 1816, the Theatre Royal was then in the management of Mr.
Crisp, of the Shrewsbury and Worcester Theatres. 'At one period it
could boast of the first company out of the metropolis; at present,
however, it may be said to have one of the worst. It has furnished for
the metropolitan stage its Austins, Cookes, Mundens, Cherrys, Bel-
lamys, Conways, etc., but those days are past, we fear never to
return.' The theatre, he tells us, had originally a proprietary company of twelve, but in 1816 the shares were divided among six or
seven. The house contained about £120 on any one night and the
record benefit to date, but soon to be surpassed, was Mr. Gordon's
£115.10s. There was seating and standing room for about a thousand
people. Hanshall evidently thought the theatre was in decline. But
not yet. He could not have been present on that tremendous
Saturday night, September 23, of the previous year, when Edmund
Kean, on tour from Drury-lane, played Richard the Third – his most
celebrated part – with unrestrained passion. Although not more
than five feet four inches tall, Kean had an extraordinary power of
command on the stage. According to the paper's account, the Chester audiences were held in thrall, except for some sensitive spectators
who had to quit their seats, so fearful and dismayed were they by the
great actor's projection of unmitigated terror. 'It was one of the
strongest approximations to realized villainy we ever saw depicted
upon any stage', wrote the marvelling Chronicle critic. In a voice 'by
no means melodious', Kean appears to have croaked the unspeak-
able thoughts of the 'crook-back'd tyrant'.

Mrs. Glover, another queen of Drury-lane, played at the Theatre
Royal for three nights under Crisp's management in October, 1816.
She, too, excelled in Mrs. Jordan's comic part of Widow Cheerly in
The Soldier's Daughter, and gave it at the request of the local patrons.
Just to show how times had changed, the Mayor, Sir John Cot-
greave, knighted during his year of office for having the presence of
mind to present a congratulatory address on the marriage of Princess
Charlotte, bespoke 'a fashionable night' on Saturday the 12th, and
Mrs. Glover and Mrs. Townley combined in the comedy of *The Pro-
voked Husband* before his Worship and the Corporation. The theatre

was now, at long last – and ironically at the start of a slow decline – high in official esteem. No more knocking on the door by the Beadle and the Watch with orders to forbid the performance. For the three nights of the popular Miss O'Neill in October, 1816, the management doubled the price of admission. The paper made a point of printing the box-office receipts: Thursday, £130, Friday, £140, Saturday, £155, and a grand total of £425, a record surpassing even Mrs. Siddons's. And the actress received £100 a night – 'how ill-founded must be the complaint of the scarcity of money', observed the Chronicle enviously. Miss O'Neill played Juliet, Belvedira in *Venice Preserved*, and Mrs. Oakley in *The Jealous Wife*. The following week brought the famous clowns, Grimaldi and Bologna, from Covent Garden to Chester to play in the pantomime *Mother Goose*.

In 1817 there was a lighting revolution. Gaslight superseded the flambeaux, candles and oil lamps of Garrick's time, and for the October season, 1818, the new 'element' was proudly announced at the Chester Theatre. But the famous good days were coming to an end. There was a respite for some years after 1828, when Mr. Lewis, lessee of the Liverpool Theatre, moved in and raised the ceiling once more, to make room for an additional tier of boxes, increasing the possible takings of the house to £170 a night. Hemingway described the theatre thus altered as 'altogether one of the most elegant and commodious outside the metropolis'. Here in January, 1832, appeared the astonishing figure of Paganini. The paper said that the demonic virtuoso looked remarkably like his own violin. Again the box-office was besieged: 'some people had their coats literally torn off their backs, their faces scratched, and their money snatched.' On the Friday night there was 'a brilliant and numerous audience, but the house was only thinly attended on the Saturday'. We search the columns in vain for a critique of the wizard's performance. The Chronicle had more important matters on hand: 'We had prepared a notice of the performance, and of this extraordinary being himself, which we are obliged to displace to make room for the proceedings of the Adjourned Sessions yesterday.' From this time the theatre appears to have gone steadily downhill. There were occasional flashes of the Promethean fire, but the flame was going out. In the middle of the century the building, and the boxes and the stage, had become tarnished, decayed and dirty. The character of the audience also changed, and the place was frequented by the dissolute of both sexes. Respectable people stayed away. In May, 1853, the lease expired, the properties were disposed of, including the forlorn gilded chair of state, formerly used to represent the throne of royalty, and the old theatre reverted to the custody of its former masters the Dean and Chapter, whose first concern must have been to exorcise it! Presumably, after reconstruction by the local architect James Harrison, who took out the theatre encased in the original church walls, it was leased again, this time as a Music Hall, with a grand organ 'and all'.

When Charles Dickens appeared on the Music Hall platform on the night of Tuesday, January 23, 1867, and stood by the little reading table with its crimson cloth, did he, I wonder, recall his prentice days as a reporter and Parliamentary shorthand writer for the Morning Chronicle? The days when he roamed London and the country with a luminous and phenomenally memorising eye. The days when, as the observing Boz, he began collecting characters and wrote the biography, at once humorous and pathetic, of Grimaldi the clown. Although all the great novels had come from his pen since then, it is possible that he recollected the White Lion across the street and the market-place as the scene of the Grimaldi-Bologna suppers after the fall of the curtain on *Mother Goose* in 1817. Dickens's dramatic readings of scenes from the novels were by this time famous throughout the country, and in Ireland. His opening tours were in 1858 and 1861, the itinerary including Chester, and after this second appearance at the Music Hall in 1867, he had a 'season' in America. The constant travel and change of lodgings and the energy consumed in these performances – which were as much acting as reading – shortened his life, and three years after the Chronicle reported him at length at Chester, Dickens was dead, at the age of 58.

Those who have seen the readings as presented by Emlyn Williams, the Flintshire-born actor and playwright, in our own time, have some idea of the profound impression that Dickens himself must have created by projecting his own characters on a stage which was in shadow save for a single spotlight. Dickens also presented himself, the creator, and that was the unique fascination for that Chester audience on the severely cold night of January 23, 1867. They came partly out of curiosity to see the greatest writer of the day, but chiefly, as the Chronicle said, to divine the mystery of 'the author's original conception of his creations – to descend into his brain, in fact to see how Mr. Pickwick and Mr. Weller, Mrs. Bardell and Serjeant Buzfuz existed there'. They wanted, in short, 'to enjoy the treat of having Charles Dickens the novelist interpreted by himself'.

Every reader had his own notion of the characters, but, said the Chronicle writer, any man's notions 'might be as different from what they were meant for as Bottom and Snug are from Macbeth – one could not help be struck, in fact, in the course of the entertainment, with the frequent illustrations of this difference'. Here is the reporter's impression of Dickens's reading of the trial scene, Bardell v Pickwick:

> Nothing was better brought out than the character of the stupid old judge, especially where he reproved Mr. Winkle for calling himself 'Daniel Nathaniel' and threatened to commit Mr. Weller senior for interrupting the business of the court. Mr. Winkle's nervous confusion was capitally done, and so was the impersonation of the inimitable Sam Weller. Sam, as Dickens thinks of him, is not the slangy, dried-up cockney who jerks out his drolleries with a consciousness of their force and gives a self-satisfied smirk when he sees how they sting, but rather a pleasant, smart young fellow, shrewd as he is quick of motion, ready with his flooring joke as he is amusing with his comical smile, but doing it all with a perfectly natural and almost artless air.

Sam Weller to the life, surely, and as most of us have pictured him ever since.

The Music Hall, whatever its merits – and it was used for operas, concerts, festivals of music, ballets and political meetings – was no substitute for the old Theatre Royal, and the professional stage as such went dark in Chester for some years. Modern Theatre may be said to have had its origin with the coming of the railway, just as the earlier theatre had been sustained by the 'fast' coaches. When City-road was made from the Bars in Foregate-street to the new General Station – an innovation which wrought the destruction of John Wesley's Octagon Chapel, standing as it did on the line of the new road – a wooden building was left, probably by the contractors, on the east side, on the site now occupied by the Royalty Theatre Club. From about 1866 this place was used occasionally as a theatre and for small visiting circuses. On November 16, 1878, the Chronicle reported that this unpretentious wooden structure, 'of late empty and falling rapidly into decay', had been refurbished and improved and opened the previous week as the Prince of Wales Theatre. Mr. Brinsley Sheridan, lessee of the Warrington Theatre, had obtained a theatrical licence from the city magistrates for three years. A good audience saw the first productions there, *Miriam's Crime* and *The Wandering Minstrel*.

The Prince of Wales, then, was the first successor to the old Theatre Royal and the nucleus of the Royalty Theatre. For in the paper of February 4, 1882, under the heading of 'The New Royalty Theatre, Chester', the announcement was made that the undertakers had arranged with the lessee of the Prince of Wales to 'erect on the same site an elegant and substantial brick and stone building – a new Temple of the Drama'. Sheridan's three-year licence had expired and that was the beginning and the end of the Prince of Wales Theatre. He sold out to Messrs. Walker, Custor and Chalton, who built the New Royalty, which had a 'grand opening' on Saturday, December 23, 1882, with the pantomime *Aladdin*, to which the Chronicle gave a column notice. The splendour of the 'new electric light' was the subject of admiring comment. Mr. Dacroy was the first acting manager. (Whether this meant that he was an actor-manager I do not know.) This house, as the Royalty Theatre, became the principal place of entertainment for many years afterwards. To my contemporaries it is the only theatre they knew in their youth. Mr. Rigby, the owner in 1896, sold it to Mr. J. W. Carter, who announced in the Chronicle of March 7 of that year, his intention to form a limited company with a share capital of £7,000 in £20 shares, one-third reserved for local subscribers. 'The Royalty is more fortunate than many provincial theatres,' commented the paper, 'owing to there being no opposition and the management are enabled to keep open all through the year. We believe that up to the end of October, 1897, the whole period with few exceptions is booked with excellent companies.'

In that week Mr. and Mrs. Kendal brought their London company to perform in a four-act play *The Ironmaster* and a three-act comedy *A Scrap of Paper*. The Chronicle described Mr. and Mrs. Kendal as 'this distinguished pair' and Mrs. Kendal was indeed an actress-manager of much fame at this time. Her company had many touring engagements and could remain only three nights in the smaller towns. 'From the appearance of this house on Thursday,' said the paper, 'there is little room for doubt that they would fill the Royalty for a week and longer.' Henry Irving acted at the Royalty in this its first phase, probably in his popular adaptation of *The Bells*, but I have not been able to trace the date. About 1904 the Royalty passed into the control of Messrs. Compton and Milton-Bode and then began its colourful 'music hall' period of variety, revue, melo-drama and farce. MacDonald and Young's *No, no, Nanette* took a record £900 at the box-office in the 1920s. Frank H. Fortescue's reper-tory company, with Mr. Kimberley, were a frequent draw, present-ing *Ignorance, Should a Wife Tell?, Maria Marten, East Lynne, Not Fit to Marry, Midnight in Paris*, and *The Face at the Window* – surely all true successors of the Theatre Royal's farces of a century and a half before. Hamilton Deane came on tour with *Dracula, The Fake, Fran-kenstein*, and *At the Villa Rose*; Lew Lake with *Sweeney Todd*; and Alfred Denville's stock company once ran for thirteen weeks. I do not know if Sir Frank Benson's Shakespearian company was at Chester when they went to Flint Castle to perform *Richard the Second* in the summer of 1899, but they were at the Royalty in the 1920s and afterwards, pre-senting Shakespeare and Sheridan. Benson I can see now in the mind's eye, a spare, scholarly figure. His Shakespeare was urbane and well-spoken. He could not summon up the furies like Cooke or Kean, and perhaps he was not the equal in his own time of Henry Irving – but for thousands of young people he took the plays agree-ably out of the schoolroom into the theatre. He was a kind of Henry Wood or Malcolm Sargent of the theatre.

A new company acquiring the management in 1932, plans were made some five years later to enlarge the theatre and improve the ac-commodation. But the Second World War intervened and com-pletion of the work was deferred until 1957. The Royalty was reopened on July 8 of that year. The Chronicle invited patrons to note the wide sweep of the extended circle and the replacement of 'the gods' by the upper circle. By cantilevering the two circles it was possible to remove the pillars which, until then, had obstructed the view of the stage from some parts of the pit. 'Our aim,' said the man-ager, 'has been to retain the old-world atmosphere of the Royalty, and we feel that our patrons will agree that here is a theatre with a history to be proud of, offering a homely welcome and still worthy of the city which it hopes to continue to serve.' It continues to serve today but no longer as a 'straight' theatre. Mr. W. Macqueen Pope, reopening the theatre in 1957, acknowledged the new competitive challenge to the live stage. The Chronicle reported his saying: 'Tear yourselves away from the miracle of television for one evening a week and visit the live theatre instead of sitting in the dark looking at a window frame.'

The story of the Royalty's eventual conversion into a popular theatre club is the story of many smaller-town provincial theatres, in the 1960s and after, faced with increasing costs, the decline of the stock companies and road shows, the eclipse of the touring leading man or variety star, and the counter-attraction of the cinema and television. Such theatres, unsubsidised and living entirely on their public attraction, were obliged to change with the times and the audience. And so there was the 'bingo' period as a means of livelihood, and now there is the theatre club, with its ballroom dancing and cabaret and other social facilities: its visiting club comedians, bands and old-time music halls. With these last, the Royalty revives something of its old self – for was not Albert Chevalier on its boards in November, 1921, and Marie Lloyd, with *The world's love story* and *My old Dutch*? Forgotten now perhaps, but they are in the Chronicle file. The paper has always been a good friend of the theatre, from Cowdroy's time to our own. The Royalty can claim also that it served repertory well and has been a lavish presenter of pantomime.

The Royalty having continued the tradition of the Theatre Royal for the best part of a century, and made a gallant last stand for the touring commercial theatre, it was time, if the drama was to survive in Chester, for a fresh start. The opportunity came with the civic redevelopment in the Northgate-street area adjoining and at the rear of the Town Hall. Here, in Hamilton-place – within loud-hailing distance, so to speak, of the site of the Theatre Royal – a small, compact, neatly-designed and well-appointed civic playhouse, to be called the Gateway, was opened on November 6, 1968, with a 'world première' of *The Double Case History of Dr. Valmy*. The author, the Spanish playwright Antonio Buero-Vallejo, his wife and an interpreter were in the audience, and after the last of four curtains the Mayor gave a civic reception. The Gateway is the property of the Corporation and is managed by a trust company financed by a City Council guarantee (from which the rent is first deducted), grants from the Arts Council and the North-West Arts Association, and box-office receipts. There is seating for 500, and prices range from 40p to 65p, which, when you think about it, compares favourably in these times of high inflation, with the price of seats at the old Theatre Royal in its great days.

None the less, the Gateway pays its way. With its studio theatre, companionable foyers, and club, it is at once a social centre, a forum of the arts, a place to enjoy the classical and modern drama, music, poetry, and dance, a workshop with excellent backstage equipment

and a school. The Chronicle gave the entire enterprise a cordial welcome from the beginning. The first director, Julian Oldfield, asked
for honest, intelligent dramatic criticism rather than mere puff and
reporting, and he has had it from the pen of the paper's music and
drama critic, Maureen Nield. Mr. Oldfield had the task, and the
challenge, of establishing the Gateway at a time when all theatrical
art was in the convulsion of almost total restatement. There was a
new drama, a new criticism, a great deal of experimental excitement,
and, inevitably, some pretentious nonsense as well. The ferment is
still working and some great things have come out of it, with a freedom of writing and performance unparalleled in the history of the
stage. The drama, like the novel, belongs to its own time (or, if it is
good enough, all time), and Mr. Oldfield's six years at the Gateway
established the little theatre as a liberally-minded, lively contemporary playhouse, reinterpreting for an impressionable modern
audience of all ages the great drama of the past, and introducing the
ideas, forms, and pressures of today. The director once explained to
me for the Chronicle, quite simply, what he was trying to do. 'For
me,' he said, 'the theatre is a means of expression, a basis for communication. The basic aim of any theatre should be to entertain.
However, along with this main objective go several secondary ones,
and with the right mixture one can not only entertain but also stimu-
late and (dare one say it without risk of being labelled pretentious
and patronising?) educate.'

And that policy has been put into practice with much skill and
understanding of what the audience ought to like and enjoy, from
pop to pastiche. The Gateway is indeed the portal of the theatre for
many young people who are instructed even as they are entertained.
It discovers talent, encourages participation and sustains the amateur drama in the city and for miles around. All the arts come together here. The 'mix' of the provincial audience may sometimes
leave the theatre still bemused by what some contemporary playwright has been trying to say. Better luck next time, and there is
always something new, original, challenging, exotic to see and hear,
with from time to time people famous on stage, television, and radio
taking part as individuals or groups. In this way Michael MacLiam-
moir, John Alderton, Pauline Collins, Beatrix Lehmann, Bill Simpson, Rodney Bewes, John Dankworth, Cleo Laine, Annie Ross, Cy
Grant, Julie Felix, George Melly, Cyril Fletcher, Ken Dodd, David
Kossoff, the Paul Taylor Dance Company, the Northern Dance

Theatre, Phyllis Sellick, Larry Adler, Max Jaffa, the Spinners, and many others have entertained on the Gateway boards. In many ways, it is the old Theatre Royal updated, radically changed, wonderfully varied, but essentially the same in intention.

After its opening, and a Christmas pantomime, the Gateway gave a taste of its quality and aspirations with a production of *Macbeth* in February, 1969. 'I have imagined,' said Oldfield, 'that our audience is coming to see it for the first time, and we have therefore concentrated on the story and the relationship between the characters.' Fair enough, wrote the Chronicle critic, 'although one may argue the calculated risk to the stature of the whole if one reduces Shakespeare's tragic hero to the popular local boy makes good and his partner in greatness to a ruthless social climber'. Here at any rate was recognition that the company was not afraid to engage in adventure. In the succeeding autumn the company took a different kind of risk with *A Streetcar Named Desire* and carried it through many tense moments to 'a magnificent final curtain'. A compelling, imaginative performance by Margaret Ollerenshaw (afterwards director of the Tramshed in London) was praised by the Chronicle. 'A revival in the fullest sense of the word – Shylock swops his Jewish gaberdine for a morning coat,' said the paper of *The Merchant of Venice* (February, 1970), 'acted on a superbly adaptable, literally swinging set.'

A famous play of the 'sixties, Harold Pinter's *The Caretaker*, was another 1970 production: 'Julian Oldfield seems happy to let the piece speak for itself – if that is not too ludicrous a way to refer to the interpretation of a work that is about, among other things, noncommunication.' In the autumn of the same year the Gateway essayed Arnold Wesker's *I'm Talking About Jerusalem* and a year later another Pinter play, *The Birthday Party*, in which, said the Chronicle critic, 'the art does not quite conceal the artifice'. Plays by Dylan Thomas, John Osborne, Shaw, Wilde, Coward, Becket, Eliot, Maugham, Emlyn Williams, Arthur Miller, have gone into the repertory, and the Studio has its own adventures. Continuing the Chronicle tradition of writing for as well as about the theatre, Maureen Nield, the paper's drama critic, won the Gateway Club's playwriting competition with *Poet and Peasant*, which was performed in March, 1973, and in the same year she was commended in the national competition for the John Bourne Memorial Award given for the most stimulating newspaper criticism of the amateur drama. In 1970–71 the Chronicle, in conjunction with the Gateway and the

Cheshire Community Council, sponsored a play-writing competition in which a local teacher, David Fitzsimmons, was joint first prize winner. In 1974 he had a play produced in London's West End. The example of the Gateway has stimulated all amateur art in the city and its region, including the Cheshire Community Council's annual drama competition (for which the Chronicle has awarded perpetual trophies) and given a new point of focus to the city Festival of the Arts. Another good result of all this activity is the promotion of an Arts Centre, with the theatre as a nucleus. The arts in Chester are fostered also by other theatre, operatic, and music clubs and societies, and outlying in the changing scene of old Newtown, the Little Theatre in Gloucester-street continues its good work of social comment and theatrical amenity with the new high-flat dwellers on the fringe, and the last of the Victorian terrace tenants round about.

I began this chapter with the eighteenth century, when the drama threw off the Puritan inhibitions and recovered some of its earlier Elizabethan pride. But there was a people's drama in Chester long before that, and it has been left to this century to rediscover the mystery or miracle plays first acted in the city streets at Whitsuntide in the fourteenth century. Authorship of the twenty-four plays of the Chester cycle is attributed to Ralph Higden, a monk of the Abbey of St. Werburgh, and because they were intended for acting by the citizens and the trade guilds there is a lot of local colour in them and particularly in the famous *Noah's Flood*, given by the Water-Drawers of Dee. For three hundred years the plays were performed as moveable pageants in the streets until the custom fell into disuse. The first revival of which I have note in the paper was in June, 1906, when the English Drama Society performed the three Nativity Plays in London, under the direction of Mr. Nugent Monck. A repeat performance was given on November 29 of the same year at the Music Hall, but a staging of the complete cycle was considered infeasible. At last the opportunity came in the first Chester Festival of 1951, when part of the cycle was performed, and again in 1952, when Beatrice Tunstall, the Cheshire novelist and author of *The Shiny Night*, reported for the Chronicle a two-weeks' season in the Cathedral Refectory. She wrote in the paper of June 14, 'It is believed that before the Festival revival last year the complete plays were last performed in 1660', which may very well have been so. Possibly the most memorable account of the old playbooks was given as part of the Festival of the Arts in July, 1967, by a company of amateur performers, some 170 strong, acting on the Cathedral Green and at moveable stations in the streets.

I wrote about this in the paper at the time, remarking upon the proximity of the Cathedral Green to the cloisters, where Ralph Higden created, revised, or translated the original scripts. The street stations attracted citizen curiosity, laughter and serious attention. Surprisingly, the plays were alive and relevant. But something was missing: 'the thought remains that our ancestors never saw the plays so decorously and devoutly performed. Missing and echoing only in the mind is the clamour of the throng in the narrow, high-gabled streets, the jonglerie, the fantastication, the mingled squalor and high faith of the mediaeval scene.' What was the point of it all now? Maureen Nield, under the headline 'The Mystery at the Heart of the Mystery Plays', discussed the meaning, intention and relevance of the plays when they were once more attempted in the Festival of 1973. The director and adaptor, James Roose-Evans, claimed that 'the vision of the old story remains alike for believer and unbeliever, so that our task has been to create imaginatively the great truths and insights of the mystery plays'. Housewives, teachers, students, doctors, civil servants, engineers, managers, a farmer and a variety of citizens took part in the presentation. Somehow, this time, the spell did not work. As the city buses swept past the acting-platform at the Cross, the words were lost on the air and the mystery left unresolved. Observing the scene, a colleague said to me: 'What's all that about?' It was a good question, and we shall have to wait for the answer.

Part 3

13

The middle years of expansion

The day is Friday, January 16, the year 1835. The first issue of the Chester Chronicle following the death of its proprietor John Fletcher has gone to press and the Editor, John David Barry, is sitting at his desk in Fletcher's Buildings thinking about the future. For the time being his own name appears in the imprint as editor and printer, and that of Samuel Berrington – he and his brothers Joshua and Walter are Chronicle compositors – as the publisher. But this is only temporary. The old man's nephew and successor Thomas Fletcher is expected in the office any day now. As the only kin, he has inherited the paper and his uncle's estate of £20,000, and he knows nothing about the business of conducting a newspaper. Astonishing, muses the Editor, that John Fletcher, a scrupulous man of affairs, far-sighted in all his dealings, should have died without making a will and a great pity that he had had no son trained up to succeed him. The Chester Chronicle is now a considerable undertaking rapidly increasing in circulation and influence. How is Thomas Fletcher, by all accounts a simple labourer, to manage it? The Editor is in doubt and perplexity, not least about his own position. There had never been any uncertainty in old John's long reign. Having chosen his editor and made sure of him – and he had picked some of the best journalists of his time – he never questioned the editorial discretion or authority, concerning himself with the business management and his own separate affairs and enterprises. But he was always there to consult and advise, and always primed with ideas and information. And now he was there no longer.

The only trouble with old John had been that he was somewhat parsimonious in the matter of salary. But now? The lawyers winding up the estate had hinted to him, John Barry, in the darkly confidential manner of their kind, that there could be difficulties ahead. To begin with, they had had some trouble finding the nephew, at last tracking him down in a Runcorn stone quarry where he worked as a common labourer and was recommended by his employers and his mates as a reliable man and a cunning poacher. A man, it would seem, of little education – or none – and of no particular trade, and totally unfitted to assume his uncle's responsibilities and place in life. True, John Fletcher himself had been of humble origin, but then he had proved himself a man of immense capacity. Advised of his fortune and the new duties attendant upon it, Thomas had expressed no surprise, no curiosity, no sentiment, except to say that he knew very little of his uncle. Advised to make an early and decent appearance in the office at Chester, he thereupon asked for money in hand to buy new clothes, since he had no other than his working outfit. The lawyers had hinted also of some sort of arrangement to be arrived at between the editor and the new proprietor. How else was the concern to be carried on?

Arriving in the office a week later, the Editor finds a stockily-built stranger lounging in his chair, dressed country-style in drab breeches and leggings, and turning over the leaves of the weekly account-book. Says he without ceremony, 'I'm Tom Fletcher. Who are you?'

'John Barry, editor of your newspaper, at your service.'

'I know naught about editors and suchlike, but it says here that you're paid three pounds a week. And that's sadly too much by my reckoning. I can get a man to hedge and ditch for twelve shillings a week. What d'ye say to that?'

John David Barry – afterwards described as a man of high education, probity, and honour – is painfully affronted. He says nothing, but resumes his tall hat and his stick and with deliberation quits the office.

A year later he left for good. Whatever accommodation was reached between them in the interval, it did not work. That first encounter was the death of any partnership. Thomas Fletcher's imprint appeared in the paper for the first time on February 13, 1835, and by June 12 he was sufficiently confident to announce: 'Thomas Fletcher, nephew and successor to the late Alderman Fletcher, begs to return his best thanks to the public for a continuance of the favours conferred for a long series of years upon his late respected uncle; and to announce that, having recently purchased a great variety of beautiful and modern types and printing materials, he is now enabled to execute posting bills, circulars, pamphlets, bookwork, and letter-press printing of every description, at the Chronicle Office, in a superior style and on terms that will challenge comparison with any other office.' An announcement quite in the old style. Thomas Fletcher's relations with the last editor appointed by his uncle might not be very cordial, and certainly not good enough for their success-ful joint conduct of the paper, but he was evidently learning the printing and publishing side of the business, just as his uncle had had to learn it fifty years before. It was later said of Thomas that he came to Chester, moved into his uncle's house in Further Northgate-street, 'entered upon a new and improved sphere of life, and under all cir-cumstances, with the good common sense of his relative, carried on by well qualified agents the Chronicle paper'. Thomas Fletcher's 24 years' ownership was unremarkable save for one thing. He had ap-parently inherited his uncle's flair for selecting first-rate editors, and in 1837, when John Barry departed, probably for Manchester, he came to terms with the first of the 'well qualified agents', John Trevor, who edited the paper until the 1860s, continuing the tra-dition of notably good writing and sound journalistic practice estab-lished by Cowdroy, Hanshall, and Hemingway.

There was, however, a significant difference. For some twenty-five years John Trevor was in virtual command of the Chronicle. It was the editor's paper rather than the proprietor's, and, allowing for the unusual circumstance of Thomas Fletcher's accession, it was fortu-nate that Trevor proved to be the right man for the job at the right time. He was more of a political journalist and man of affairs than any of his gifted predecessors; he had more authority and self-reliance than John Barry, and, like John Fletcher, he served as She-riff and was twice Mayor of Chester. He had many of the old man's attributes, including a head for business and the management of money, and above all a capacity to understand the movements of his time and the dynamic changes taking place around him. The paper's leading articles of all this period are soundly Liberal Rad-ical and accompanied invariably by extensive reporting of the more important Parliamentary debates. This had been a characteristic of the Chronicle since 1775 which distinguished it among provincial weeklies, most of which, with the honourable exception of the old rival the Courant, were content to look no farther than the local hor-izon. Few concessions were made to easy reading. The news columns were close-packed with solid paragraphs running into hun-dreds of lines and the art of headline writing was almost unknown.

News-gathering extended throughout Cheshire, Lancashire and North Wales. Important matters, national and local, were reported at great length. Only the light-minded and sophisticated city of Chester was treated to gossipy paragraphs with sub-heads.

For the rest, the Editor, burning the midnight oil over his weighty, well-considered leaders, assumed in his readers a capacity for political study and a maturity of judgment that a good many of them, I am bound to think, could not have had. But perhaps it was different in those days, still long before universal education. The newspaper was the educator and the Chronicle accepted the responsibility with high seriousness. At the same time, it must not be forgotten, the franchise was being gradually extended – not without reluctance in some quarters – and the people looked to the Press for political guidance and information, and this could be had more accessibly, at this distance from the capital, in the Chester Chronicle than in The Times or The Morning Post or The Morning Chronicle – justly famous and respected as those daily papers were. Thus the Chronicle had less space for triviality than at any previous time, but it continued to report in gross detail the more sensational criminal trials of the day. No evidence was considered unfit to print. The Assize Courts and Sessions afforded education of a different kind.

Thomas Fletcher receded into obscurity after his appointment of John Trevor to the editorial chair. What salary inducement was offered is not known, but Trevor understood money, as we shall see, and Fletcher must have profited from his misadventure with Barry and learned the value of a good editor. The fact was that he had little choice, but posterity will allow that at this significant stage in the progress of the paper, Tom Fletcher did indeed act with the 'good common sense' of his uncle. He served his purpose, continued the Fletcher interest (while the rival Courant had changed hands in 1832), and retired into the background. John Trevor's father lived in Chester for some time but he himself was born in Bolton in 1800. In his youth he had a Dick Swiveller flirtation with a law apprenticeship but soon slipped off the high stool in the outer office to try his hand on the Press. He became a reporter on a Manchester paper, and we hear of him next as Editor of the Caernarvon Herald in 1834. Four years later he moved to Chester as Editor of the Chronicle.

In 1843 he published his *Panorama of Chester*, an up to date guide book based on Hanshall and Hemingway, and in style and content entirely in the Chronicle tradition of local history and contemporary comment and information. Memory of the 'closed Corporation' before the first Reform Bill in 1832 was still fresh, and in the last words of his introductory essay Trevor stirred the embers of the fire first kindled by the paper for citizen rights: 'To be a freeman of Chester is prized more than gold; and to the honour of that patriotic body be it said that in all the arduous contests of bygone days, whether for parliamentary representatives or the municipal authorities, not all the power of wealth, nor the blandishments of high rank, could subvert their independence.' But there were battles to come and the Chronicle was to stand up again for its old principles. The *Panorama* is a document of social change in that it reported the decline of the high days of the stage-coach and the coming of the railways. The principal city inns – Royal, Albion, Green Dragon, Feathers, Blossoms, Hop-pole, and White Lion – were still serving the coaches but providing also horse buses to and from the station.

On August 17, 1838, cutting of the Chester and Crewe line had been started near the Spital Locks, Boughton, and surveys of the Holyhead line began less than a year afterwards. The Chester and Birkenhead railway was opened on September 23, 1840, followed by the Chester and Crewe line on October 1. So that by 1843 the stations of the Chester and Crewe branch of the Grand Junction Railway and the Chester and Birkenhead railway, communicating with Liverpool, were in full operation. 'In addition,' wrote Trevor, 'there is now every prospect of the speedy accomplishment of the Chester and Holyhead railway as the principal line of communication between London and Dublin.' The 'celebrated Mr. Stephenson' had surveyed the line for the Chester company and recommended Chester via Holyhead as the best line and best terminus on the Welsh coast. In 1848 the line was opened to Bangor and later in the year the Shrewsbury and Chester railway was opened throughout.

In the advertisement columns of the paper, coach time-tables, each with a woodcut illustration of the coachman on his box and the guard or postboy up behind, which had been a regular feature since the first issue, were now accompanied by the railway operators' time-tables and fares, and, after the first inevitable fatal accidents, by announcements in the name of the Railway Passengers' Assurance Company offering cover in the event of death at the rate of 3d. first class (£1,000), 2d. second class (£500), and 1d. third class (£200). Thus the social gradations, scrupulously cherished by the railways for so many years afterwards, were firmly fixed from the start. The first railway advertisements adopted the stage-coach practice with the device of a puffing billy, tender and passenger coach at the top. The prudence of some sort of insurance cover was dramatically demonstrated on the night of May 24, 1847, when John Trevor and his reporters were summoned to the scene of the latest kind of news story. Stage-coaches overturning and the horses fouling the traces, outsides pitching from the roof on to their heads, and other hazards of the road such as highwaymen, they were familiar with, but 'a desolating spectacle' was before them that night at the new Roodee railway suspension bridge over the Dee.

'We shudder to record,' said the Chronicle of May 28, 'that a passenger train to Wrexham and Ruabon was suddenly precipitated into the river while passing over. Four dead bodies were taken out of the water and carriages, and fourteen persons taken to the Infirmary with dislocated and broken limbs and various concussions of the brain.' The train was the 6.15 p.m. out of Chester and was on the bridge when the third arch parted. There were 30 passengers aboard. The engine got over, the carriages plunged 34 feet into the river. The death toll was eventually five: the guard, the stoker, and three passengers, one of whom died afterwards in hospital. That was the first fatal rail crash in Cheshire and because it was the first and because of the 'dire evil' of the circumstances – the broken bridge, the river deeps below, the driver thrusting the engine across – it is remembered even now. Dread of another kind – collision in a tunnel – was awakened four years later. The Chronicle gave a harrowing description of what happened in Halton tunnel on the night of Chester Cup day, 1851, when the last of three passenger trains carrying returning racegoers to Manchester crashed into the unlighted rear of the second train with its single engine, the first and second trains having been slowed down by the gradient and insufficiency of water. Again five people were killed, but this time many more were badly injured. The steam age of quick and convenient transport of people and goods had begun, gathering speed as the years went by – 1848, Chester-London via Crewe, 6½ hours, 1851, five hours 35 minutes, 1860, four hours 55 minutes – and inevitably there were the great railway accidents, of which the most disastrous have occurred in the twentieth century, and two of those in Cheshire, coincidentally on the same line at Minshull Vernon a few miles from Crewe Junction, in 1948 and 1962.

John Trevor's editorship coincided with the beginning and development of the first railway age, Chester ranking second to Crewe Junction as the north-west hub of the system. As Telford and Fletcher's canal started the steady growth of Netherpool into Ellesmere Port, the railways created, much faster, the town of Crewe out of the Cheshire hamlet of Monks Coppenhall. Before the 1830s Crewe simply did not exist except in the name of the Jacobean mansion Crewe Hall. Then came the station (1837) and the locomotive works of the Grand Junction Company (completed in 1843). The first houses were occupied in 1842, the population of Monks Coppenhall rising from 200 to 1,000 like lightning. Christ Church – first patrons of the living, the Grand Junction directorate – dates from 1845, but was many years a-building. On December 8, 1843, the Chronicle reported: 'The large locomotive carriage and wagon manufactory of the Grand Junction Railway Company, at their station and village of Crewe, having been recently completed, and for some time in active and successful operation, the directors gave the superintendents, clerks, workmen, their wives, families, and acquaintances, a grand dinner, tea, and ball on Saturday last.' The festivities were held in a splendidly decorated engine shed. The village beauties were all there, and so were the neighbouring farmers, some of whom had made a substantial profit from the sale of their land to accommodate the coming of the iron road. Absent were the Nantwich hereditary landowners whose determination to keep the railway out caused them to put a prohibitory price upon their acres. That is one reason why Crewe Junction is where it is today.

By the standards of the time – indeed, far in advance of them – the railway founders were socially paternalistic in their single-minded creation of Crewe. At the inaugural celebration they provided a lavish feast, with copious draughts of hot negus to follow; and with the same intention of keeping a contented work-force in good living conditions, they planned the town, its streets, houses, and social services from scratch. It was a total act of public enterprise privately initiated and financed by the powers of steam. At the same time a modern legend was in the making – the legend of Crewe Station itself, the junction of arrivals and departures in people's lives, a tide of trains in the affairs of men and women, and the platform of poignant meetings and farewells in the two world wars of the present century, to say nothing of the platforms of endless patient waiting. In 1843 all this was in the future, and the time was not far off when the newly organised workers would begin to resent the disciplined running of their lives by the railway capitalists protecting their million pounds investment. Schools, churches, the Mechanics' Institute, welfare and everything provided, that was all very well, but basic things like sanitation and public lighting were minimal, and after a time the model town began to look scruffy and mean. It was as if the railway directors, having willed the town into existence, thereupon left it to look after itself. At best it was a master and servant relationship which inevitably caused political and industrial conflict from the 1880s and culminated in the first national railway strike of 1911. But to old-established Chester in 1843, its trade withering in the silted river, the new towns of Ellesmere Port and Crewe were portents of irresistible, ordered mercantile progress. The Chronicle reported the installation of the floating dock at Ellesmere Port and commented that the sturdy artisan dwellings of Crewe were a reproach to the slums of Chester and Nantwich. From that time the paper fixed its attention, political and social, on the rising railway settlement, and this attention some years hence was to take an even more positive form, and by then those artisan dwellings were less ideal than they had seemed to be.

In 1844 John Trevor, then living in Seller-street, was elected to Chester City Council and entered upon a career of public service which was almost a continuation of John Fletcher's. Like Fletcher, he was Sheriff of the city (1849), alderman (1859), and twice Mayor (1860 and 1861). He was a magistrate, chairman of the Finance Committee of the Council, chairman of the Board of Guardians, and a governor of the Infirmary. And in addition, from 1847 he discharged the lucrative and trusted office of County Court Treasurer for Cheshire. His capacity for public business was such that it was said of him that the management of the city finances was almost exclusively in his hands. For some years after his appointment to the County Court Treasurership Trevor accepted no 'fee or reward' for editing the Chronicle, and about 1860, because of the demands of official duties upon his time, he had the assistance of an associate editor, John or James Price, who eventually succeeded him. Trevor, however, continued to write for the paper and contributed two articles on the Bala Lake water supply shortly before his death, which came unexpectedly on September 5, 1866, and made news. He was the second victim of the Asiatic cholera epidemic in the city.

Having lost its editor by this untimely stroke, the Chronicle examined the onset of the visitation in some detail and attributed it in part to the cattle plague which afflicted the county in the previous January, when 40,000 animals died or were destroyed. Cholera, it was suggested, had been induced by drinking water contaminated by surface drainage from places where diseased cattle had been buried. For the first time doctors began the slow job of inoculating Cheshire's vast diary herd against foot-and-mouth disease, but their work was overtaken by the cholera spreading into the county. The paper reported a City Council meeting of May 13 at which concern was expressed about the filthiness of some parts of Chester and the danger arising from a hundred open middens. In July cholera struck in Nantwich and Winsford and on September 1 in Chester. The first to die was a young woman named Brett. The second was John Trevor. Preparations had been made for the conversion of a farm house, on land which eventually became the Grosvenor Park, into an emergency hospital, and of this as the cholera spread in the city and district Miss Frances Wilbraham, a lady known for her good works, took charge. The hospital was not closed until December. Miss Wilbraham's selfless night-and-day service was honoured by the City Council and the first Duke of Westminster afterwards called her 'the Florence Nightingale of Chester'.

Trevor's editorship was a time of change and development at the Chronicle Office and in the local newspaper world. Iron rotary presses were developed in the first decades of the nineteenth century, and in August, 1851, a steam power press of the Cowper design was installed in Bridge-street Row by Tom Fletcher to complement the Stanhope iron press in use since 1809. The issue of August 2 (number 4065) was the first to be run off on the new machine, and the old wooden press, having served its turn for 76 years, was finally discarded or relegated to the 'jobbing' shop. There were now eight pages, 24″ × 17″, instead of four even larger broadsheets, and forty-eight columns instead of twenty-eight. Since 1815, when Stamp duty was raised to 4d a sheet, the paper had been at its highest selling price of sevenpence, reduced in 1850 to fivepence. Fletcher and Trevor were at pains to explain the purpose of their new press power: 'The encroachment of advertisers on the news department of the paper have so steadily increased that, in justice to them and the general reader, we are bound to provide means that the interests of both shall be fairly consulted.' At this point I imagine the Editor taking over, for the notice went on:

> 'Every successive week, in order to make room for the advertisements,
> we are compelled to curtail interesting articles of news, to pass over
> matters with the most meagre notice where details would be accept-
> able, or to pretermit them altogether, to the prejudice of that universa-
> lity of intelligence, and that regular narration of events which
> constitute the claims of a journal to public confidence and support. . . .
> We have adopted the only proper remedy by presenting an ample sheet
> which shall justify its title of a newspaper in the fullest and most liberal
> acceptation of the term.'

They wrote like that in those days. It was the first, and most grandi-
loquent, acknowledgment of a problem that has exercised successive
managements of the Chronicle, and of every popular and widely circulated paper, to this day – how to provide sufficient space for all the
news and all the advertisements. The Times newspaper, pioneers in
printing progress, installed the first Cowper rotary in 1847, and here
was the Chester Chronicle keeping up to date four years later. The
Courant, now moved from Newgate-street to Northgate-street,
owned by John Ramsden and edited by John Hicklin (a noted anna-
list of the city), made the same change two months later. For a transient period from about 1840, the established rivals had another
hopeful competitor in the Chester Gazette, published from an office
in Eastgate-street. It did not survive. A lasting venture, significant as
it was to prove in later years for the Courant, was the start in May,
1854, by Henry Mills, of the Cheshire Observer, published 'at No. 3
Black Dog Passage in the Parish of St. Michael'.

Before John Trevor died so suddenly at his home, 19 White Friars,
cut off in the midst of an exceedingly busy and useful life, there were
two changes in the Chronicle proprietorship, the first of which
brought the Smiths into the Fletcher family business. Thomas
Fletcher's daughter, Ann, married William Smith, a stage coach
proprietor and farmer, of Kop House, Sealand, and afterwards of the
Warren, Broughton. Fletcher published the paper until 1859, when
he was succeeded by his son-in-law. Upon William Smith's death
four years later the management was carried on by his widow, who
was fortunate to have for three more years the editorial support and
business counsel of John Trevor, at a time when newspaper costs
were high. The Chronicle in 1851 had paid £609.4s.6d. in duty on advertisements and £361.17s.6d. in Stamp duty – a large part of its revenue. But Trevor was to live long enough to see the 'taxes on
knowledge' gradually repealed and finally abolished in 1861, after

which advertisements multiplied and more pages were printed with improved press capacity at less cost to the readers. Circulations, too, began to run into the thousands. Trevor saluted the lifting of the impost with a resounding editorial, and the way was clear for the Chronicle expansion of the next two decades.

Of John or Joseph Price, editor in the late 1860s, nothing is known except his name. It was Price, however, who moved like a shadow through Chester and afterwards across the water to Dublin – where the paper still had residual contacts from its old-time association with the Irish linen trade – trying to search out the mystery of the frustrated Fenian 'Raid' on Chester Castle, the raid in which not a shot was fired, although the plot was supposedly deep and well prepared. The paper's reporting of the events of Monday, February 11, 1867, is vivid and circumstantial. An informer, one Corydon, had tipped off the city authorities that the Fenians, dedicated to an independent Ireland, were to arrive in the city in small batches until some 600 were infiltrated, and their job was to capture the stand of arms in the Castle cockpit and hold the citadel until 2,000 reinforcements turned up.

As the night wore on the 'invaders', deciding after a meeting in Liverpool-road that the game was up and that the plot, if there was a plot, had been smoked, began to drift away through crowds of jeering citizens and a tight Police cordon to the railway station. Was there really an Irish plot to capture the Castle and its arms? Or was it a demonstration by discontented Englishmen bent on making a riot in patrician Chester to draw attention to their grievances of unemployment or hard toil, low wages, and bad housing? Tradition dies hard and social improvement was hard to get in the land ruled by a new aristocracy of grim-faced industrialists. Two thousand mysterious 'visitors' were reported counted out of Chester that night, whatever their purpose, but most of them were on their way back not to Ireland but to Liverpool, Manchester, Stockport, Stalybridge and Preston, known towns of industrial and social unrest. The Editor of the Chronicle, wearing (as he wrote) his meanest clothes, moved among them until the last group had gone before midnight, and next day he went to Dublin to get more light on the affair. The Chronicle never got to the bottom of the business and it remains a mystery to this day. When the Militia Barracks in Castle Esplanade were taken down in our own time, the Fenian 'Raid' was an almost forgotten story. But the Irish trouble never goes away.

John (or Joseph) Price's part in our story, aside from the bizarre Fenian affair, is that he quietly and competently prepared the way for Frederick Marshall, perhaps the most distinguished of the editorial line. Marshall, succeeding to the chair in 1870 or earlier, consolidated the Chronicle's Gladstonian Liberalism and the religious Nonconformity that, in Cheshire, was another expression of it. The paper went on to support the 'straight' Liberal Radicals like John Brunner, founder with Ludwig Mond of the chemical alkali firm at Winnington, Northwich, which was the beginning of the giant Imperial Chemical Industries of today, and it opposed the Whig remnant and the hybrid Liberal Unionists who, following the lead of the first Duke of Westminster, parted company with Gladstone and fell in with the Cheshire Tory squirearchy over extension of the franchise and Irish Home Rule. The Weaver Valley, until then the domain of the Salt Union, and South Cheshire, until then mostly agricultural with old Nantwich as the centre and market town of the richest dairyland in the country, were the sites of new industries and new working populations. Rural Cheshire was undergoing a change even more significant than the enclosures of the previous century.

In Crewe the railway workers were beginning to organise in trades unions – engineers, boilermakers, iron founders, and coach-makers, and the Amalgamated Society of Railway Servants – and these 'red hot radicals' were seeking political expression. (That genteel Victorian title of 'Railway Servants' was swept away in the battles to come.) In 1874, Alderman James Briggs and Alderman W. McNeill, representing the Liberal Party in the town, went to Chester to wait upon the Editor of the Chronicle. Their purpose was to persuade him to provide Crewe with a Chronicle of its own. Ann Smith, her son Richard Fletcher Smith (eldest of nine children), and the Editor, Frederick Marshall, took the decision to establish a new paper, the first of the Chronicle family and associated newspapers of today. Marshall had on his staff a questing, energetic reporter in his twenties named Frederick Coplestone who had come to Chester from the Hereford Times. Upon this young man the Editor laid much trust and responsibility, for he himself had been called to the Bar at the Inner Temple and was preparing to lay aside his journalistic duties for a new career in the law. The editorial chair would presently fall vacant. Was Coplestone the man to be entrusted with it? There was one way to find out. He was sent to Crewe charged with the daunting but challenging task of starting a paper in what must have seemed to him a raw frontier town.

Moving into a rudimentary office in the High Street, Coplestone appointed correspondents and advertisement agents, canvassed the traders and made personal contact with all the leaders of this vital, aspiring community. And the Crewe and Nantwich Chronicle was published for the first time on March 21, 1874. The inclusion of Nantwich in the title and the area to be covered was important, for the Chester Chronicle had been reporting news of the old town for a century and had much good will there because of its interest in agriculture – so much so that it was now widely accepted as the farmers' paper. It would be some years before Nantwich could 'accept' Crewe, but it could never ignore it, and upon that mutual interest and latent neighbourliness the new paper was built. By 1890, however, Crewe had grown so much in population and importance that a single edition was given to it, and the Crewe Chronicle and the Nantwich Chronicle separately titled, date from July 12 of that year. The Sandbach edition of the Crewe Chronicle was from the start identified with the industrial enterprise of the famous Foden family.

A personal account of that time has fortunately been given by the young Coplestone's companion and assistant in the Crewe venture, one S. Sleigh, Marshall's stepson, afterwards of the East Anglian Daily Times. Thirty years on he recalled the 'little wooden shanty office, with its rude counter, small fire stove, and couple of chairs. Prominent tradesmen were in the habit of dropping in, wanting to know how we were getting on'. And there were also homely and eccentric characters about, in new Crewe just as in old Chester, like old Mr. Moon the photographer across the way from the office, who had an interesting past, having been concerned in the Chartist disturbances of 1848, and Johnny Kay the chemist, who kept live snakes in a glass case and was addicted to spirit rapping. Alderman Heath, prematurely reported dead, came into the office one day brandishing the Chronicle and declaring that he was not satisfied with his obituary notice. The youthful Mr. Sleigh also never forgot another hazard of a reporter's life. In the old Police Court at the rear of the Royal Hotel he was sitting at the solicitors' table, with a prisoner charged with burglary standing behind him. 'Suddenly he whipped from his pocket a piece of glass with which he inflicted a terrible gash in his throat, besprinkling my clothes with some of his blood. Mr. Speakman, the magistrates' clerk, fainted right away.'

There were at least ten pubs in the High Street in the vicinity of the office, and they opened at 5 a.m. and did not close until nearly midnight. Here the furnace workers slaked a consuming thirst.

Coplestone and Sleigh had been a year at Crewe and Nantwich when Ann Smith, the Chronicle proprietor, died at her home in Barrel Well Hill, Boughton, and was succeeded on July 24, 1875 – the centenary year of the Chester Chronicle which strangely was passed over without celebration – by her son Richard Fletcher Smith. He and Marshall (for the next three years) and for long afterwards Coplestone, continued the direction of the paper, which in the next decade was acknowledged as the champion of Liberalism throughout Cheshire and North Wales. As we have seen, the paper's line of march out from Chester was given direction first by increased printing power, the capacity of the compositors at head office to set up more copy (the linotype machine was still to come) and the press to machine more editions; by the appearance on the scene of powerful industrialists like the railway directors, Brunner and Mond, W. H. Lever, the first Viscount Leverhulme, who established Port Sunlight in the 1880s, and Henry Hall Summers who, also towards the end of the century, started Hawarden Bridge Steelworks on 10,000 acres of marsh land in the Dee Estuary (see Chapter Nine); and by the rise of a new artisan or working class which looked, before the advent of the Labour Party in 1906, to the Liberals for social betterment and political representation.

Frederick Marshall about 1878 or 1879 resigned the editorship to take up the law career for which he had long and industriously prepared himself. Law books were the companions of his early life and hard study alternated with his journalistic work. Afterwards the paper said of him: 'From his store of classical scholarship, wide range of information, and acute understanding of men and affairs, he was a ready and cultured writer on the variety of topics that adapt themselves to contemporary journalism, but the law, and not success in journalism, was the goal of his ambitions, and much of his time while connected with this newspaper he devoted to study for the Bar.' Marshall, who came to Chester from Northampton, took his B.A. degree at London University in 1862 and in 1870 the degree of LL.B. Having been called to the Bar, he left the Chronicle and his home at Curzon Park in Chester to take chambers in London, establishing a large practice and becoming one of the leading junior barristers on the Chester and North Wales Circuit. In 1893 he took silk and in 1900 he was a bencher of the Middle Temple. As a K.C. he had

Top Lord Thomson of Fleet with Mr. Walter H. Annenberg (centre), the former U.S. Ambassador to Britain, reading the Declaration of Independence as it was first printed in the Chester Chronicle of August 23, 1776 (issue number 70). A facsimile of this edition was presented by Lord Thomson to Mr. Annenberg at the U.S. Embassy in Grosvenor Square. On the right is Mr. John Long, managing director of the Chester Chronicle. *Bottom* The 18th-century Eaton House on the site of the Grosvenor ancestral home dating from the Norman Conquest.

Top The Victorian Eaton Hall, taken down with the exception of the Clock Tower, and now replaced by a modern version. *Bottom* Famous visitors watching the world go by from the Watergate Row – Charles Laughton and Elsa Lanchester.

a high reputation in cases of civil law and rating disputes in particular, and several times when on circuit he acted as Commissioner of Assize. The Liberal Party, mindful of his earlier eloquent advocacy in the Chronicle, invited him more than once to contest a Parliamentary seat, but he always declined. He died at Herne Bay on August 1, 1910, aged 71. The Chronicle summed up the two interests in Marshall's life thus: 'He was a very able journalist, but those who knew him are aware that his one aim was the Bar.' So Marshall was one Chronicle man who got away – and there have been many others, but none so distinguished in after life as this one. A son, Hugo Marshall, also became a barrister on the Chester and North Wales Circuit.

Young Mr. Coplestone was recalled from Crewe as Marshall's assistant and a year or more later was installed as Editor. Installed is the appropriate word, for he exercised the editorial command for the next 51 years. At the beginning it was a demanding job for so young a man – the editorial chair is not customarily reached without a long apprenticeship – but the Chronicle was exceptional in this matter of its editors. Coplestone had the Crewe experience behind him, he had energy and journalistic flair and a talent for writing, and he had learned a great deal from the scholarly Marshall. After a few years it was time to establish another commercial and politically influential base in the rapidly changing county, with the Crewe and Nantwich success as the example. In 1884 Fletcher Smith and Frederick Coplestone received another politically-inspired call from the outlands, this time mid-Cheshire, where Brunner and Mond, both of whom had had to contend with deeply entrenched county conservatism, were building their empire. On April 11, 1885, another Chronicle was born, the Northwich and Winsford paper. The first local editor was probably J. S. Boddington, described as journalist and artist, who had succeeded Coplestone at Crewe and was now transferred to Northwich. Appropriately the second new paper put in its appearance a few months before a general election in which John Brunner was making his first bid for the Northwich seat which he held, with the exception of a few months, for 25 years. About this time also the Chester Chronicle shortened its lines of communication in North Wales – these had formerly extended as far as Anglesey – and concentrated on Flintshire with the edition known as the 'Flint and Denbigh' until 1974, when the two counties coalesced into Clwyd under local government reorganisation.

The character of the provincial Press was subtly changing. There were more big papers in London and the centres of population, communications were faster, and the local papers of a lineage much older than some of the great metropolitan sheets were constrained to mark out their own territories and discontinue the wide-ranging but somewhat haphazard record of earlier times. It was, paradoxically, a time for expansion and contraction. But almost to the end of Coplestone's editorship the Chronicle took itself seriously as a political and social influence. On the 150th anniversary, May 2, 1925, he was boldly writing: 'Of the Chronicle two things can be claimed – that it has never compromised its principles nor corruptly sold its columns. Purely localised papers with limited circulations are no doubt struggling for existence, while a great many dailies which refused to recognise the need for change, have disappeared. It is to the merit of the Chronicle that its strength and influence have increased as the years roll round.'

From the 1880s to the turn of the century the paper fought for Liberalism and reform on several fronts, taking issue in turn with the Chief Mechanical Engineer of Crewe Railway Works for denying political liberty to his men and with the Duke of Westminster for dividing his own party and 'handing the safe Liberal seat of Chester to the Tories'. Earl Grosvenor's association with Mr. Gladstone began in 1852 and there were always neighbourly relations between Eaton Hall and Hawarden Castle. In 1866, the Earl, for reasons which he honestly stated in the House, opposed his leader's further reform of the franchise. In 1869 he succeeded as the third Marquess of Westminster and in 1874 Gladstone, in the Queen's name, offered a Dukedom to his old friend and supporter. Gervas Huxley, the excellent biographer of the Grosvenors, has written in *Victorian Duke* that the Marquess's opposition to Gladstone's Reform Bill in 1866 'had long been forgiven and during his first ministry Gladstone had come to regard the Marquess as one of his most valued supporters, even though he had declined to accept ministerial office.'

But the friends were to part company again over disestablishment and Ireland and the Chronicle in the general election of 1885 hinted at the coming breach in this comment: 'To be a Whig nowadays is to be a Tory sailing under false colours. We Liberals would gladly wash our hands of the whole party of Whigs. Every Liberal measure for the past few years has been a compromise in consequence of the retrograde action of the Whigs in the Cabinet.' Instead of giving his traditional open support to Dr. Foster, the Liberal candidate in Chester, the Duke declared his neutrality. But the Liberals won in Chester, Crewe, Northwich, in Flintshire and in the Flint Boroughs. 'The domination of Toryism in Cheshire has come to an ignominious end' claimed the paper on December 5 after the poll. 'The democracy of Cheshire is now enfranchised against landlord domination.' The Tories, however, won Wirral and Eddisbury, the latter a rural constituency later to be visited by Mr. Lloyd George and which now no longer exists. In the contest at Crewe the Chronicle stalked a different enemy, not the Tory landlords but the Tory 'intimidators', the railway bosses and Mr. F. W. Webb, the great Mechanical Engineer and genius of steam, in particular.

There was, said the paper, terrorism in the town. 'Walking down the street a few days since, we met a mechanic whom we knew to be an earnest Liberal, and we ventured to observe that the Press was taking cognisance of the condition of things in the works. 'Yes,' he replied, 'I wish to God it could be stopped. We dare not openly attend the Liberal candidate's meetings or assist him. If we did, we should be spotted. Dismissal means absolute ruin. We have to think of our wives and children. Sir, you cannot appreciate the misery it is to live as we do. No man's sentiments, except they are Tory, can be heard outside or inside the works.' The Editor asked Mr. Webb what he thought he was up to. 'Do you think it manly, not to say honest, to force your views down the throats of men to whom they are abhorrent? Mr. Webb is a powerful unscrupulous partisan who apparently regards the mechanics as part of the vast machinery which he controls, and whose minds and bodies are to be placed at his beck and nod.' In the Northwich contest the Chronicle did not spare a magistrate, Mr. Christopher Kay, who said the paper had inflamed trouble by reading the Riot Act because of a trumpery disturbance at the declaration of the poll. 'Who is Kay? An active Tory and would-be candidate himself who because his party is beaten commits this deplorable act of petty tyranny.' A bit unfair, perhaps, but those were the days of embattled politics. No shadow boxing as in the television age.

In the Home Rule for Ireland election in 1886 Gladstone himself rebuked the Duke of Westminster for refusing to endorse the Liberal M.P. in the Chester contest. 'The Duke,' wrote Gladstone to Dr. Foster, 'says it is time for Liberals and Conservatives to work together as they have never worked together before. But the Duke forgets that he is not altogether a novice in working with Tories against Liberals. In 1866 he was the ornament and the head of a body which worked with the Tories to oppose a most moderate Reform Bill of a most moderate administration, and that zealous co-operation, on which they can now hardly improve, succeeded in destroying at once the Bill and the Government. I am doubtful, therefore, about the Duke's fitness to advise the Liberals of Chester' – although, he added, he had the highest estimate of the Duke's personal character. At the same time the Chronicle leading article appealed to the working men of Chester to support their M.P., adding 'We have confessed heretofore that the people of Chester were under many obligations to the House of Eaton, but his Grace on Tuesday sponged them all out. The Duke has a perfect right to his opinions, and he was quite justified in giving expression to them in a legitimate manner, but he ought not to have allowed his sons to canvass his tenantry in Chester. We can appreciate fair fighting, and we can also condemn cowardly influences of this sort in equally explicit terms. We fairly tell the Duke of Westminster that the Liberals of Chester will not follow him whenever he takes a freak into his head to bolt. This is the second time he has deliberately laid himself out to defeat his party.' The Conservative, Mr. Yerburgh, won by 66 votes, and at Northwich Brunner surprisingly lost the seat he had won the year before.

The battle was renewed vehemently at Northwich in 1877, when the death of Robert Verdin, the Conservative M.P. returned in the previous contest, caused a by-election in which Lord Henry Grosvenor, the Duke of Westminster's third son, was put up as a Liberal Unionist with Conservative support to fight Brunner, the redoubtable 'straight' Liberal Radical. It was said at the time that the Duke's disaffection had gone so far as to cause him to turn Gladstone's portrait at Eaton Hall with its face to the wall, and in a thorough-going polemic the Chronicle brought in this detail and also reminded his Grace to whom he owed the Dukedom:

'The Duke is a public benefactor; he has done much for Chester, but

Rich gifts wax poor when givers prove unkind.

Secure in the possession of almost unlimited wealth, enjoying a title conferred upon him by the influence of a great statesman, the presence of whose portrait he cannot now tolerate, and basking in the smiles of royalty, why must he needs spoil the gratitude of the people by pushing upon them this immature scion of his house as their representative in a Parliament which is called upon to do the most serious work? At the Duke's bidding Chester has returned a nonentity – a mere Tory voting machine labelled Liberal Unionist – and now Northwich is asked to do the same.'

The Courant, in which the Duke had recently acquired a financial interest, was roundly told to mind its own business. The veteran rival paper had scolded the Chronicle for forgetting that the Duke had been a staunch upholder of Liberalism in the past. 'If we read all history backwards we might have come to such a conclusion', retorted the Chronicle, and the Editor wrote to Gladstone advising him of Lord Henry's pretensions and claims at Northwich. Gladstone replied in a letter to the paper saying that the young nobleman had not the smallest knowledge of what he was talking about. Brunner won hands down by 1,129 votes and became a fixture at Westminster. These political storms blew more fiercely on paper than in actuality, although words could still lead to blows at election times. The friendship and mutual respect of Mr. Gladstone and the Duke was too strong to be irrevocably broken by political difference. The Chronicle, too, made its peace once again with the House of Eaton and with Mr. Webb at Crewe. After the incorporation of that borough, and the election of Mr. Webb as the second Mayor, 'the hatchet was buried between us,' said the paper, 'and everybody who is anybody worked with might and main for the development of the town', a task in which the Chronicle sought the aid of the Cheshire County Council, set up in 1888, and its distinguished chairman, Sir William Hodgson.

I noted in an earlier Chapter that the Chester Chronicle's circulation from 1775 to 1800 was estimated at 20,000 copies a year, and these were passed from hand to hand and read by many more people. In 1851 the figure was given as 80,048 a year. In 1875 a cryptic announcement was published to the effect that the circulation 'has doubled in the last 15 years in spite of competition with the national dailies', and thereafter the new editions in Cheshire and Flintshire were continually adding to the total. In 1882 an experiment was made with a bi-weekly edition, published every Tuesday 'for the early country trains'. It was discontinued after a few weeks. From 1890 Richard Fletcher Smith's name as printer and publisher was

replaced in the imprint by John Ward Jones, who continued to act as
general manager until some time before his death in 1914. He started
as a printing apprentice and served the paper altogether about seventy years. His first innovation was to reduce the selling price of all
the Chronicles to a penny and then to improve their appearance with
new type faces, announcing on January 17, 1891: 'This week our
readers will note the manifest improvements in the paper. From
headline to imprint it is set entirely in new type. The encouraging
reception given to the Penny Chronicle has induced the proprietors
to make it not only the largest but the best paper of its class in the
North of England.' Always up to date with new printing techniques
the Chronicle published a half-tone block on August 29 of the same
year. Old-fashioned woodcuts continued to be used for some little
time longer in advertisements. The paper was also the first in its area
to set its type by Linotype machines, two Model Ones being installed
in 1896 by the manufacturers at Altrincham.

With Frederick Coplestone in the full vigour of middle life, the
Chronicle steadily pursued its political aims and kept a close watch
on Mr. Gladstone at nearby Hawarden. The village became famous
throughout the world as the home of the great statesman and it was a
constant source of news for the London papers. Coplestone and his
young assistant editor, Frederick William Parker, were the accre-
dited correspondents of The Times, and many of the anecdotes
about Gladstone, such as his tree-felling exploits in Hawarden Park,
were given currency by them. The London papers as well as the
Chronicle went in for verbatim reports of political speeches and
Coplestone and Parker were kept busy until late in the night or early
next morning transcribing their Hawarden 'copy' for dispatch by
telegraph. There was the occasion when The Times wanted a full
account not later than 3 a.m. of a Gladstone speech at Hawarden on
a big question of the day, the Bulgarian 'atrocities'. The great man
finished speaking at 10 o'clock after going at it for nearly two hours.
Three harassed reporters took carriage to Chester, arriving at 10.45,
and 'we each had over two columns of notes to transcribe. We finished our task at 3.15, and the next morning – or that morning – The
Times appeared with a leader and a seven-columns report. They had
been as smart at their end as we at ours.'

Soon the heavy black reversed column rules were to be brought
into use. The Chronicle went into mourning first for the death of Mr.
Gladstone on May 19, 1898, and published a pictorial supplement as

well as many columns of biography and tribute. Memorial services were held in the Cathedral and at Hawarden and the Duke of Westminster organised a fund for a national memorial, of which St. Deiniol's Library founded by Gladstone at Hawarden is now part. The black rules were required again when the Duke died on December 22 a year afterwards. A family memorial service was held in the private chapel at Eaton on Christmas Day. Absent was the Duke's heir, Hugh Arthur Richard Grosvenor, who was serving against the Boers in South Africa. A great congregation attended the Cathedral service, and the first Duke's memorial in Chester was to be the restoration of the Cathedral south transept. Thirteen months later, on January 22, 1901, the old Queen died. The Victorian age was over and things were never to be the same again. At the opening of the twentieth, the Chronicle was advanced a quarter of the way into its second century.

14

From 1930 to the
bicentennial

The year is 1930, the scene the all-purpose editorial room in Fletcher's Buildings along the passage from Bridge-street Row. It is at the top of the iron staircase leading to the composing room door opposite, from which issues the soothing shuttling hum of the lino-type machines. Eight people occupy this exiguous chamber, but not all at the same time. There is space only for six, but since the reporters come and go after the manner of their kind, there are usually enough gaps at the table. The window on to the passage won't shut, summer or winter. It is propped at the bottom by an old Debrett's Peerage and at the top by Kelly's Directory of Cheshire. There isn't much security. The single wall-bracket hang-up telephone is in constant use by the reporters pursuing their inquiries. Presiding at the table is Frederick William Parker, the assistant editor, at his side the sub-editor, Hubert Smith, son of Richard Fletcher Smith, the former proprietor and publisher who died in 1912. Littered all across the table is a great pile of 'copy' which as the day wears on is transferred from time to time by a printer's devil to the composing room across the iron staircase and replenished by news parcels arriving by train and bus from Crewe, Northwich, Winsford, Sandbach, Runcorn, and Mold in Flintshire. The head office men 'write up', nonchalantly throw in their contributions, and depart for the next assignment on the day's diary.

Every now and again the foreman printer, James Lilley, a stern master in his own domain, clatters across the staircase to consult the assistant editor or to give warning that the compositors' cases of Pica and Long Primer type exclusively used for headlines are running low. Mr. Parker I see now in my mind's eye, a tall figure, at this time in his middle fifties. He wears a dusty black Homburg-type hat and keeps it on all the time. He commands authority, respect, and affection, and his word is law, in some ways more binding than the editor's.

Having marked up the diary of reporters' engagements for the day and the night with due deliberation, remarking as he always does that the morning 'calls' must be made personally and not by telephone, he patiently sorts the 'copy', passes half of it over to Hubert Smith, and together they start with scrupulous care upon the reduction of a mountain of work. Occasionally there is a shout from the bottom of the iron staircase. It is the Editor calling for proofs or the assistant editor's presence in the sanctum below. All the Chronicle editors have occupied this room since John Fletcher moved the entire concern from the yard of the Hop-pole Inn. Although spry enough, Mr. Coplestone is now a very old man indeed – nobody knows how old but well into his eighties – and he rarely climbs the iron staircase. He is a small man, somewhat stooped, dapperly dressed in a pepper-and-salt suit, with a silvery Vandyke beard, very sharp and shrewd, but with a pair of humorously twinkling eyes behind pince-nez. Only a few weeks before he has given me, a youth from school, the entry to journalism by apprenticeship at five shillings a week, with the adjuration to work hard and read everything I can lay my hands on.

'Read Dickens, boy,' he says. 'He knows about life and was a reporter once himself after he left the blacking factory.' I am already a little better acquainted with Dickens than he supposes, and it strikes me that there is something Dickensian about Mr. Coplestone himself. When some time later I pluck up enough courage to ask for a modest rise he refers me benevolently to Mr. Parker, and Mr. Parker, duly applied to, benignly refers me back to Mr. Coplestone. Just like Spenlow and Jorkins in *David Copperfield*. The old-fashioned Chronicle Office is still in many ways not so far away from its distant origins. The pace of the day's work is deliberate but unhurried. The Editor arrives punctually at 9.30 in the morning, takes a turn before the scanty fire in the grate, and sits down to write in pencil a couple of the 'leaderettes' which by the publication of the Crewe paper on Thursday will occupy two columns of the back page. Mr. Coplestone has written so much and so rapidly in his many years that the editorial hand needs the co-operation of an experienced and crafty linotype operator to decipher. This expert is Jack Dunning, grown grey in the service of the paper, and he performs the like office for Mr. Parker, who writes the City and County Notes in a hand scarcely less secretly codified than the Editor's. Only the reporters use typewriters, and then only on sufferance, because of the distraction of three-finger tapping.

His 'copy' despatched with the readiness of a long lifetime's practice, Mr. Coplestone confers first with Mr. Parker, then with Mr. Charles Smith, the portly managing director, and departs for the Town Hall to sit on the City Bench of Magistrates (he has been a J.P. since 1907) or to the Royal Infirmary, where he is on the Board of Management, or to the Rotary Club, of which he is a founder. As one of the original members of the Lancashire, Cheshire, and North Wales branch of the British Empire Cancer Campaign, the Editor has done much valued service for the Infirmary, where, with the help of his own personal efforts and the agency of the Chronicle, radium and X-ray equipment have been provided. Lately he has been immersed in the promotion of the appeal for the King George Thanksgiving Fund, to be used for a new theatre and pathology block, and arrangements are in hand for the royal opening by the Duke and Duchess of York in March, 1931. Another of Mr. Coplestone's humane interests has been the founding of the Chronicle Crippled Children's Fund, by means of which, and by the help of surgeons and voluntary collectors, surgical appliances have been provided, and many children entertained to a festive party at Christmas.

It will be seen, then, that the Editor has lost little of the legendary vigour and enthusiasm that he brought 56 years before to the founding of the Crewe and Nantwich Chronicle. And since the turn of the century he has pushed the Chronicle newspapers into Lancashire with the Runcorn and Widnes edition and started also a Saturday Evening edition of the Chester Chronicle. Structurally John Fletcher's old printing office is very much as he knew it, but it is getting too small for the battery of linotypes and other modern machinery which it now contains. Down below there has been since 1924 a three-deck Victory-Kidder press printing a 12-page paper at 10,000 or 15,000 copies an hour in place of the single-reel 8-page press in use since 1919 or earlier. Gone are the days of annual computation of the circulation. It is now running at over 40,000 a week and steadily rising. The editorial claim of May 2, 1925, on the 150th anniversary, that the Chronicle's 'strength and influence have increased as the years roll round,' is demonstrably true, so that on June 29, 1927, the company of the Chester Chronicle and Associated Newspapers Ltd. has been incorporated, with the Editor as chairman of directors and Charles Smith, a younger brother of the late Richard Fletcher Smith, as managing director and publisher. Thus the Fletcher and Smith family interests of two centuries have been consolidated.

As I am writing now from personal recollection as well as research, some of the readers of this book will share in the story as it goes forward from about 1930 as above to the present day. But more changes have come about in those 45 years than in all the former time. I will try to keep the chronology, with deviations here and there. When Mr. Coplestone died at his home, Richmond Hill, Boughton (somewhere near Ann Smith's old house), on November 19, 1932, the Chester Chronicle had ceased to be a paper of national record and its great political days were over after the First World War and the decline of the Liberal Party. But years before I first saw the venerable Editor he had fought a notable battle at Chester in the famous election of 1906. The Liberal candidate was Alfred Mond, son of Ludwig Mond, John Brunner's partner in the great concern at Northwich, and with the aid of the Chronicle and a young eloquent Welshman named David Lloyd George who came to speak for him he defeated Mr. Yerburgh, the Conservative, by 47 votes after a dramatic challenge on the count. In this contest Mr. Coplestone formed a friendship with Lloyd George which he sustained by frequent correspondence and by splendid patriotic writing in the paper during the latter's war-time leadership. After the war Mr. Coplestone was invested by King George V with the C.B.E. for service to the national cause. The war brought to the Editor two private sorrows. He lost his son, Lieut.-Commander Lewis Coplestone, in Submarine D2, and his son-in-law, Commander Alfred Coplestone-Boughey, of H.M.S. Defence, at the Battle of Jutland. When Mr. Coplestone himself died in 1932 Lloyd George remembered 'my old friend' in a letter of sympathy to the family and the paper.

To me and my generation Frederick William Parker was 'the Editor', and I always think of him as in the true Chronicle tradition and the last of the distinguished old line. His succession in 1932 was preordained. He and his old chief had shared so many news vigils and adventures for the benefit of Fleet Street and the Chronicle that he was the successor by right. He, too, was a Gladstonian, although, like the victor of Chester, Sir Alfred Mond (afterwards the first Lord Melchett), he sought later to liberalise the Tory Party. We knew him as the Editor, but he had been a resourceful reporter in his youth, and recollections of Hawarden and of Eaton Hall in the last years of the first Duke and the first two decades of 'Bendor', the famous, popular, newsworthy second Duke, never left him. He would recall the two-horse wagonette that operated from Chester every Sunday, chiefly to carry American visitors anxious to catch a glimpse of the 'G.O.M.' on his way to church or chipping away at trees in Hawarden Park. (This last diversion was the subject of a celebrated satirical speech by Lord Randolph Churchill on Chips in the Park.) Mr. Parker was on reporting duty in Hawarden Church when the Archbishop of Canterbury (Dr. Benson) collapsed and died during morning service. There were no telephones in those days to aid the reporter and he had to engage a local farmer's horse and trap to return to Chester to have his 'copy' telegraphed to London.

At Eaton Hall one day he met a Fleet Street sleuth named Edgar Wallace. The second Duke of Westminster was entertaining the King of Spain and his entourage. Wallace, afterwards famous as a writer of thrillers, did not get to know until Mr. Parker told him that the Duke had arranged a bullfight for the entertainment of the royal guest. Edgar Wallace had been 'scooped', but he took it in good part, advising the local man to send the story to his (Wallace's) paper as well as to the others. It was front-page news next morning. And the Eaton house parties on occasion included Winston S. Churchill, known to the electors of Chester as a Conservative and then as a Liberal. Mr. Parker was in the chair until his retirement in 1957 and in all that time the Chronicle Office was a model school of journalism. He saw the Chronicle through the Second World War and an almost total revolution in newspaper practice, and some aspects of the newer journalism he did not like at all. He died on March 6, 1963, aged 88, and there was a great congregation at the funeral service in Chester Cathedral.

As Mr. Coplestone had been the first chairman of the board of the company incorporated in 1927, so Mr. Charles Smith had been the first managing director and publisher. He was one of the younger sons of the large family of William Smith and Ann Fletcher. As a young man he played cricket for Boughton Hall, hunted with the Beagles, and stroked the Royal Chester Rowing Club to several victories, including the Thames Challenge Cup at Henley in 1882. Later he turned to gardening and the cultivation and exhibition of carnations, became known in the dog world as a show judge of collies, and had his own shooting in Montgomeryshire. There was a touch of the country squire about Charles Smith as I briefly remember him. He died on June 11, 1932, aged 75, and was succeeded by his nephew, Hubert Smith, Mr. Parker's sub-editor. Hubert, like his uncle, was a man of equable temperament and much kindness and good humour, so that his death not long afterwards, in 1935, was a sad blow to the editorial staff and to the management.

About this time there was at Flint Borough an ambitious Welshman in his thirties, John Gwyndaf Jones, who had joined the Chronicle from the staff of Mr. Coplestone's old paper the Caernarvon Herald. He was making a name for himself as Mr. Fred Violet's principal editorial colleague in Flintshire, where the paper was firmly established and highly regarded. Mr. Violet, at the Mold Office in the High-street, was for many years one of the best-known journalists in North Wales. The direct Smith succession in the management having ended with the untimely death of Hubert Smith, Gwyndaf Jones was called to Chester and given the job of manager, to which from the start he brought a drive and energy reminiscent of Mr. Coplestone's earlier time. He and Mr. Parker conducted the Chronicle through the second war years, dealing patiently with the Ministry of Information and all its restrictions and producing, with the aid of Mr. Jack Brett at Northwich, Mr. Alfred Dodd at Crewe (succeeding Alfred and Charles Childs, father and son), and Mr. Violet in Flintshire, the best papers they could with a staff in all departments drained away by war service. I was one of the many absentees. After the war Gwyndaf Jones, now managing director, introduced process engraving – halftone blocks had been up to this time made in Liverpool – and brought the entire printing establishment up to date. It was the biggest typographical revolution the old Chronicle had ever seen, and, as we shall see, was to be superseded by another in the 1960s and 1970s.

When I returned from the Army and was eventually appointed assistant editor I felt that I had to start all over again, so great had been the change in the techniques of journalism and the collection, make-up, and presentation of news. A new set of skills had to be learned, and a much bigger staff was needed. Those were absorbingly busy and exciting years, with the veteran Editor holding fast to first principles while his younger lieutenants swam with a tide of typographical innovation in which Pica and Long Primer were the first to sink for ever out of sight. The display advertisements were still tied with string, there were still some old-timer compositors around with snuff on their waistcoats, but the compositor's stick and the cases of well-worn hand-set type were at last falling into disuse. (I called for some of this not long ago and it was found tied up in an ancient bag.) The fast linotype operators were kings of the composing room, and they worked early and late, the best of them with astonishing speed and accuracy. Our famous long-lived rival the Courant was still coming out on Tuesday (as it does now, much altered, like ourselves, but full of new life), and the Cheshire Observer, with the Courant as its partner in ownership, was the principal vigorous competitor (as it continues to be). The Warrington Guardian newspapers then as now were strong also in Cheshire, but at last conceded to the Chronicle in Crewe and Nantwich. And away in the east, at Macclesfield, the veteran Courier, opposition champion in the political broils of the past, kept its standard. I remember misgivings in the office about the Runcorn and Widnes Chronicle, and it was discontinued in the 1950s after nearly 50 years' persevering publication.

From this period dates the expansion of an army of village correspondents in Cheshire and Flintshire, first recruited about the 1890s or earlier – clergy, schoolmasters, blacksmiths, postmistresses, parish councillors, club secretaries, and later the ladies of the Women's Institutes and Townswomen's Guilds, all of whom continue to contribute their weekly budgets of rural news. I recall their dismay (and patient loyalty) in the protracted printing strike of 1959, when we made do with an emergency bulletin and all the countryside sorely missed the big paper. Alderman William Gibson, 'father' of the County Council, said to me afterwards that 'after the Bible, the Country edition of the Chester Chronicle is the Sunday reading in the villages'. Although the company in 1939 had installed a Hoe Crabtree 10/50 rotary press of 24-page capacity, in the 1940s and 1950s it became clearer every week that 24 pages were quite inadequate for all the news and advertising – the classified columns were spilling over into the most unlikely corners of the paper – they were expected to contain. The big independent Crewe Chronicle, with its fast-growing circulation, was making heavy demands on the ten or twelve linotype machines and taking up more of the limited week's printing time on the press. Another battery of linotypes came into the composing room, but a big production decision would have to be taken sooner or later.

When Mr. Parker in 1957 decided to retire he called me into his room and said somewhat lugubriously 'The burden's yours from now on if you want it. There's nobody else. It's a lonely job. Keep at it and do your best, and do it your own way.' Next week's leaders I wrote with a faltering pen, knowing that he would read those fledgeling words in his own column on the back page with a critical eye;

and for eighteen years thereafter I have been trying to measure by that standard. It is hard to live with the memory of the old Chronicle masters. There are no great battles in this chapter. The cataclysmic First and Second World Wars, unlike that far-off domestic upheaval the American War of Independence in Chapters One and Two, were the world-wide chronicle of Fleet Street, and the regional weeklies were properly engaged keeping the record in their own corners of the home front. For this reason the files of the war years – and particularly 1914–18 – are poignant bound books of the names of missing generations of young men, names to be found again on all the town and village memorials. Post-war changes in the 1940–60 decades were many and far-reaching: the Chronicle's lines of communication back to that four-page folio of 1775, so small and yet so large in purpose and intent, were marked on the map of time but almost indistinguishable in places. But the determination of the founding fathers had never been lost sight of – 'to accelerate the commercial and domestic intelligence of the ancient and respectable city and the neighbouring counties upon a more liberal and extensive plan . . .' And that is what we have done all this time, and are doing now.

If history does not exactly repeat itself, it certainly gives presage of the future. About the time old Mr. Coplestone gave me my first job, across the world in Canada an extraordinary man in his thirties named Roy Thomson, ready to turn his hand to anything, was buying, for 200 dollars and 28 promissory notes, his first newspaper, the Timmins Press. It had one linotype machine and an obsolescent hand-fed press of an ancestry coeval with the Chronicle's flat-bed of the early nineteenth century. Thomson and his six employees all worked together feeding the machine and manually inserting a thousand copies into the folder to make an eight-page weekly paper. When I first read about this and about the resilience and indestructible self-confidence of Roy Thomson's early life, I thought of John Fletcher and of how he bought the Chronicle from John Poole, dealt adroitly with Mr. Monk of the Courant, kept the local politicians at a wary but respectful distance – and asked for advertisement money down on the counter.

The eventual appearance of Roy Thomson in Britain with the reputation of collecting 'a lot of little papers' (as Lord Beaverbrook said), his move into Scottish television, the acquisition of The Scotsman, of the Sunday Times and the Kemsley Press empire, and of The Times itself, is another story beyond the range of this book.

The relevance is that the Chester Chronicle and Associated News-papers are now part of Thomson Regional Newspapers, related to the same world-wide family of publications that embraces also the Moose Jaw Times Herald, the Yorkton Enterprise, and the Bangkok Post. The Courier of Macclesfield is in the family, too, renamed the County Express. Although we are senior in years to The Times (bicentennial 1985), there is one other of Lord Thomson's papers older than the Chronicle, the much-esteemed Press and Journal of Aberdeen. On March 27, 1965 (number 9,868) the Chester Chronicle front page said: 'The Thomson Organisation announce that an offer made on their behalf to purchase for cash the whole of the issued share capital of the Chester Chronicle and Associated Newspapers Ltd. has been accepted in respect of 92 per cent of the shares, and is unconditional. As in the case of all the Thomson Organisation news-papers, the Chester Chronicle and its associated newspapers will re-tain their editorial independence . . .'

After 190 years the paper had changed hands and the residual links, still represented among the outgoing directors, with the Fletcher-Smith family descent were severed. John Gwyndaf Jones became chairman of the local board of the new company and I con-tinued in the editorial chair. There was, naturally, some speculation about the future of our papers, and when I saw that one newspaper had headed its report of our affairs with 'Chronicle goes out of local hands' it was clearly necessary to make matters absolutely plain. In the paper of April 3, 1965, I wrote 'If the implication is that, quite suddenly, after nearly two hundred years, we have ceased to be true to ourselves, or indigenous to Cheshire and Flintshire, and that our operations will be remotely conducted by master minds having only a distant community of interest with the area and the life of its people, the implication is ludicrously untrue and hopelessly wide of the mark.' Change of ownership has enhanced the capacity of the Chronicle to do the job it has always done. The editorial indepen-dence of the paper and the freedom and responsibility of the editor to act upon his own judgment are as scrupulously guarded now as at any time in the past. Of the quality of the paper in the past decade I say nothing – that is for others to judge – but it is impossible not to notice that in improving ourselves we have been the cause of emula-tive improvement in other newspapers round about us.

The gradual changes of the last ten years have been chiefly com-mercial and mechanical, and on a large scale. Some of these changes were inevitable and had been prepared for by the former directors, who in 1964 at last gave way to my insistent demand that news should be restored to the front page (where it was in the eighteenth century) and the gothic lettering or so-called 'Old English' superseded in the masthead. A new title in roman was designed and a variant of it heads all the Chronicles today. In the same week in May, 1964, the Middlewich edition was given a title separate from Winsford and took its independent place with the trinity of papers in mid-Cheshire. In the 1940s and 1950s web-offset lithography was challenging letterpress as the modern printing system, the first major development in the craft for half a century. With the 24-page paper bulging at the seams, and the editor and the advertisement manager at their wits' end in the competition for column inches, thought was given to the suitability of the new printing system to the Chronicle papers. Gwyndaf Jones had seen it at work in Tokyo on his visit there as President of the Newspaper Society. He now went to the Continent to examine its operation there.

As a result the directors in May, 1963, ordered from Hoe Crabtree a 10/50 Spearhead offset-litho press designed to print 32 pages broadsheet, with a colour satellite. The premises of a wine shop next door to head office having been acquired, the deep cellar was reconstructed and made ready to receive the new press. Access was provided to the service area of the Grosvenor-Laing shopping precinct, at the hub of the commercial life of the city. (See the final Chapter for a study of this notable enterprise by the Grosvenor estate executors.) Before construction of the press was completed the paper was bought by the Thomson Organisation, and the new proprietors added a unit to the original specification, increasing the paging to 40 and extending the colour range.

Meanwhile an intensive process of retraining in web-offset techniques was going on in the composing room, in the former process department, and in the sub-editors' room, where the new system's flexibility in the imaginative treatment of page lay-outs was under study. The first casualty was the foundry, for no longer would it be necessary to cast cumbersome printing plates by means of moulded hot metal. The hour of the light sensitised photographic printing plate was at hand. Mr. Gwyndaf Jones retired in July, 1965, and handed over to Mr. James S. Adam as the first managing director of the Thomson régime in September. On July 29, 1966, the Flintshire County Herald, bought in June, 1960, was the first paper to be run off on the new press and all the Chronicles followed in the succeeding week. The rotary press in service since 1939 was afterwards sold and may still be in commission in a North Wales newspaper office. Crabtree presses have a long and useful life. Henceforth stereo was replaced by screened film, and although hot metal (lead) continued in some stages of production, pages were designed and finished in paste-up, including display headlines and display advertising. In addition to the advantages of colour in news and advertising offset-litho immediately gave to the Chronicle papers a typographical clarity and a depth and sharpness of reproduction of half-tone pictures that was never before possible.

About the same time that the Chronicle 'went web-offset' the Thomson Organisation were projecting the first computer-controlled, photo-set, web-offset paper in Britain, the Reading Evening Post, which started publication in 1966. Behind this now highly successful experiment (followed by others, the first new evening papers to be established for some years) was research by the Universities of London and Newcastle-upon-Tyne into the use of computers in printing and type composition and the American, Japanese, and Continental experience in automatic and film typesetting.

Mr. Adam, who had been general manager of The Scotsman before his appointment to Chester, became managing director of the Evening Gazette at Middlesbrough in 1969. He was succeeded at Chester by the present managing director, Mr. John S. Long, who also came from Edinburgh and The Scotsman. In 1970 Mr. Long made a fresh initiative, establishing the Chester Mail, the first free newspaper to be published within the Thomson Organisation. Towards the end of 1971, anticipating Welsh local government reorganisation and the coalition of Flintshire and Denbighshire in 1974, a second edition of the Chronicle 'Welsh' paper (it contains a regular weekly article in that language) was started, incorporating the Flintshire County Herald. I appointed a Welsh editor, Mr. Rex Thelwall, in 1972 as a signal recognition of the importance of the Welsh connection in the paper's affairs and of the developing social and industrial character of the two counties. The next move was into Wrexham and the immediate Denbighshire territory riding with Cheshire, Flintshire, and Shropshire. This edition began in February, 1974, and an editorial and advertising office was opened in Wrexham town in March. And in this bicentennial year the Chronicle has welcomed into its family the Whitchurch Herald, published on the Shropshire–Cheshire border. In printing production the logical next move into computer type-setting was made in 1973–4, when photo-typesetters with built-in computers were introduced. Teletypesetter keyboards are gradually superseding the linotype machines and the electronic keyboard operators look into a kind of small television screen and see the letters they are setting. The old black art of printing has indeed undergone a change, and the scientific advance is continuing.

The voluminous Chronicle of today, sometimes of more than 60 pages and with a series circulation of over 80,000 – rising I hope in my time to 100,000 – is an example of the utility of the provincial weekly Press as a market for goods, services, merchandise, and employment. The Chronicle carried advertisements from the first issue and was among the first papers to classify its columns. That good man of business John Fletcher would observe with astonishment and satisfaction the advertisement content and variety of his paper today. And he would also be pleased to see that in all this prodigality (compared with his own four and six pages) there is hopefully always space for the single advertiser who wants to buy or sell, or has a job to offer or seeks a job himself, and that many long-established businesses have advertised in the paper for generations. It is difficult to write about the paper in one's own time. But perhaps I may be permitted to say that the Chronicle's deeply concerned reporting of the foot-and-mouth scourge which decimated Cheshire's cattle population in 1967–8 was widely appreciated and commended and afterwards helped to start the farmers on the road back to restocked herds. The deputy editor, J. Ormsby Jones, and I subsequently wrote a book about it. Always the paper has been watchful of the welfare of the city of Chester, seeking to safeguard its unique character and historic treasures in the inevitable process of development. The next Chapter brings this under review. While recognising the desirability of reform, the Chronicle opposed the harsh dismemberment of Cheshire proposed in the Maud Report on Local Government Reorganisation and counselled constructive counter-action by the county authorities in a series of articles examining the county's historic ethnographic status, its agriculture and industry, and its leadership in educational provision, especially in secondary schools. The less draconian proposals of the government of the day were welcomed and they are now in operation for better or worse. And Chester under the new dispensation has its city status renewed (first Mayor, Sir Walter Lynnet, 1257) and draws into the Council Chamber the representatives of the surrounding countryside.

The old editors would not think much of our modern political stance, but times change as they themselves knew well enough. In the last twenty years the paper has been independent of all political parties, although the long Whig and Liberal allegiance had an echo in support for Mr. Grimond's leadership, and after Mr. Macmillan's 'never had it so good' British readers were recommended to give Mr. Wilson and Labour a turn. In the historic crisis election of 1974 we saw a Liberal revival, in which six million voters were able to return only 14 MPs, the Liberals refusing to form a coalition with the Conservatives, a virtual stalemate between the two big parties, and Labour back in minority office – after our two hundred years of the political swings and roundabouts. I wonder what some of my famous predecessors would make of all that – or of the subsequent election in the same year, with a bare Labour majority and an extraordinary splinter of parties in a House of Commons faced with unprecedented political, economic, and social problems?

15
Two hundred years of Chester
1775–1975

It is a summer's afternoon in the year 1789 and we are among a party of visitors walking about the city with William Cowdroy, Esq., Editor of the Chester Chronicle. We are fortunate to have such an excellent guide. Mr. Cowdroy, in his late thirties, I judge, is vivacious and voluble, with a glancing wit and a felicitous turn of phrase. He is also primed with information of times past and present and very willing to impart it. He tells us that, in addition to his journalistic work, he is writing some memoirs of the old city, of which he is a native, and among these are an account of bear and bull baiting at the High Cross (a brutal pastime of the citizens formerly participated in by the Mayor and Corporation as spectators leaning excitedly out of the windows of the Pentice across the way) and an anecdote of the time of Bloody Mary concerning a Dean of St. Paul's who was outwitted by the landlady of the Blue Posts Inn in Bridge-street. (This inn, now a shop, he points out to us.) We have met Mr. Cowdroy by appointment not at his newspaper office in the Hop-pole Yard but at his house, one of the quaint mid-seventeenth-century Nine Houses in the shadow of the City Wall in Park-street. From thence he conducts us on to the Wall near the Wishing Steps (the fable of which he relates) and we remark upon the width of the Wall passage-way and the remarkably fine preservation of the fabric, much of which is sandstone and perishable. How is it, we ask, that a defensive Wall of such antiquity has not become ruinous or in parts destroyed, for, miraculously, the circuit is entire?

'As to that,' says Mr. Cowdroy, 'we are indebted to the trading opulence and mercantile spirit of the gentlemen in the linen branch belonging to our sister kingdom of Ireland – a kind of murage duty of twopence on every hundred yards of linen imported into the city being paid for this purpose.' (You will see that our guide has a drily consequential way of expressing himself.) He goes on to explain that the Irish trade is carried on in some one hundred and eleven shops at the Linenhall, built some ten years before, just off Watergate-street, convenient to the Custom House and Port. Taking up our point about the defensive character of the Walls, Mr. Cowdroy says that they have not served any defensive or offensive purpose since the Civil War, although the Watergate, Northgate, and the sally-ports were walled up temporarily at the time of the '45, under apprehension of the Scotch rebels attempting to enter the city. Now the Walls are used by the citizens, and by strangers such as ourselves, as an airy perambulation the like of which for completeness can be found nowhere else in the kingdom. Two city officers called Murengers still collect the duty for the upkeep of the stonework and parapet, which need constant repair.

At the Newgate, or Peppergate, our complaisant guide tells us a romantic old tale about a Mayor's daughter eloping through the postern with her lover. We admire the handsome Eastgate, completed just twenty years before at the expense of Lord Richard Grosvenor. Here suddenly we are in the midst of the city. 'There below runs the Great Watling Street,' says Mr. Cowdroy, 'for on this site, separating the Forest or Foregate-street and Eastgate-street, stood the Roman Porta Principalis within living memory. Our highly esteemed historian and topographer, Thomas Pennant, Esq., of Holywell in Flintshire, has recently set down his recollection of the demolition of the old gate in 1768. On taking down the case of Norman masonry the Roman appeared full in view, two arches formed of vast stones, the pillar between them dividing the street exactly in two. Mr. Pennant remembers seeing the figure of a Roman soldier placed between the tops of the arches fronting the Watling Street.'

From the Eastgate Mr. Cowdroy conducts us by a stairway into the busy street below and, passing under the pillars of the Royal Hotel, informs us that in that place Mr. Beacroft's dancing assemblies are held fortnightly from November to March and card assemblies every Thursday. 'There are very brilliant assemblies of beauty and fashion and the best society in the city and the county,' says Mr. Cowdroy (sententiously, as I thought), 'held in the Race Weeks at the Town Hall Exchange in Northgate-street, and a more modest affair for the local people takes place there the first Tuesday of the month from November to April.' The most convenient way of getting about the city, especially for the ladies in winter-time, he says, is by chair for which sixpence is the common rate within the limit of the Bars at the top of the Foregate, the Maypole in Handbridge, the

Crane and the Port side of the city, and Further Northgate-street. Beyond these points the fare is doubled. 'Your chairman is a cheerful, patient fellow,' he goes on. 'He will wait for you one hour for a shilling and afterwards at the rate of ninepence an hour. Some of our modern elegant houses have the convenience of a porch at the front door for the neat accommodation of a sedan chair.'

In Eastgate-street we remark upon the mire in the kennels, the uneven distribution of the cobblestones, the jumble of carts, stalls, and wagons, and the disorder occasioned presumably by the frequent markets for fowl, butter, and cheese which are held here and in St. Werburgh's-lane and Fleshmongers'-lane leading off. St. Werburgh's-lane, as we thought, is a very mean approach to the Cathedral. We exclaim also at the extraordinary disparity of the houses on each side of the Eastgate-street, some standing high with pitched roofs, others grovelling low, and the Rows squeezed dismally through them with washing strung on a line between the stalls. 'Quaint and venerable indeed!' says Mr. Cowdroy, with a sweep of the arm towards the fantastically broken skyline. 'A model of everything antique and perhaps not much credit to our system of renovation and improvement. And yet, methinks, there is something in the variety. Even on this south side, where there are new-built houses and shops, they are so intermixed with old ones as to make the general appearance even more motley and grotesque, as you can see. But is it not like a scene of human life, made up of all kinds of characters?' Mr. Cowdroy's eye twinkles: he is about to practise a pleasantry upon us. 'Look over there. What do you see? A modern mansion, just finished, standing between two gothic structures, the youngest probably not less than two hundred years old – like the picture of a fine gentleman of the present day placed between the portraitures of a brace of beaux of the days of Queen Bess!' With which moralistic sally our guide leads us through the press of city folks and farmers and market women from the country.

'And here,' says he, 'is the Cross. While Chester stands, and the Roman street plan endures, this will be the centre, as it has been from ancient days. The High Cross, thrown down by the Parliament men at the end of the Siege, stood over against the Pentice at St. Peter's Church there.' The Pentice? – we must ask him about that. At the corner of Eastgate-street and Bridge-street – which, he tells us, continues the line of the Watling Street – we notice a curious small square stone building with a kind of basin at the top, and nearby, unmistakably, the pillory, from its appearance long disused. 'None has stood there for nearly twenty years past,' says Mr. Cowdroy. 'And as for the curious building, that is the Conduit for the city water. It was built about 1582 and is now supplemented and in part superseded by the waterworks at the Bridge Gate and by the cistern at the Exchange. Can you imagine it flowing with good Rhennish? Formerly, on festive occasions, it was the prodigal custom to turn the Conduit water into wine, the citizens freely imbibing a certain portion of the juice of the grape, properly qualified, spouting from the pipes. What a Bacchanalian debauch!'

Our guide the Editor is in a humorously musing mood as he directs our attention to St. Peter's Church. 'Seven years ago,' says he, 'St. Peter had a lofty spire steeple which, being struck by lightning, had to be taken down. For the want of it, the church, methinks, exhibits so naked and dilapidated an appearance as to give the idea, if you will pardon me, of a lady on a windy day having lost her high-crowned hat! If the citizens at large do not throw in their mite, poor St. Peter must go to bed many winter nights without his night-cap.' There is much aptness in this whimsical observation, and the neglected plight of the old church is not improved by a shanty-like structure precariously attached to its south side, fronting the Bridge-street. 'Precarious it may appear to be,' says Mr. Cowdroy, 'and like enough it has not much longer to cling on to St. Peter, but the truth is it has been there since the fifteenth century. That, gentlemen, still serves as the Town Office and the occasional seat of the magistracy. It is all that is left of the Pentice (or Penthouse, as I suppose), in former times the place of the Mayor and Corporation and the entire town government. Kings have been entertained there. Until eight years or so ago it occupied the entire south side and part of the north side of the church and, with the shops about it, was so obstructive of carriages and foot passengers converging on the Cross that, as my newspaper reported, a Corporation Assembly determined to remove all the shops and that part of the Pentice at the bottom and west of the Northgate-street.'

All parts of the city can be looked into from the Cross, and we glimpse the cavernous, heavily gabled and projecting Rows of Watergate-street leading down to the Port of Chester, the Crane wharf and the shipyards on the river. There is not much light of day in those Rows. Do the tradesmen who have their shops below also dwell in those dark precincts? we ask our guide. 'Assuredly they do,' answers Mr. Cowdroy. 'More people live within the city by far than in the suburbs of Handbridge and Boughton. And I am often asked, supposing the city to consist of 15,000 inhabitants, where are they all, for they are not visible? It is true that a stranger, on first entering the city, might think that it is but thinly inhabited, the enveloped situation of the shops, which are mostly covered by Rows, tending to hide a considerable number of citizens from the eye. The sequestered character of the Rows, I may add, also affords shelter to night-time skulkers and desperadoes who lurk in the shadow of lanes and alleys leading into the back quarters.' He tells us also of the former practice of the magistracy of licensing public stews and brothels in the city, these ill-favoured premises being white-washed to render them conspicuous – 'an outward and visible sign, though not of the inward and spiritual grace,' adds Mr. Cowdroy pleasantly. The name of Cuppin-street derives from the brothel or cupping-house that once existed there.

Turning into Northgate-street, Mr. Cowdroy conducts us through the maze of Shoemakers' Row, pointing out over the way the Theatre Royal. This, he says, is annually opened under the management of Mr. Whitlock and Mr. Munden by one of the first companies in the kingdom outside London. 'As for the building itself,' he goes on, 'though now most commodiously fitted out for its purpose, it has suffered more vicissitudes than any other place in this city, where time has wrought many remarkable changes, I can assure you. No circumstance can evince the strange mutations to which things are liable more than this place, which was originally a chapel dedicated to St. Nicholas and devoted to religion; afterwards a common hall devoted to justice; next, a warehouse devoted to trade; and now, a playhouse devoted to amusement.' This apt epitome of a playhouse and the justness of Mr. Cowdroy's words on the unpredictable chance of things make a sensible impression upon us. Chester is indeed old and strange, as if a special providence is working here. God's providence – as in the house in Watergate-street? Or the influence of the Roman deities? I soon banish such recondite thoughts, for at the end of Shoemakers' Row the town square opens out and here, opposite to the Exchange (where, since the last century, the city courts of sessions, crownmote and portmote, and the Common Council have been accommodated, a remnant of the Town Office only being left at the Pentice) is a thriving market scene, fish, vegetables, and the flesh shambles of the country butchers.

No people hidden away in Rows here! Opposite is the West Door of the Cathedral and, adjoining, the Abbey Court, where are a number of handsome new houses on two sides and the Bishop's Palace, erected about the middle of the century. Here Mr. Cowdroy consults his fob watch and excuses himself. He must return to the duties of the Chester Chronicle. He is sorry: there is so much more to see and to dilate upon, but time presses. He takes his leave with a recommendation to us to examine the statue of Queen Anne in her niche over the door of the Exchange. 'Observe how she has been defaced by the rioters in the last election. I am a Whig, but I voted Tory to spite them!' Then, as an after-thought, he says 'Go down Love-lane, as all men should. It is off the Foregate, and is celebrated for the manufacture of tobacco-pipes, the fame of which has been puffed in almost every town and city throughout England and Ireland, proving that the Cestrians are the most social and convivial set of people on earth. Adieu!' And he is gone, the kindly, humorous, thoughtful, and memorable William Cowdroy, Esq. . . .

In the foregoing I have summoned up a scene as it might have been, using (as readers learned in local lore will have guessed) William Cowdroy's *Guide to Chester* published by Fletcher in 1789, and my purpose in this chapter is to attempt to picture the city as it was in the paper's first decade and then to trace the changes of two hundred years, slow enough to begin with but rapidly accelerating as we near our own time. As Poole, Fletcher, Cowdroy and their successors went about the business of the Chester Chronicle and one century turned into another, in what familiar scenes did they move? And how many of those scenes are familiar to the citizens of today? As the years go by, there is no lack of contemporary description. It is there in the files of the paper and in the studies I have made from them linked to a wider reading of the historical development into the present day. It is there also (as I have said in Chapter Three) in the books written by the Chronicle editors, beginning with Cowdroy's *Guide* and ending fifty-four years later with John Trevor's introductory essay to the *Panorama of Chester* based on Hemingway's great *History*. In quoting any of these I feel I am at home: they are prescriptively a Chronicle copyright, so to speak, in perpetuity. In addition there are the writings of Thomas Pennant, John Broster, William Bingley, the brothers Lysons, Thomas Hughes, and, of course, George Ormerod, each of whom added touches to the picture.

If in the night-time the shades of the Chronicle founding printers and journalists revisit what is left of the Hop-pole Paddock and our own Fletcher's Buildings (where the shell of the old structure is preserved within the many modern accretions and is appropriately listed as of historic significance) and haunt the city centre, they will not fail to recognise the landmarks, familiar to them as to us, but how changed! To them, two hundred years ago, the city had all the marks of extreme antiquity – the streets narrower than they are today because of the overhanging gables, the Rows darker and more mediaeval, the Cathedral sandstone incredibly time-worn and in parts ruinous, the Walls retaining more of their frowning Civil War aspect, with the old Bridge Gate and its water tower and the Dee Mills, the forbidding Northgate and its infamous dungeon – and everywhere cobblestones. Marvelling in the midst of the modern city, they would think, somehow it looks the same and yet it is not the same at all – it is not two hundred years older but two hundred years younger! And the illusion would be created mostly, of course, by the repetition in the nineteenth century and after of Tudor styles and motifs in new buildings and by very skilful restoration of old ones. For some well-remembered places our ancestors, revisiting the glimpses of the moon, would search in vain, including the site of the first Chronicle office and the Hop-pole Yard itself. The coaching Inn survived until this century, a dwindling shadow of its former self, and the Yard or Paddock occupying the rectangle within Foregate-street, Frodsham-street, the City Wall, and the Kaleyards is mostly now shopping precinct and car park. Where the printing office was I have never precisely determined. It could have been where Messrs Phillipson and Golder had a printing establishment until recent years. Or it could have been nearer to Foregate-street to which it had access by a passage, as I have imagined in Chapter One.

Cowdroy, as we have seen, saw the Pentice at St. Peter's Church in its last days. It was finally swept away in 1803 and the last court to be held there, the Sheriffs', removed to the Exchange. This building, brought into use upon its completion in 1698, was well known to our first scribes, and it was here that John Fletcher read the Riot Act in the election of 1826, as we have seen in Chapter Five. It was the headquarters of the city government, the law courts, the place of election of the Mayor and officers, and the chamber of the Common Council. It was, in fact, the Town Hall, the civil and social centre for 165 years.

Pennant, writing in the early 1780s, noted the civic administration as still divided between the Pentice, where the Sheriffs, Recorder, and aldermen determined civil cases, and the Exchange, where in the Common Hall the courts of crownmote and portmote, distinctive to Chester, were held, the Mayor presiding, assisted by the Recorder. The Common Council, consisting of the Mayor, two Sheriffs, Recorder, and 40 Council men, met in the Exchange. Our next informant is Bingley. He saw the Exchange in 1798 as an elegant fabric supported on five columns and containing a large Common Hall, a mansion house for the Corporation assemblies and entertainments, and a subscription library. The west side was filled up with shops. Cowdroy mentioned Queen Anne's statue on the top of the south front – the Exchange faced south, not east, as does the present Town Hall – and the indignities she had suffered from the rioters in the election of 1784. According to the account in the Chronicle, her Majesty received further injury in the election of 1812, when she lost part of her hands and the globe and sceptre were broken off. Near to the Exchange stood the Engine House where the fire engines were kept, with the keys at the Coffee House next door. Broster in 1795 described the Engine House as a neat building with Corinthian columns.

On the spot as they were, the firemen were unable to save the Exchange when it caught fire on December 31, 1862. We turn to the Chronicle of January 3, 1863 (number 4653):

TERRIFIC CONFLAGRATION AT CHESTER
Destruction of the Town Hall and Exchange

On Tuesday evening last this city was the scene of a terrific conflagration. Shortly after six o'clock the attention of the chief constable, inspector of police, and several other persons who were in the office of the former at the Town Hall, was arrested by a crackling noise overhead, and on proceeding to the Sessions Court to ascertain the cause, it was perceived that the north end of the room was on fire . . . The hose reel was quickly brought into play, and no time was lost in bringing the Corporation engines (three in number) to the spot . . . Before the engines could be got to work (and when they did work the supply of water, we are told, was not equal to the emergency) the fire had taken such hold on the building that all efforts to save it became hopeless . . . The engines played until six o'clock the following morning, when the fire was so far got under that the three of them ceased, and the new engine belonging to the city was deemed requisite to put it entirely out, which it did several hours afterwards. It is scarcely necessary to state that the New Market Hall and the neighbouring property were exposed to great danger and fears were entertained of their safety, but happily, through the active exertions of the fire brigade and others, the damage was confined to the Exchange . . .

The inside of this building was surrounded with portraits of civic celebrities, and in the Pentice Court there was a full-length portrait of George III, presented to the Corporation by the late Marquis of Westminster. In this room there were also numerous portraits of benefactors to the city charities. We are glad to say that all the portraits, with the exception of about three, are saved; as well as all the muniments, Corporation plate, furniture and other property of value. The Exchange with its contents was insured for £5,000 in the London Union Office. A figure of Queen Anne fixed in a niche at the south side of the building is entirely preserved.

Good Queen Anne, who had survived the election mobs and the Exchange fire, eventually found another niche between Bonewaldesthorne's Tower and the Water Tower on the Walls, only to be completely destroyed by the mindless vandals of our own time. The city's treasures, including the archives, are safe enough today in the Record Office of the present Town Hall, which was opened by the Prince of Wales (afterwards King Edward VII) on October 15, 1869. It was after a fire here in 1897 that the existing handsome Council Chamber was redesigned by the Chester architect T. M. Lockwood. You will remember that Cowdroy in his catalogue of the various stages in the life of St. Nicholas's Chapel (the Theatre Royal in his time) said that in its second transformation it was a Common Hall devoted to justice. It was a Music Hall when the Exchange went on fire, and, entirely in accordance with its strange history, it reverted for a short period to its former use as a hall of justice. Sir Horatio Lloyd, one of the more distinguished of the city Recorders, has related how, upon the destruction of the Exchange, the Courts were homeless and were obliged to sit temporarily in the Music Hall, the Cathedral Refectory, and the Corn Exchange in Eastgate-street. 'When I became Recorder in 1866,' he said, 'the foundation-stone of the present Town Hall had just been laid; and as it was not to be completed for four years, the late Duke of Westminster (then Member for the city) was good enough, at my request, to pilot a Bill through Parliament enabling the City Courts to be held for five years at the Castle . . . and the sittings were held at the Castle until the present Town Hall was made ready in 1869.'

The 'old' Market Hall was nearing completion when its neighbour the Exchange was burnt down and luckily was not involved in the conflagration. In the fire-fighting conditions of over a century ago ('the supply of water, we are told, was not equal to the emergency') the Market Hall could have been destroyed before it was opened to the public, an event which took place on March 10, 1863. Built on a sociable site (the White Lion, often mentioned in these pages, stood here), the Market was a cheerful, friendly place, a common hall for town and country for just over a century. For the first time it took within doors the street markets which had been held almost since trading began in the open space outside. And on its main east front it had a remarkably erratic public clock which, in harmony with the unhurried business within, frequently allowed time to go slow or stand still. In place of the old Market there is today the Forum, rearing its aggressive, twentieth-century tiered front like a challenge to the Town Hall Gothic next door. Large and lively, it has a spacious approach to the stalls area, but (as I see it) the façade is alien to the scale and style of Chester. (Doubtless, however, as the twentieth century turns into the twenty-first, the Forum will be considered as out of date as its predecessor.)

In all the old prints of Chester the mass of the Dee Mills are seen looming through the arch of the Bridge Gate. In one form or another the Mills existed from the Conquest to the twentieth century.

> I care for nobody, no, not I,
> And nobody cares for me

sang the Miller of Dee, and for such defiance the Fates burnt down his Mills four times. Fire and water were their elements. The Chronicle of Friday, October 2, 1789 (number 749) reported the fire which broke out at midnight on the previous Sunday: 'The whole building and its extensive appurtenances were entirely consumed, leaving a part of the walls only standing. The loss is believed to be little less than £4,000, the principal part of which must be sustained by Mr. Orford, the tenant, who is universally pitied as a worthy, industrious character.' The Mills were rebuilt once again. Then, on Saturday, March 6, 1819, again a little before midnight, the citizens, wondering at the wheeling lights in the sky, were drawn pell mell to a fantastic, macabre scene down by the river and the Bridge. The fire began in the upper storey of the Mills. 'The progress of the flames was extremely rapid,' wrote the Chronicle reporter (March 12, number

2279), 'the night mild and calm, and in half an hour the entire fabric presented one vast volume of flame. There was a great quantity of corn, both barley and wheat, on the premises, and the flames, ascending to an immense height, illuminated the country through-out a circuit of several miles – presenting a magnificent but terrific spectacle . . . Every endeavour was used to save the property in the mill, but about one hundred bags of corn only were thrown out. Mr. Frost with much difficulty and appalling risk contrived to snatch his books from the general ruin; but a man considerably advanced in years, named Davies, fell a victim to his intrepidity. He was burnt literally to a cinder, and when found, about 11 o'clock on Sunday morning, merely the body, shoulders, and thighs remained, parched into one indistinguishable mass, not three feet in length. The un-fortunate man left a widow and eight children, for whom a sub-scription has been opened . . .' That fire, you would suppose, was death to the Dee Mills. But not so. On the rock of tradition (and the insurance money) the great mass of the building rose yet again, and once more was partially burnt down in 1847.

Some time after 1910 the Mills were removed for ever and on the site now is an electricity sub-station. Fire danger in Chester has always been very great. In all periods from the Middle Ages the city has been compactly built, full of timber, and interlocked by Rows and shops in depth. An unchecked outbreak could indeed spread like wildfire. 'There is scarcely a town in England,' wrote Hemingway, 'where old buildings are so closely huddled together as in the central parts of our city.' The city fire brigades in our own time have devel-oped a high skill in containment of fires that threatened the core of the city.

Because the Cathedral is within the Walls and therefore in the midst of the city and not set apart on a hill as some other Cathedrals are, many changes have taken place round about it in the past two hundred years and many changes, too, in the great Abbey church itself since Poole and Cowdroy, Fletcher, Hanshall, and Hemingway all in turn expressed their concern about the condition of the fabric. After Bingley, who beheld the Cathedral in 1798 as 'one of the most heavy, irregular, and ragged piles . . . its exterior seems fast moul-dering to decay', Hanshall in 1816 described the outer walls as in a very ruinous state and recommended that the whole outside should be 'chipped'. 'We see many structures much older than this with less mournful evidences of decay,' wrote Hemingway in 1831. 'It is built of red soft sandstone from some of the neighbouring quarries, which on exposure to the air soon becomes friable and gradually wastes. It is greatly to be lamented . . . that owing to the low state of the Chapter revenues the whole building was suffered to fall into a serious state of dilapidation before it was attended to. In consequence of this, some of the most distinguished and excellent parts were so completely ruined that no art could repair or preserve them. A subscription was however set on foot throughout the diocese about a dozen years ago and a handsome sum was collected, though insufficient to restore the grandeur of its former architectural dignity.' Hemingway was referring to the calling in by the Chapter of Thomas Harrison, architect of the Grosvenor Bridge and the reconstructed Castle. Fittingly, as we may think, he was the first rejuvenator of the Cathedral, for the south and west sides were refaced according to his advice.

Alterations to the Lady Chapel and the Choir followed, and from 1868 to 1876 George Gilbert Scott was engaged in rescuing almost the entire building, and so vigorous was the restoration that he undertook that I have heard the Cathedral as we know it today described as 'Edwardian'. In a famous lecture to the Chester Archaeological Society in 1870 Sir Gilbert Scott explained the magnitude of his task. 'The decay of the external stonework throughout the Cathedral is most lamentable – probably no building in England has suffered so severely. In many parts, in fact, it is impossible to retain any portion of the old stones, so that restoration means renewal. Such has been the case with the eastern clerestory, with almost the whole of the Lady Chapel, and with the central tower. The decay had gone deep into the stone and left its courses projecting, rounded, and shapeless, like the layers of a mouldering rock . . . It is a distressing kind of work, yet if conscientiously carried out it is the saving of the old design, even though the old material gives place to new . . .' The Cathedral's beauty had been sadly dimmed by decay and barbarous repairs, said the architect, and had come down to that time a mere wreck of what it once was, 'a melancholy relic of former ages and a reproach to our own.'

The work was continued by Sir Arthur Blomfield and into this century by Charles James Blomfield and by Giles Gilbert Scott. F. H. Crossley's hammer-beam roof over the Refectory was completed in 1939. When Sir George Gilbert Scott's major renovations were going on the Cathedral had a famous visitor in the novelist, Henry James, whose impressions of Chester I have quoted in Chapter Three. He sat in the choir stalls to hear what he regretfully described as a disappointing sermon by his fellow writer Charles Kingsley, then a canon of the Cathedral. But he did not stop there. He committed to paper a characteristically Jamesian piece of fine writing and even finer perception: 'The vast oaken architecture of the stalls, climbing vainly against the dizzier reach of the columns, the beautiful English voices, the little rosy "King's scholars" sitting ranged beneath the pulpit, the light beating softly down from the cold clerestory . . . every element in the scene gave it a great spectacular beauty.' And he noted the intonations and cadences, resonance and melody of the service, and the affirmative presence of faith in a structure 'darkened and devoured by time.'

In 1969 the Chronicle and other newspapers helped to launch an Appeal Fund for £300,000. In an editorial of January 10 (number 10,065) I wrote: 'Another century has gone by since Sir Gilbert Scott's restoration. There are more remedial jobs to be done: repair of the stonework, including the central tower and turrets, re-roofing of the Cloisters and Chapter House, installation of modern heating systems in the Refectory and Chapter House, a major renovation of the organ, and the construction of a separate Bell Tower.' The earlier announcement of the Bell Tower plan invoked some criticism in the paper – criticism of the design, of the removal of the bells from the Central Tower to a separate new structure in the south-east precinct, and of the wisdom of consuming funds in this way which could be devoted to more immediate practical Christian causes. In answer, the Dean's practical argument for the separate Bell Tower was that it will remove the stress of change-ringing from the Central Tower, provide a centre for the diocesan bellringers, and cost less than putting the re-cast bells back into the old Tower. 'As for the rest of the criticism,' I wrote, commenting on the letters we had received in the newspaper office, 'has the Cathedral's Christian witness of eight centuries no longer any meaning for us? To think so, surely, is to subscribe to the self-conscious hedonism of our time, in which a kind of militant idealism goes together with the most corrupt cynicism . . . It is our turn to honour our trusteeship for the ever-continuing care of the Cathedral.' I had the feeling that my predecessors would approve of those words and of the ever-continuing care bestowed on the Cathedral since their time. Hanshall's hope that measures would be taken to 'preserve the building some centuries longer' has been fulfilled.

The first major 'redevelopment' of Chester began in the Chronicle's second decade, when, about 1786, Thomas Harrison submitted plans for new county buildings, Shire Hall, courts, and prison, to be erected on the site of the old Castle, and continued until 1832, when Princess Victoria opened the Grosvenor Bridge. This period may properly be described as Chester's Harrison period. The Castle complex, the Grosvenor Bridge, the Northgate, the City Club in Northgate-street (originally the Commercial News Rooms), Watergate House, St. Martin's Lodge in Nicholas-street, Dee Hills in Boughton, and the Sessions House at Knutsford are all his. Impressed by the site, and the views to be obtained from it, he also prepared several designs for the tower to be erected on the summit of Moel Fammau, high point of the Clwydian range of hills, visible from most parts of Chester, to mark the jubilee of George III. One of the less elaborate designs was accepted, the first stone was laid on October 25, 1810, but the structure, intended to rise to 150 feet, was never completed. In 1896 a great storm brought down the masonry. Wind and weather over a century and a half had reduced the tower to a ruinous pile when in 1970 the schools, foresters, and conservationists of Flintshire and Denbighshire decided to restore it as a project for the Prince of Wales's Countryside Award in European Conservation Year. The restoration won the award, and on November 2, 1970, Prince Charles, in his dual capacity as Prince of Wales and Earl of Chester, climbed the mountain to inspect the work. Chronicle reporters and cameramen were in the Prince's party, following the same path taken by the paper's reporter on October 25, 1810.

Although he never visited Greece, Harrison brought the Greek Revival to Chester and in doing so added to the extraordinary diversity of the city architecture. Thomas Harrison (1744–1829), a master of the monumental, was, from all accounts, a man of much personal modesty, honoured in Chester, North Wales, and the North-West in his lifetime but not fully acknowledged until today as one of the greatest architects and engineers of the first quarter of the nineteenth century. His designs were bold, large, and lasting. He imposed the first big changes which were to transform the eighteenth-century city

into the Chester we see today. The eight-storey monolithic block of
the County Police Headquarters, built 1964–7, now stands over
against the Grand Entrance of Harrison's Castle, but instead of
dwarfing it only serves to enhance the authority and unity of the
Castle concept. The new building does, however, shut off the view of
the Castle and Bridge from St. Martin's Lodge (now an office of the
County Council) which Harrison designed and built for himself so
that he could superintend the progress of his great works on the spot.
Harrison's work in Chester occupied some forty years and from 1820
until his death he watched over it from this house, which is an elegant
example of his domestic style. Thomas Harrison and Joseph
Hemingway were friends and the architect contributed much information about his plans to the Chronicle of the time, and that part of
the editor's History of Chester which deals with the Castle was written by Harrison himself. Both were buried, I believe, in St. Bridget's
Churchyard and upon its removal in the making of the Grosvenor-
road roundabout the interments were transferred for reburial in the
suburb of Blacon – but of this I have no certain knowledge.

For one of the last descriptions of the Norman Castle, which
Harrison's plans dismantled with the exception of Agricola's Tower
(including the Chapel of St. Mary de Castro), we go back once more
to our indispensable guide Thomas Pennant. (You will remember
his account of the fearsome old gaol, given in the Chapter headed
'On Gallows Hill and Tyburn Tree'.) He saw the Castle as in two
parts, upper and lower, each with a strong gate defended by a round
bastion on each side, with a ditch and drawbridge. 'Within the upper
ballium are some towers of Norman architecture, square. The hand-
somest is that called Julius Caesar's . . . On the sides of the lower
court stands the noble room called Hugh Lupus's Hall, in which the
courts of justice for the county are held: the length is near ninety feet,
the breadth forty-five; the height very aweful and worthy the state
apartment of a great baron. The roof is supported by woodwork, in a
bold style, carved . . . Adjoining this Hall is the Court of Exchequer,
or the chancery of the county palatine. The Earl of Chester is the
present chamberlain . . .' The old Castle gateway, with its towers
and drawbridge, was taken down in 1807, and presumably Hugh
Lupus's Hall – the loss of which we may lament – was destroyed at
the close of the eighteenth century.

The several stages of Harrison's work were reported in the paper
as the years of building went by. In 1788 a start was made on the new

gaol, Exchequer Court, and Grand Jury Room; in 1791 on the Shire
Hall; in 1797 on the erection of the Shire Hall columns; in 1800 on the
barrack blocks on either side of the courtyard; and in 1811 on the
Grand Entrance or Propylaeum, which was not completed until
1822. In the entire grand design there are 84 columns, each formed of
a single stone, and the erection of the first of these, in the portico of
the Shire Hall, was a ceremonial affair reported with fitting panache
in the Chronicle of October 13, 1797 (number 1165):

> On Monday se'nnight, on the occasion of the erecting the first of the
> large columns of the portico of the New County Hall, building here, the
> Loyal Chester Volunteers assembled in the Abbey Square, and from
> thence marched with their colours and accompanied by the band of
> music belonging to Lord Falmouth's regiment of Cornish Cavalry, to
> the Castle Yard. There a double guard was drawn out to prevent the
> large concourse of people who were assembled to see the operation
> from approaching too near the workmen: among whom were several of
> the acting magistrates, with a number of ladies and gentlemen, and
> also the young gentlemen of most of the schools in Chester.
>
> The column being previously brought to its situation, and all the
> machinery prepared, several coins of his present Majesty in a small urn
> of Wedgwood's ware, enclosed in another of lead, were deposited with
> a suitable inscription. This being done, the machinery began work, the
> band playing 'God Save the King', and in about twenty minutes the
> column was raised, upon which the Volunteers fired three excellent
> volleys, the field pieces firing likewise three rounds, and the cannon
> upon the battery; together with three cheers from the whole of the
> corps, workmen, etc.
>
> These columns are of excellent stone of a good colour, and were
> brought from Manley about eight miles from Chester upon a carriage
> with six wheels, built on purpose, drawn by sixteen horses, and when
> in the rough weighed from fifteen to sixteen tons each. They are three
> feet six inches in diameter and without the capitals measure twenty-
> two feet six inches long, being considerably larger than those in front of
> the New College in Edinburgh. There will be twelve of these columns
> in the portico in two rows of the Doric order, without bases, and twelve
> more likewise of one stone, something smaller, of the Ionic order, form-
> ing a colonnade round the semi-circular part of the inside of the hall.

In August, 1813, when the first column of the Grand Entrance was
reared on its plinth, the Royal Denbighshire Militia paraded with
their Colonel, Sir Watkin Williams Wynn, who deposited coins in a
cavity cut in the plinth, and over them a brass plate recording 'the
signal victory gained over the French by Field-Marshal Lord Wellington, near Vittoria, in Spain, June 21st, 1813 . . .' Round the plate,

upon the stone plinth, was cut a memorial of 'the last triumph of the Marquis of Wellington, victory of the Pyrenees, July 30th 1813.' The inscription writers were doing their best to keep up with Wellington. The Chronicle report added 'The Castle Yard was crowded with an assemblage of fashion rarely witnessed.' Having been sand-blasted clean in 1973, in preparation for this European Architectural Heritage Year (1975), the excellent stone of a good colour (as the paper's reporter of 178 years ago noted) glows in the westering sunlight. I have heard it said that the Castle strikes a false note in the style and scale of Chester. But Dr. Pevsner, for example, sees more incongruity introduced by later buildings. Of Harrison's Castle he has said (1971), 'One of the most powerful monuments of the Greek Revival in the whole of England . . . the Shire Hall is of great beauty.' A later addition to the Castle area is the modern County Hall, facing the river and at the rear of Harrison's work. Started in 1938, the County Hall building was halted by the Second World War, and the work was not finished until 1957. Successive County Architects designed the County Hall and the Police Headquarters.

Harrison did not live to see the completion of the Grosvenor Bridge. Begun in 1827, when the first stone was laid by Earl Grosvenor on October 1, it was finished in 1831, two years after the architect's death. 'This stupendous structure, though not completed at the time I write (November, 1830)', said Hemingway, 'is rising into magnificence; the centres all fixed and several courses of stone laid upon the arch.' The bridge cost £36,000, of which £7,000 was for the approaches, and was at the time the largest single-span stone arch, 200 feet, in the world. There have never been any critics of the 'incongruity' of the Grosvenor Bridge. It continues to serve its purpose and spans the river with grace and strength. From the day when the young Princess Victoria passed over it in her carriage, the bridge has been the principal highway into and out of North Wales, relieving the Old Dee Bridge of most of its burden. If Thomas Harrison could see the weight and volume of motor traffic ceaselessly borne today by his stone arch, he would, I imagine, after reflecting how well he had built, approach the drawing-board and offer to design another masterpiece the necessity of which he would so clearly see.

In conjunction with the bridge, and to secure its approach, Grosvenor-street was cut diagonally from the foot of Bridge-street, about 1828–1830. This was the first departure in all the centuries from the Roman street plan, and today Grosvenor-street continues the southwestern line of the Inner Ring Road, constructed in the 1960s and 1970s. The building of the bridge cut into the City Wall and created the Little Roodee (until then part of the big Roodee) and gave the opportunity, taken in about 1900–2, to continue the promenade road round the Walls from the Northgate to the Bridge Gate, from which it follows the riverside to the Groves. The Grosvenor Bridge scene from the childhood of Queen Victoria is worth recalling. When most of us think of the Queen the picture that comes to mind is of the revered matriarch, the Widow of Windsor – such a long time ago since she was a young girl! But on Wednesday, October 17, 1832, the Chronicle reporter at the opening of the bridge saw 'the interesting little Princess, dressed in white, her hair combed back and plainly adjusted behind her ears, with bright blue eyes and pleasing countenance.' The Princess Victoria was 13 years of age. It was a kind of little royal progress for her when she and her mother, the Duchess of Kent, came into Cheshire from Wales, remaining for a week as guests of the Marquis of Westminster at Eaton Hall. On the Tuesday of that week the Mayor and Corporation went in fifteen carriages to Eaton to present respectful addresses, and next day a cavalcade set out from Eaton to Chester, the Princess having agreed to open the bridge by driving across it in her carriage and to name it at the invitation of the Mayor, the Corporation, and the citizens. As the carriage approached the Royal Standard was hoisted above the keystone of the bridge and a 21-gun salute was fired from the Castle Yard.

The second Chester 'redevelopment' was the black-and-white renaissance dating from about 1850, evidence of which can be seen today in all the principal streets and at its best perhaps in St. Werburgh-street. A handful of local architects determined the character of 'old Chester' in the nineteenth century – they pretended that it was unchanged from the sixteenth and seventeenth centuries by reproducing, more elaborately, the earlier domestic town style of half-timber gables. In many instances the height betrays the fiction even to the untrained eye. But there is no doubt that generations of tourists have been happily 'taken in' by the Tudor of T. M. Penson, T. M. Lockwood, and John Douglas. With an original exception here and there, Eastgate-street as we see it today is largely their creation, from the Grosvenor Hotel to the Cross, and wonderfully atmospheric it all is, Visitors take away memories, reinforced by ciné pictures, photographs and postcards, of Chester Cross and the Eastgate clock. These are the folk symbols of the old town known throughout the world. Lockwood created the Cross as represented by the corner buildings joining Eastgate-street and Bridge-street Rows, and Douglas designed the setting and ornamentation of the clock for Queen Victoria's diamond jubilee. In Northgate-street there are Douglas and Lockwood again: the arcaded west Row, replacing the true Shoemakers' Row about 1897: and in St. Werburgh-street all the east side is Douglas's, and splendid work it is in its own right. Dominating Bridge-street, east, is Lockwood's St. Michael's Buildings, an earlier Grosvenor estate development, at first surprisingly faced with white faience, later altered to traditional black and white at the behest of the second Duke of Westminster.

Traditional Chester, that is how we should describe the work of these architects, and it is only in the 1960s and 1970s that contemporary architecture of differing degrees of quality has been allowed to displace the tradition. Not only did the traditionalists put up new façades in the old manner; they restored and touched up the true old buildings such as Leche House (James Harrison), God's Providence House (James Harrison), and Bishop Lloyd's House (Lockwood), all three in Watergate-street, and now (with the treasured leaning gable in Lower Bridge-street) regarded as the last and best of genuine Chester domestic. As the ownership or tenancy of these historic buildings changed, so also changed their usage and some valuable oak panelling and other irreplaceable fitments and embellishments disappeared in the process. Bishop Lloyd's House was once in danger of being bought up for removal to America. Least restored are Leche House and Bishop Lloyd's. God's Providence, however, if you compare the former prints and descriptions with the modern evidence, is a House very much altered. There was a lot of controversy in the Chronicle in the 1860s about the alterations required by the owner at that time for the convenience of his business. James Harrison, it appears, did his best to mitigate the more drastic of these and to keep some semblance of the original façade. This Harrison (overshadowed by his more famous namesake) contributed to modern Chester in other ways. He restored the Church of St. Mary-on-the-Hill, rebuilt St. Michael's Church, rebuilt Holy Trinity Church (now the Guildhall), but did not live to see the spire finished, designed the Savings Bank next door to Lockwood's Grosvenor Museum, and took down the Theatre Royal in Northgate-street and put a Music Hall in its place, the original foundation courses of St. Nicholas's Chapel being exposed in the side passage-way, as may be seen today. (Cowdroy would be vastly interested in the latest apotheosis in the life of St. Nicholas's Chapel: after the Music Hall it became a cinema for silent pictures and then talking pictures, and it is now a Supermarket.)

The black-and-white restorers had a field day in 1935, when Stanley Palace in Watergate-street, town house of the Stanleys of Alderley, was vigorously reconditioned. Seven gables are full in view today, and the mass of the house looks up Watergate-street across the ring road instead of as formerly into a dismal courtyard. It is in good use and care and has the appearance if not the actuality of the sixteenth century. There is much to be said for restoration and even reproduction. Is it not now all called conservation? In the 1960s there was some perturbation about the activities of commercial developers. At about this time began the frequent alterations of shop façades and internal arrangements in the more fashionable Rows. Could the old town successfully absorb all this innovation, some of it vulgar and garish?

There were genuine fears about the accelerating process of change, and the paper reflected them all through the 1960s. On June 17, 1961, the Chronicle announced the plans of the executors of the Eaton estate for a shopping mall or precinct appropriately linking up with their earlier St. Michael's Arcade, and this precinct, with the inner ring road and the modernisation of the civic centre, was to form the third large redevelopment of Chester. 'The gathering ruins of old Newtown and the desultory destruction of once-proud Pepper-street in the remorseless grip of the ring road that is to be . . .' That is a comment in the paper of about the same time, and how quaintly and plaintively it reads now. (Ask a citizen who remembers old Pepper-street to describe it, or any other place that he knew well in the recent past, and he will have a visual difficulty.)

The inner ring road swept away Egerton House in Upper Northgate-street and that perfect period piece, the Unitarian conventicle or meeting-house known as Matthew Henry's Chapel, a simple shrine of Chester Nonconformity; and it pierced the City Wall, which is now carried over it between Pemberton's Parlour and Morgan's Mount by St. Martin's Gate, for which the City Engineer of the time, Mr. A. H. F. Jiggens, was chiefly responsible. Although the old street was seedy and pretty much decayed, the section of the inner ring which replaces Pepper-street and is now called Pepper Row is not (in my view) entirely satisfactory. Here is the long southern aspect of the shopping precinct, with a sort of street-level Row or arcade, which could perhaps have been better managed. For the rest, the visual damage caused by the road – which, as it rises and curves, commands a new set of town vistas – is less than was feared. It has, indeed, been skilfully inserted into the city, and without it, of course, there could be no traffic truce such as we now have in the centre. But at the time even the local architects were wondering what Chester would be like in the next five years. In an editorial of April 27, 1963, the Chronicle said

> 'In these innovating times our task, in ordering the changes that are inevitable, is to preserve something of the old city's character. To do this are we to shut out the ideas of our own time and go on repeating Tudor? The answer must be firmly No. But I am pondering what kind of pattern there will be in Northgate-street with a modern Market, a Victorian Gothic Town Hall, the mellowed sandstone of the Cathedral, the black-and-white reproductions here and there, and the contemporary investment-lot style . . . Chester is not Coventry. We are not starting afresh here with a free hand at an entirely contemporary and experimental design for modern living. The planners, architects, and developers must not be permitted to alter the whole character of the place as a sort of exercise in commercial convenience.'

In May, 1963, the Grosvenor-Laing partnership published its plans for the shopping precinct and the Chronicle offered this first comment:

> 'To the custodians of Chester a change of ownership, the falling in or foreclosure of a lease, are matters of moment. The agents of change are the motor-car, the Corporation (with its market, north-west central development, and inner ring), the private developers (office blocks and shops), and Grosvenor-Laing (with their £3m plan for a covered shopping precinct). This last scheme is "new townish" in conception and open to objection by the more conservative on that ground alone were it not for its imaginative extension and adaptation of the idea of the Rows as existing pedestrian precincts. The Grosvenor-Laing scheme is a modern treatment of an original and unique Chester notion.'

In 1965 the paper published articles by Peter Scott, of the Town Planning Institute, on Mr. Grenfell Baines's Plan for the Central Area of Chester (which, with Mr. Donald Insall's later working study, is the basic blueprint for the developing new-old city) and opposed the admission of tower-block buildings into the townscape. A panoramic picture of the skyline as seen from the Roodee was contrasted with a lithograph of the same scene in the last century, when the Cathedral Central Tower stood almost alone as a modest eminence.

The theme was taken up again in August, 1966, with the publication of an aerial picture and this comment:

> 'You see that to the historic street map converging upon the Cross has been added the inner ring road still under construction, and clearly dominating the townscape now are no longer the Cathedral and the Town Hall but the tower-blocks within and without the Walls. What you do not see, because it is only fragmentarily in existence after years and years of talk and delay, is the outer ring road with a new bridge across the Dee to link all the radials which now serve the South, Manchester, Wirral and Liverpool, and North Wales. Experience has shown the inner ring road as a useful artery of traffic flow but also at peak times in itself the cause of congestion, delay, and confusion.'

Pressure on the inner ring had been by this time increased by the opening of the shopping precinct in November, 1965. This unobtrusive re-use of a substantial segment of the city behind the south-east Rows deserved a special edition and the Chronicle on November 5 (number 9,900) produced with the normal big paper the first of its many subsequent supplements devoted to a particular aspect of life and affairs in Chester and the two counties. In a front-page comment the paper said:

> 'For centuries Chester has had what the modern town planners call pedestrian precincts in the shape of the Rows; and there was some fear that when the time inevitably came for extensive commercial redevelopment in the city, the Rows might in some way lose their character. The fear has proved groundless. In the event the architects, Sir Percy Thomas and Son, in their revitalisation of the backlands of East-gate-street South and Bridge-street East, with Pepper Row or the inner ring road as the enclosing arm, have incorporated the existing Rows into the precinct and extended the idea – which simply is a covered gallery with interior level of shops above the street – into a continental-style piazza itself. So that the Grosvenor-Laing development, though conforming to twentieth-century concepts of town planning, is uniquely a Chester adaptation. Altogether it is an imaginative piece of design with a wholly functional purpose.'

In this way the precinct is seen to be a logical sequence in the Chester story of the past two hundred years. It might, with less thought and care, have been otherwise. Shopping precincts are common enough throughout the country, and some are common indeed.

The immediate success of the precinct brought more car-borne shoppers into the city and the twin problems of traffic containment and dispersal were not by any means solved by the high-level parking system incorporated into the scheme and by the opening of civic and other perimeter car parks. A typical Chronicle comment of the late 1960s was this:

> 'One first battle against the admission of tower blocks within the Wall has been fought and lost, with the Royal Fine Art Commission and the Chronicle on the losing side. But not all was lost. After the Police building, there has been a more thoughtful consideration for the city's architectural scale. But the tide of motor traffic will eventually engulf Chester if its main streets are not, some time in the ensuing decade, converted into pedestrian precincts and the motor-car banned from them, or the outer ring road and new bridge hastened.'

Articles by John Sargent and others, reflecting the collective and individual views of the Chester Society of Architects, were published from time to time, commenting on the various one-way street and other systems experimentally adopted by the authorities and examining other fresh aspects of town planning and amenities. There were imaginative proposals for bridges linking the Rows in Bridge-street, Eastgate-street, and Watergate-street, in the context of a central pedestrian precinct, and to illustrate how well this latter amenity could be made to work, socially and commercially, the Chronicle sent a photographer to Norwich in April, 1971. Here was the first traffic-free precinct in a busy city centre. The photographer came back with a picture of Norwich's 'foot street' full of people moving about unimpeded by cars. This was published and headlined 'Traffic-choked Chester could be like this.' In the succeeding week, to drive the message home, a contrasting picture of the confusion at Chester Cross, in which only the exhaust fumes were not seen, was headlined 'The running battle.' These two pictures, as I have reason to believe, helped to concentrate public and official opinion on the lifting of the traffic siege from the Cross and the main streets which we now have. This major improvement enabled the authorities also to consider the restoration, first suggested and illustrated in the Chronicle, of the reconstructed High Cross, preserved in the Roman Garden outside the Newgate, to its original position opposite St. Peter's Church.

Thousands of visitors come from all parts of the world every summer to see the antiquities of Chester, to savour the past, and to enjoy the modern amenities. The streets are a stratification of all our history, and the bottom layer, the indestructible foundation put down by the Romans, keeps on coming to the surface. In the intensive redevelopment period of the 1960s and 1970s sites have been cleared that for centuries were built over successively. The archaeologists seize the chance to move in before the bulldozers and make the most of the precious time they have before the rebuilders take over again. Passers-by may see nothing more than a sizeable hole in the ground, oblivious of the presence there of the ancient world. The base of a pillar, a frieze, moulding, cornice, hypocaust, the distinctive shape of an altar, domestic pots, ornaments, coins: all are glimpsed briefly in situ, then (if removable) are carried off to the Grosvenor Museum or recorded and covered up for another long night of buried time. (A cliché, I know, but very true in its application to Chester.) The Chronicle's first report of a Roman 'find' was on January 29, 1779 (number 197): 'Last week, on digging foundations for a range of new houses in the field now called the New Linen-hall Field, fronting Watergate-street, a considerable quantity of Roman antiquities were discovered about three to four feet underground, particularly two Roman hypocausts or sweating-baths, in pretty perfect repair.' John Trevor, Editor of the Chronicle about the middle of the nineteenth century, included a comprehensive account of the Roman discoveries in Chester in his Panorama of Chester up to the time of its publication in 1843. In the later nineteenth century Professor F. Haverfield enriched our knowledge of Roman Deva. He was followed by Professor R. Newstead, Mr. W. J. Williams, Dr. Graham Webster, and now by Mr. D. F. Petch.

When the shopping precinct area was under excavation there came to view the foundations of what conjecturally was a massive gymnasia, bath-house, and exercise hall for the use of the 20th Legion Valeria Victrix, quartered in the fortress of Deva on and off for the first three centuries A.D. At the same time substantial foundations of a large Roman building with colonnades were uncovered on the adjacent site being developed for the new printing press hall of the Chronicle. In 1968 the removal of the old Market Hall enabled the archaeologists to explore another part of the site of the Praetorium, the grand headquarters building, evidence of which first came to light in 1897, and again in 1948–9, when excavations in Goss-street revealed the foundations of the 244 feet wide colonnaded west front. Unquestionably, however, the most significant discovery this century was of the Roman amphitheatre. One day in June, 1929, a workman excavating a heating chamber for a new wing of the Ursuline Convent School outside the south-east corner of the City Walls came across a coin of the Emperor Hadrian. He showed his find to Mr. W. J. Williams, who went to the site and saw stones 'of a size unsurpassed in Roman Chester' built into a great wall eight and a half feet thick with two massive buttresses. To the archaeologist's dismay, the solid ashlar was being demolished with crowbar and hammer. He arrested the destruction long enough to record that the wall was constructed of huge blocks of sandstone with a filling of sandstone rubble. Pottery evidence fixed the date of the structure as the first century, and the wall of the amphitheatre then recently excavated at Caerleon in South Wales under the direction of Sir Mortimer Wheeler, but more monumental in character. Thus a casual encounter in the street between the workman and the scholar led to the identification of the amphitheatre of Chester the existence and site of which had been for many years the subject of conjecture only. More than forty years elapsed before the site was cleared, excavated, landscaped, and opened to public view. August Bank Holiday visitors in 1972 saw it for the first time after the 'official opening' by Mr. John Bell, representing the Ministry of the Environment. One half only of the arena and seating-bank has been exposed. The other half still lies under the Convent School, awaiting another Architectural Heritage Year . . .

In this chapter we have come a long way from our perambulation of the city with William Cowdroy in 1789 and in all the changes since then there is a kind of pattern, fortuitous or logical or predetermined, in whatever light you choose to see it by. In Cowdroy's time the pattern was for the citizens to live in the city, above or at the back of their shops or other business premises in the Rows. The city had thus a continuous interior life of its own. And this went on for a long time until the growth of the suburbs and the revolution in transport changed the pattern. Mr. Donald Insall's Historic Town study of Chester in 1968, with its accent on the conservation of buildings in relation to their neighbours, to the general stock of buildings in the city, and to their commercial and domestic use, has encouraged the authorities and the private owners to return to the old concept of the city as a dwelling-place as well as an emporium. Because they were no longer in domestic use, upper storeys tended to fall into disrepair, and when the roof is neglected the house is in danger. Evidence of such rot at the top was to be seen almost everywhere within the Walls and much timely rescue work has been undertaken. Some historic units – Gamul House and the Dutch Houses, for example – have been looked to before it was too late. Lower Bridge-street's slow decline into seediness has been arrested and the whole area down to the Bridge Gate reconsidered as a neighbourhood of much interest and diversity in which, also, city and county have a mutual interest.

Intelligent conservation rather than destruction or, worse, acquiescence in wasteful and irretrievable decay: upon this advice, given in the Insall survey, Chester is acting. In some other historic towns the damage has been done. In a notable passage, touched with irony, Mr. Insall asked: 'Should we remove the Cathedral to ease traffic movement? Few would permit the actual destruction of what people come to see merely to make accessible the place where it used to be. Yet there are other more subtle forms of destruction. The modern road to hell is paved with tarmac and lined by buildings . . . The most insidious enemy is lack of thought; the next is planning by rule-of-thumb.' And so, with generous Government grants, self-help by the local authorities (including the famous original 'penny rate' levied for the purpose) and private owners, the official commitment to progress on the outer ring road and new bridge across the Dee, and a renewed civic awareness of inherited treasures, Chester leads the Historic Towns of Britain into European Architectural Heritage Year. There will be no award other than satisfaction in discharge of the trust that is laid upon each generation of Chester citizens and the pleasure of visitors in a Wall-girt city so full of ancient renown, so different from the brutalism of other human settlements, and yet so much at home in this century as in all that have gone before. That is the abiding charm of Chester – a long-continuing homeliness. And the Chester Chronicle, in its modest two hundred years, has helped to honour and sustain that priceless tradition.

Bibliography

The Chester City archives
The Grosvenor Family archives
Files of the Chester Chronicle
Files of the Chester Courant
Files of the Crewe and Nantwich Chronicles
Files of the Northwich and Winsford Chronicles
Journals of the Chester Archaeological Society
Canal documents in the Public Record Office
    (British Transport section)

A Tour through England and Wales. Daniel Defoe (1724)
Tours in Wales. Thomas Pennant (1778)
Journey from Chester to London. Thomas Pennant (1783)
Directory and Guide to the County and City of Chester.
    William Cowdroy (1789)
Guide to Chester. John Broster (1795)
Life of Dr. Samuel Johnson. James Boswell.
The Adventures of Sir Launcelot Greaves. Tobias Smollett
Miscellaneous writings of Dean Swift.
North Wales. W. Bingley (1814)
The Stranger in Chester. J. H. Hanshall (1816)
History of the County Palatine of Cheshire. J. H. Hanshall (1823)
History of Chester. Joseph Hemingway (1831)
Directory of Printers and Printing. C. H. Timperley (1839)
Panorama of Chester. John Trevor (1843)
The History of Wirral. W. Williams Mortimer (1847)
Chester and its Environs Illustrated. J. Romney (1853)
The Stranger's Handbook to Chester. Thomas Hughes (1856)

English Hours. Henry James. (Heinemann. 1906)
Mary Davies and the Manor of Ebury. C. T. Gatty. (Cassell. 1921)
Alfred Mond, First Lord Melchett. Hector Bolitho. (Martin Secker. 1933)
English Social History. G. M. Trevelyan. (Longmans. 1942)
A History of the English-Speaking Peoples. Winston S. Churchill. (Cassell. 1957)
Lady Elizabeth and the Grosvenors. Gervas Huxley. (Oxford University Press.
    1965)
Victorian Duke. Gervas Huxley. (Oxford University Press. 1967)

Chester. A Study in Conservation. Donald Insall and Associates. (Her Majesty's Stationery Office. 1968)

Sir John Brunner, Radical Plutocrat. S. E. Koss. (Cambridge University Press. 1970)

Buildings of England. Cheshire. Nikolaus Pevsner and Edward Hubbard. (Penguin Books. 1972)

Farewell to the Assizes. The Honourable Sir Basil Nield. (Garnstone Press. 1972)